D0906315

THE GOTHIC TRADITION IN FICTION

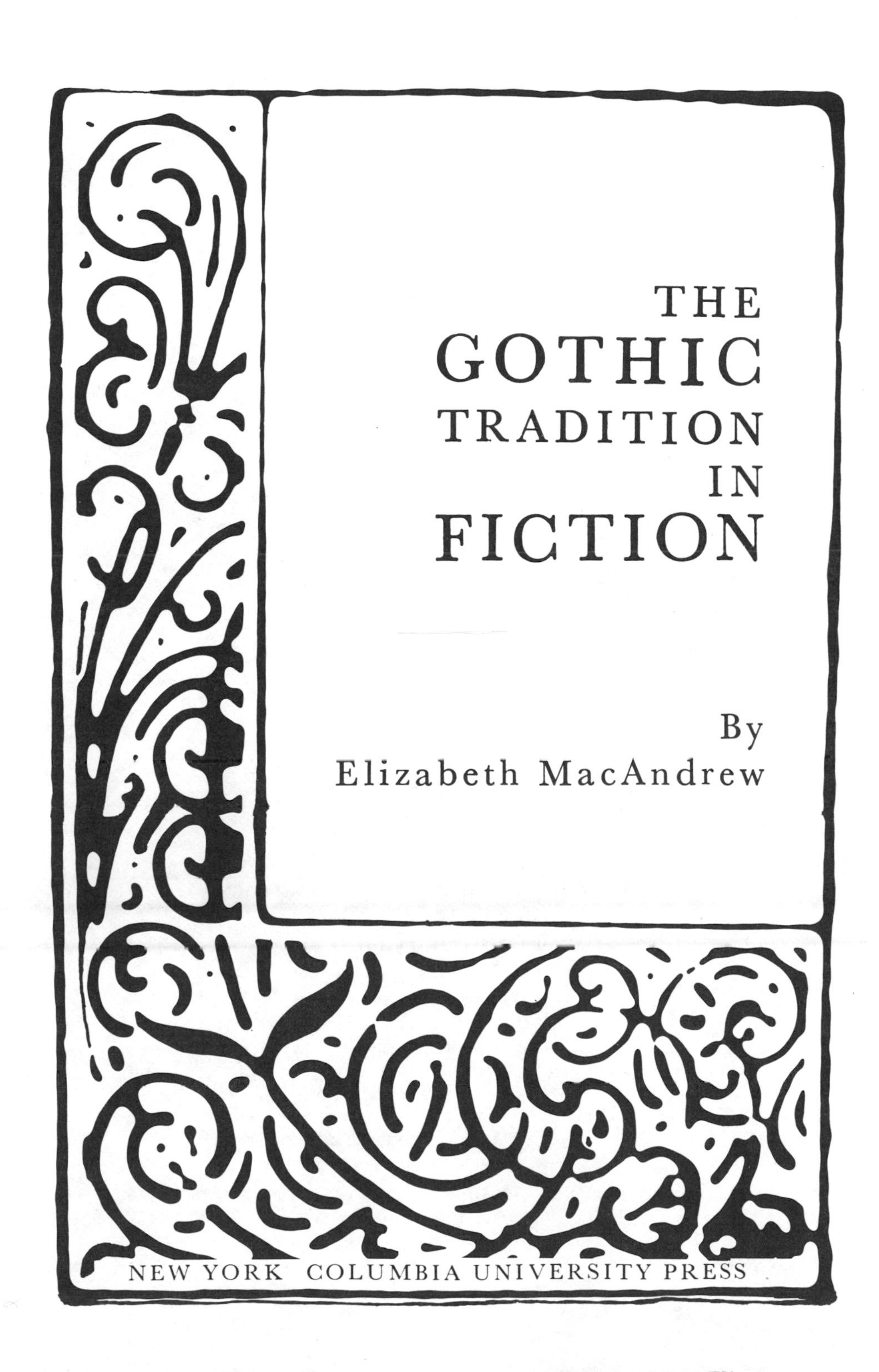

THE GOTHIC TRADITION IN FICTION

By
Elizabeth MacAndrew

NEW YORK COLUMBIA UNIVERSITY PRESS

LIBRARY OF CONGRESS CATALOGING IN PUBLICATION DATA

MACANDREW, ELIZABETH, 1924–
THE GOTHIC TRADITION IN FICTION.

BIBLIOGRAPHY: P.
INCLUDES INDEX.
1. GOTHIC REVIVAL (LITERATURE) 2. ENGLISH FICTION—
HISTORY AND CRITICISM. I. TITLE.
PN3435.M3 823'.0872 79-9447
ISBN 0-231-04674-X

COLUMBIA UNIVERSITY PRESS
NEW YORK GUILDFORD, SURREY

PRINTED IN THE UNITED STATES OF AMERICA
9 8 7 6 5 4 3 2

TO
JOSEPH KISSANE

whose generosity in sharing ideas
and patience in advising upon their execution
lead me to dedicate this book to him in
gratitude and friendship

CONTENTS

PREFACE

THIS BOOK is a study of a convention. It traces the appearance and continued use of certain literary devices through two hundred years, showing that authors writing in the Gothic tradition employ the same structures, imagery, and methods of characterization because their works have a common purpose—the exploration of human nature.

The first work in a conventional genre is not itself conventional, but an innovative break from the past. The first in the tradition under study here, Horace Walpole's *The Castle of Otranto,* was subtitled "A Gothic Tale," providing the entire convention with a descriptive term. At the time—1764—"Gothic" still retained some of its old connotative aura of "barbaric" and things "Gothic" had only recently come to be seen as romantic and interesting, not just ugly and forbidding. A "Gothic" setting and "Gothic" events, consequently, were a suitable means of filling the reader with pity and fear in order to engage his "sympathy," to involve him emotionally in the work. Walpole uses such means to make his readers experience ideas about human nature and the place of evil in the human mind. Other authors, following him, used the same devices—closed worlds, mediated narratives, ancient houses, dark villains, and perfect heroines—for the same purpose, so that, for instance, a ghost became the conventional means of symbolizing a sense of guilt. New devices were added, but the convention remained basically unchanged, because the need to materialize these ideas in fiction did not change. In tracing this use of convention I have sought to show how the connections between one work and another add to meaning, for the use of a convention is allusive in a special way. It is a means of alerting the reader to the kind of work he is engaged with, of guiding him toward interpretation.

Since my purpose has been to show continuity and connection in the Gothic tradition, I have first briefly discussed the conditions—literary and philosophical—that gave rise to the earliest Gothic tales. Then I have delineated the characteristic features of these tales—methods of characterization and structure—which, with gradual accretions, have continued in use to this day. I have not divided my study into chapters on individual authors, groups of authors, or works. Instead, throughout a broadly chronological treatment, I have referred to works and their authors as they serve to illustrate the point under discussion. As a consequence, I have frequently made slight reference to a work in relation to others before discussing it more fully in a later section, and vice versa.

Because "Gothic literature" is a vast subject, I have limited this study in various ways. I have confined it to narrative prose fiction because that genre lends itself best to the demonstration of the special purpose of Gothic literature. The same purpose, however, lies behind much poetry and drama in which the same literary devices are used. I have also centered the study on British works, while bringing in examples from American literature and introducing some German, French, and Russian works when they have provided striking instances of the use of the convention. And I have ended the study with the close of the nineteenth century, treating the twentieth in an epilogue only, because cultural changes in the twentieth century demand a separate study.

The analysis of Gothic works raises one particular critical problem—it is necessary to discuss the works in relation to the reader despite the obvious problem of subjectivity and the "dangers of the affective fallacy." The evocation of "terror" is a feature shared by all Gothic literature, and Gothic authors employ their techniques with the effect on the reader in mind. It is therefore necessary to consider this effect in interpreting the tales. The literary effect of a work is not the same thing as its purpose, however, and my aim has been to discuss the features and the effects of Gothic literature in order to uncover its purpose.

I wish to thank Cleveland State University for the Research Initiation Award which enabled me to do the preliminary research for this work and for the typing service which it has provided. I wish also to express my gratitude to my friends and colleagues who have helped along the way. Louis T. Milic provided initial encouragement. Judith Firemen, Frederick Keener, Robert Maguire, and Leonard Trawick read and commented helpfully and constructively upon a penultimate draft. Susan Gorsky added useful last-minute suggestions and Jeffrey Ford provided advice on revisions. Zita McShane and Jay Wootten read the manuscript, made useful comments, and suggested corrections. I have discussed the subject of this study with Joseph Kissane off and on for several years until "rightful ownership" of our ideas about it can no longer be determined. My gratitude for his support and advice is expressed in dedicating the final product to him.

THE GOTHIC TRADITION IN FICTION

"I know not, Madam, that you have a right, upon moral principles, to make your readers suffer so much."

Samuel Johnson to Frances Sheridan

Thus, waking from a midnight dream of horror, one hastily turns on the light and lies quiescent, worshipping the chest of drawers, worshipping solidity, worshipping reality, worshipping the impersonal world which is a proof of some existence other than ours.

Virginia Woolf, "The Mark on the Wall"

PART ONE

THE SHAPE OF IDEAS

CHAPTER ONE

INTRODUCTORY GOTHIC LITERATURE— WHAT IT IS AND WHY

For Poesy alone can tell her dreams—
With the fine spell of words alone can save
Imagination from the sable chain
And dumb enchantment.
Keats, "The Fall of Hyperion"

OTHIC fiction is a literature of nightmare. Among its conventions are found dream landscapes and figures of the subconscious imagination. Its fictional world gives form to amorphous fears and impulses common to all mankind, using an amalgam of materials, some torn from the author's own subconscious mind and some the stuff of myth, folklore, fairy tale, and romance.[1] It conjures up beings—mad monks, vampires, and demons—and settings—forbidding cliffs and glowering buildings, stormy seas and the dizzying abyss—that have literary significance and the properties of dream symbolism as well. Gothic fiction gives shape to concepts of the place of evil in the human mind.

It was a new literary form in the late eighteenth century. At that time, the purpose of Gothic fiction, like that of the Sentimental novel, to which it was closely allied, was to educate the reader's feelings through his identification with the feelings of the characters; to arouse his "sympathy," as the aesthetics of Sensibility demanded, by evoking pity and fear; and to explore the mind of man and the causes of evil in it, so that evil might be avoided and virtue fostered. The earliest Gothic romances are literary fantasies embodying, for didactic purposes, ideas about man's psychology that were the culmination of a century of philosphical speculation on the subject. In them, good and evil are starkly differentiated absolutes, but as succeeding works delved deeper into the idea of evil as psychological, evil quickly began to be seen as relative and, in no time, its pleasures were being explored. All these works were based on accepted views about the human mind. Later authors, employing the same literary devices as the early works, introduced changes that both reflected and developed modifications of these views. As tales of the weird and horrid persisted through the nineteenth century, using the same stock characters and settings again and again, they gradually pieced together among them a picture of evil as a form of psychological monstrosity. The original querying into the origins of evil shifted to ambiguous presentations that questioned the nature of evil itself.

The highly conventionalized nature of the settings and characters, structures and imagery of Gothic fiction has always been recognized. All too frequently, however, these features have been dubbed "Gothic machinery" or "claptrap" because, like other forms of popular literature, Gothic fiction has been seen as fare for a sensation-seeking audience and not, therefore, worth literary analysis.[2] As a result, the course of the convention has not been traced. Instead, Gothic fiction has been called escape literature, intended to inspire terror for terror's sake. Such descriptions have concealed the important ideas these tales contain. The view of the early Gothic romances as "just" a form of escape does not adequately explain why they appeared when they did or why their appeal was so immediate and so strong. Descriptions of the genre as a literature of violence reflecting a violent age, or as a literature of sensation needed to perk up a jaded age are circular as well as contradictory. Recent attempts to treat Gothic literature as an aspect of Romanticism also fail to see its significance as a convention.[3] When we see that Gothic tales have continued to appear for two hundred years, and that the convention has been put to use by major writers as different from each other as Emily Brontë and Henry James, it is evident that something more is involved than a continuing taste for a ghoulish kind of bedside reading, and that these works are not confined to a single period of literature.[4]

From Walpole's maddened and murderous princeling in *The Castle of Otranto* to the self-tormented scientist in Robert Louis Stevenson's *Dr. Jekyll and Mr. Hyde,* the same conventional features keep reappearing because ideas of the same kind lie behind these works. That is, these and other writers chose the Gothic tale as a vehicle for ideas about psychological evil—evil not as a force exterior to man, but as a distortion, a warping of his mind. Walpole's slight romance yields such an interpretation, so does Stevenson's novel, so do the Gothic tales that appeared in the long stretch of time between them.

This is not to say that Stevenson and Walpole held the same view of evil, or of man's psychology in general. Indeed, their ideas on the subject form a sharp contrast. The great interest in tracing this literary convention lies in the changes that take place within it, which correspond to the changes in thought on the subject that have occurred since Locke first set forth his theory of the workings of the mind. What seems to have happened is this: following Locke (who was to the eighteenth century what Freud has been to the twentieth), eighteenth-century thinkers had devoted a great deal of their energies to the study of the mind, the nature of perception, the means to knowledge, expanding, adapting, and modifying Locke's ideas. It was the first era in which the mind was studied inductively, and the changes in world view, especially in ideas about the moral nature of Man, that such thinking reflected and also helped bring about were given literary expression in a number of different genres, but most directly in the Sentimental fiction of the time, of which Gothic literature is a part. Within this general literary development, Gothic fiction first made its appearance when Horace Walpole, his head full of a romanticized, eighteenth-century medievalism, awakened from a dream of which he could remember only a scrap and, under its influence, turned out *The Castle of Otranto,* at white heat. Though he himself felt the importance of this slight work, which, to the end of his life remained his favorite among his writings, he expected his fellow literati would scorn it as a "romance." Instead, his anonymous tale received high praise from literati and reading public alike. He had given fictional treatment to some of the major preoccupations of his time that were also his own concerns, and, after an interval, others began to copy his work—many a castle, many a tyrant, many a hero and heroine of perfect virtue and courage appeared. Naturally, however, Walpole's successors each took his devices and used them a little differently. Clara Reeve declared *Otranto* was too extravagant and confined herself wherever possible to the "Natural"; William Beckford, romping off into the Arabian Nights, introduced the grotesque into the genre; Matthew Lewis added the tormented monk who was immediately picked up by Ann Radcliffe, herself the chief among terror-mongers, whose villains had influenced Lewis in the first place.

In this rush of authors making use of and modifying one another's devices, there is more than a simple desire to share in the latest literary fad. Different though they were as personalities, these writers recognized the possibilities of the new genre for the expression of some of the prevailing views of their age, which they all shared, views not previously given fictional form. Each uncovered the implications of preceding works, recognizing the intuitions behind them. Thus, each delved deeper into the common subject, adding new devices to the convention as they were needed and producing works whose further implications could again be picked up by a successor to add a new round to the developing spiral of the genre.[5] This process continued throughout the nineteenth century, as writers embodied the views of the later age in the same way. Thus, Mary Shelley, Edgar Allan Poe, and Nathaniel Hawthorne added twisted scientists to the mad monks of Lewis and Radcliffe. Among distorted human shapes inherited from the eighteenth century, monsters and demonic animals appeared in the nineteenth. The ghosts and devils of Walpole, Reeve, Lewis, and Radcliffe reappeared considerably modified in Maturin, Le Fanu, Brontë, and James, and to them and Beckford's Giaour were added vampires and witches. Settings were changed from medieval to contemporary, a man's house turned out to be still his Gothic castle and his soul, already reflected in paintings and statues, began to look back at him from mirrors and, worse still, from his double, a living, breathing copy of himself.

Gradually, if we follow the course of the convention as it winds through the nineteenth century, feeding its weird tales into the mainstream of realistic fiction, we can trace changes in ideas about the place of evil in the mind. The moral absolutes of eighteenth-century thought crumble before a shifting, relative morality. Soon Edgar Allan Poe is playing with ideas of evil and madness. By mid-nineteenth century, Emily Brontë has evoked a primitive *spiritus loci* to confound earlier notions of evil as unnatural; by the 1890s Henry James is placing evil in the eye of the moral arbiter. In tracing the convention, we can see the developing ideas that preoccupied the late eighteenth century and obsessed the nineteenth. In Gothic literature of those years, with its monsters and madmen, we find suggested imaginatively writers' intuitive understanding of human evil.

Thus, within this literary convention, as in any other, changes and developments have occurred while it has retained its basically stable and recognizable outlines. Individual works within the convention embody the particularlities of the author's thought in the devices common to the whole convention and thereby reveal both the ideas of the particular moment and the overall purpose of the convention itself. That common purpose, which ties these works together, emerges from the peculiar form of symbolism found in Gothic tales. In this literature, the entire tale is symbolic. In analyzing it, one has to speak of storms that "stand for" the villain's anger or heroines that more closely represent a concept of virtue than flesh-and-blood women. Unlike the artfully buried symbols customary to a realistic work, the flagrant, all-pervading symbolism of a Gothic tale is almost, though not quite, allegorical. This literature is not allegory because its referents are deliberately hazy. The surface fiction is full of vague, unexplained horrors designed, not to render a precise meaning, but to evoke the emotion of "terror." Yet, these effects of "terror" in Gothic tales refer to something beyond the fictional devices that produce them. The quasi-allegorical effect derives from what lies behind the terror-inspiring fictional devices. These tales make use of the realization that monsters in fiction frighten because they are already the figments of our dreaming imaginations.

They are the shapes into which our fears are projected and so can be used in literature to explore the subterranean landscape of the mind. Terror is evoked when the ghost, the double, or the lurking assassin correspond to something that is actually feared, known or unknown. The fictional beings of Gothic fiction, whether they be human or animal, or manifestations from the "Beyond," whether they be universal archetypes or the pettiest of childhood bogies, symbolize real but vague fears that the reader recognizes as his own and all men's. Beneath the surface fiction there is a probing of humanity's basic psychological forces, an exploration of the misty realm of the subconscious, and the symbols correspond to psychological phenomena that yield to literary analysis. Yet it is probably this quasi-allegorical nature of Gothic symbolism, with its meaning lying almost entirely outside the fictional surface, that has caused this convention to be read only for its surface fiction, about which, it is true, little more can be said than that it evokes fear for fear's sake.

The authors of Gothic fiction, in writing their symbolic fantasies, necessarily chose a deliberately artificial form, for which they took their materials from earlier literature. *The Castle of Otranto* has several immediate antecedents—works that show an early use of historical setting, a ghost here and there, occasional sinister and supernatural happenings, and it has remote ancestors in Shakespeare and medieval romance. These and other predecessors have, of course, been traced. Thorough studies have been made of the relationship of Gothic fiction to the graveyard poets, to Shakespeare and Spenser, and to the combination of antiquarianism and the movement of Sentimentalism that swept the late eighteenth century.[6] But all this is mere learned lumber unless it shows how Gothic fiction does something new.[7] Since Gothic fiction was, as has been generally recognized, a new genre, it follows that it was doing something different with the materials of its predecessors. To discover what that is, it is necessary to uncover the ideas and aesthetic principles that gave rise to these works by analyzing them as symbolic constructs and to trace the convention with all its accretions through time and space. When this is done, the heritage on which Gothic authors drew throws further light on the meaning and purposes of their works.

The source and fountainhead of the entire Gothic tradition, Walpole's *The Castle of Otranto,* appeared in 1764, twelve years before its first important successor, Clara Reeve's *The Old English Baron* (1771), twenty-two years before William Beckford's *Vathek* (1786), and nearly thirty before the first works of Ann Radcliffe. It is a rather frothy little romance, so crammed with events and relationships that it reads like a plot summary of itself. If Walpole had set out to stock a warehouse of Gothic materials for his successors, he could hardly have done better. *Otranto* is peopled with two-dimensional characters embodying virtue and vice;

its setting constitutes a representation of the villain's character; it is an indirect narration, a story mediated through two voices before it reaches the reader; and its imagery and supernatural events lead to an interpretation of its meaning as an eighteenth-century psychological tale. All these features reappear in later works. Thus, an examination of *Otranto* tells a great deal about the convention to which it gave rise.

The medieval setting, the thunderous villain, the sensitive hero and heroine, the ghosts and other wonders that identify *The Castle of Otranto* as a Gothic tale were at least supposed to have been adopted from medieval romance. Here and elsewhere the relationship is tenuous at best, as the eighteenth century probably knew. A Gothic novel is to a medieval romance what an artificial ruin in an eighteenth-century garden was to a genuine one, and Walpole's romance is like his house, consciously fanciful in its medievalism. He himself said of Strawberry Hill, the house he transformed into a "Gothic" mansion: "Every true Goth must perceive" that the early rooms "are more the works of fancy than of imitation."[8] The medieval setting of *Otranto,* too, is largely a creation of its author's imagination. Walpole uses his medieval tale to make a fictional reality of evil as a psychological state; not for historical accuracy, but to appeal to eighteenth-century sensibilities. He employs it in accordance with the late eighteenth century's aesthetic concept of the sublime as evoking pity and terror to draw the reader out of himself.

The first Gothic characteristic of *Otranto* is its presentation as an ancient manuscript rediscovered. This produces an indirect, mediated narration that imparts an air of strangeness to the exotic setting. Medieval Italy is already distant from the reader in time and space and, when he is asked to suppose himself imaginatively to be reading a manuscript of shadowy authorship unearthed and presented to him by an unidentified "editor," a sense is imparted that he is about to delve into a world that will be difficult to understand. In the preface to the first edition,

Walpole's "editor" surmises that the story, the work of an unknown chronicler, is possibly by "an artful priest."[9] He speculates about the date of composition, establishing a sense of obscurity by preventing the reader from pinpointing the origin of the manuscript and by remarking on the quality of the original Italian of which his "translation," he says, is a poor rendering. All this puts us on notice that a mysterious world is about to be revealed.

Sentimental and Gothic novelists frequently use fictitious editors of this sort. They are more than just a means for the author to conceal his identity. The statements these "editors" put into their "prefaces" must not be taken at face value. Rather, they are the first of many signals alerting us to the kind of reading required of us. For instance, by setting the "editor" between us and the "chronicler," who is himelf relaying the story and, besides, is presented as suspect, Walpole guards against our rejecting the story because of its blatant artificiality, by putting us on notice that we must follow it according to its own rules.

Thus alerted, we can see that the "editor's" criticism of the writer's "moral" and his surmise that the suspect monk was attempting to "confirm the populace in their ancient errors and superstititions" is not a straightforward statement but a device of irony designed to attract our attention to that "moral." The "editor" remarks that the benighted medieval chronicler has erred in basing his work on so flimsy a precept as "that *the sins of fathers are visited on their children*" (Walpole's italics). Yet, in fact, the psychological aberration of incest—also a staple item in Gothic tales—is Walpole's central theme and he is using the editor's words to attract our attention to it. The plot is, in fact, an unravelling of the effect on children of their fathers' deeds, good and bad. From the crushing of Manfred's frail son Conrad under the giant helmet and Manfred's murder of his daughter to the hero Theodore's fulfillment of the prophecy, the children's lives are affected by their fathers' lives. And Manfred himself is driven by the demon of inherited evil. He is presented as not intrinsically wicked but as ruled by passions aroused by his obsession with the prophecy that his line will not retain its unlawful rule over the princedom. He was, we are told, naturally humane, "when his passion did not obscure his reason," but it does, in fact, obscure his reason throughout the novel. Like a medieval Oedipus, he tries to prevent the prophecy from coming true and his own evil deeds and his downfall are the result of his desparate effort to maintain the position he holds through his grandfather's crimes. Thus, the sins of the fathers are visited on the children in his case, too, but not in the sense that Manfred himself or his children have the divine wrath visited upon them. The awareness that his deeds are wrong and the sense that he is forced farther and farther down the path of evil maddens him and is actually the cause of his crimes. Thus, in this first of the Gothic novels, the problem of evil is already presented as a psychological problem created in the ambience of the family.

The characters who must carry the burden of this theme of inherited evil are also typically Gothic, being highly simplified figures useful for the embodiment of ideas. They are eighteenth-century, not medieval, figures, and, like the characters of Sentimental novels, their physical appearance corresponds to their spiritual state. The hero Theodore, his noble nature shining through his peasant's disguise, represents the Right and the Good. A handsome physical reincarnation of his grandfather Alfonso, the virtuous usurped prince whose giant ghost is haunting the castle, Theodore is nobility itself. The three women, all perfectly virtuous, are also perfectly beautiful. The son and heir is physically weak and puny, representing the weakness of Manfred's usurping claim in the face of just retribution. Manfred has more substance than they, because he is a figure torn by the conflict of good and evil within himself, but he is still a beetle-browed villain, also drawn without subtlety. These romance characters are like figures in a crowded tapestry. They talk in declamatory, set speeches that make the novel, crammed with action though it is, seem slow-moving, almost static. Hardly effective as a tale of adventure, it envelops the reader, as in a dream, a sort of symbolic nightmare.

Otranto has a considerable stock of stage effects that became typical of Gothic fiction, not just in themselves, but in the way they are used. The portrait of Manfred's grandfather is not a Gothic device just because it supernaturally steps out of its frame and disgustedly slams a door in Manfred's face. It is typical of Gothic fiction because its gesture of scorn shows us Manfred's degeneration. It reveals that he has slipped lower morally than his grandfather. His ancestor's sins weigh so heavily upon him that they torment him into evil greater than his grandfather's original usurpation. The portrait serves as a reflection of Manfred, just as the statue of Alfonso reflects Alfonso's grandson Theodore. Typically, the device that gives us the reflection of the villain is a distorting mirror, giving the wicked man a monstrous shape, while the hero is mirrored faithfully. The way the statue shows signs of life, bleeds when Manfred stabs Matilda, is an example, like the action of the portrait, of the way the quasi-allegorical aspect of Gothic fiction works. These supernatural happenings are "translatable"; for example, the significance of the statue's bleeding can be restated as: "the spirit of Goodness (Alfonso) bleeds metaphorically in compassion at the piteous sight of Virtue (Matilda) destroyed." (It is unfortunate, but beside the point, that Walpole chose to make it a nosebleed.) The other supernatural phenomena in the novel work in the same way.

The central device in *Otranto* became the most famous of all Gothic devices: the identity of the castle or house with its owner. The castle in Walpole's novel *is* Manfred. The wife and daughter he dominates so completely are confined to it almost entirely, as if they lived and breathed and had their being within his personality. The comings and goings of other characters, demanding entrance, fleeing secretively, appearing suddenly, directly reflect their relations with him. And finally, as the novel ends in Manfred's moral collapse, the castle, disobeying the laws of nature, collapses too, disintegrating into rubble as other such buildings would do in later novels.

The identification of castle and man make the castle a manifestation of Manfred's mind. In turn, this causes the giant ghost, with which Walpole again risks making the reader laugh, to render its meaning. Appearing in pieces though it does—first the enormous, sable-plumed helmet, then an arm, then a leg—it is the ghost of Alfonso, a manifestation of "the real owner . . . grown too large to inhabit [the castle]" mentioned in the prophecy. Haunting the castle of Manfred's mind, it is his own awareness of the right and the noble that have been usurped by evil. The animated pieces of the giant suit of armor, unintentionally comic though they are, have a signifiance in relation to the overall meaning of the novel. Thus: the helmet crushes the weakling Conrad; that is, the first sign that Manfred's unlawful claim is to be wrested from him—the helmet—kills the son through whom that claim was to be maintained. The helmet is too big for ordinary princelings, that is, Manfred's and Conrad's heads are figuratively too small to bear their responsibilities as princes. Conrad is too feeble physically to sustain even the first blow of retribution; that is, Manfred's claim to the castle is too weak to endure. The successive appearances of the giant mailed hand and the leg in armor and, finally, the full armored figure of Alfonso continue this theme.

Conrad's death renders Manfred more frantic than ever and so more villainous, showing how he continues to spin the web of evil out of himself. Because this event leaves him without an heir he sets in train the other dire events of the novel, all of which ultimately add pieces to the central portrait of Manfred himself. Other features of the tale also serve to characterize him. Theodore, the hero, for instance, embodies not merely nobility in the abstract but that noble sense of honor that Manfred has had to repress in himself to commit his evil deeds. It makes sense, consequently, that the villain should try to imprison the hero under the same giant helmet; that is, the threat of retribution makes Manfred aware of the unlawfulness of his position. This, in turn, awakens his sense of honor (Theodore speaks up from among the bystanders), which he immediately tries to repress. Theodore escapes temporarily through the hole the helmet has made in the paving of the courtyard, bringing him into the subterranean passages. That is, as Manfred's honor, he is confined in the dark recesses of the castle or Manfred's mind. And here he helps Isabella, the heroine, to escape from Manfred's lustful and incestuous pursuit, Manfred's sense of honor being, indeed, the only impulse that might lead him to spare her. The evil in Manfred, however, is more powerful than his honor, as we see when he angrily imprisons Theodore again, or in other words, again shuts up, represses, his sense of honor.

These correspondences between the characters and abstract qualities give this and other Gothic tales their quasi-allegorical air, but in the scenes that yield this kind of interpretation there is also a great deal of sexual symbolism that adds a rather different dimension, turning the interplay of abstract qualities into an exploration of Manfred's aberrant psychology. Much of the sexual symbolism revolves around Isabella. The daughter figure, who was to have married Conrad, becomes the object of Manfred's incestuous lust, and eventually marries the hero. When, fleeing Manfred, she comes upon Theodore in the subterranean passages, Isabella directs Theodore to open a secret lock in a trapdoor leading to a tunnel, although both are strangers to the place and the only light is a single moonbeam. Should we miss the sexual undertones to this scene, we later find her, in that incident frequently cited by critics, refusing out of maidenly modesty to follow Theodore into the depths of the caves, where they may take refuge from imminent danger. This moment in the novel is often pointed out as an example of the ridiculous lengths to which the authors of Gothic tales go to emphasize the "purity" of their heroines. But the whole scene has sexual significance. Isabella's refusal to go deep into the caves with Theodore can be seen as a refusal of sexual advances rendered symbolically in a tale in which actual sexual advances by these embodiments of Virtue would be impossible.

As a result of her refusal, her father finds the two of them at the mouth of the cave and there is an immediate clash between him and Theodore, who almost kills him—with a sword. Thus, the handsome, youthful hero has been brought into direct conflict with both the father figures in the novel, Manfred and Isabella's father, who are contending for both Isabella and hegemony over the principality to which Theodore is, in fact, heir. The story reenacts the myth of power wrested from the old king by the young prince. In its association with the incest theme, the conflict over the daughter figure between the boyish hero and the two father figures suggests an Oedipal struggle between son and father for sexual possession of the woman. We should note here that the open conflict between the young and the old man is precipitated by the "over-niceness" of the young woman in her relations with the young man. This sort of subtlety pervades the entire Gothic tradition. There are many other features of the novel that have distinct sexual overtones, such as the stabbing of the second daughter figure, Matilda, the giant sword, and more.

The rest of the novel also lends itself to this sort of interpretation. In summary, the cardboard characters of *Otranto,* moving through improbable supernatural events, tell us that Manfred, a good character at heart, has been driven and twisted into evil in his attempt to maintain his inheritance, which is the character (castle) passed on to him from his grandfather whose enthroned wickedness usurped the place of the Good (Alfonso) within him. Driven wild by his sense of his own impotence (his barren wife Hippolyta and his feeble son who is destroyed), Manfred descends to incest. This sin, which mirrors the self, is presented first explicitly in his attempt to marry Isabella then symbolically when he stabs his daughter Matilda. This is again a self-destructive impulse to repress all goodness within himself, for Matilda, an entirely spiritual being who wished to devote her life to God by entering a convent, represents goodness itself, divorced from the entanglements of worldly life. She recognizes Alfonso in Theodore, instantly loves him (the Good), and so releases him from the prison in which Manfred has confined him. Thus, Manfred's good daughter, whom he spurns when his evil is upon him, releases his sense of honor again, but it only plagues him the more. As a consequence, after many a complication, Theodore (Manfred's honor) again rescues Isabella (the object of Manfred's incestuous lust). Honor, however, is once more negated when Manfred kills Matilda, mistaking her for Isabella as she talks with Theodore before the statue of Alfonso. This murder of his own spiritual being brings about both the collapse and the regeneration of Manfred. When the enormity of the deed bursts upon his consciousness, Manfred and the castle collapse simultaneously. The spirit of Alfonso (Manfred's spirit of Goodness) is translated into heaven as Manfred recognizes his own evil and the destruction he has brought on himself, and retires to a spiritual life in a monastery.

As the successive generations of Manfred's line have become increasingly degenerate under the distorting pressure of evil, so the descendants of Alfonso have grown increasingly noble through suffering. The spirit of nobility bursts asunder the walls of the castle, the closed world of Manfred's evil, and Theodore stands forth, not as the inheritor of a crumbled ruin, but as the personification of triumphant nobility above and greater than the worldly power represented by the principality of Otranto.

Thus, the apparently tragic ending of the novel is symbolically optimistic. The view of good and evil it conveys is consonant with the deistic outlook of Walpole and many of his contemporaries and the otherwise incongruous comic resolution in the final paragraph, in which Theodore and Isabella decide on marriage to be sustained by contemplation of the beloved spirit of Matilda, makes sense as a symbolic rendering of moral order restored.

It may be objected that this sort of interpretation reads more into Walpole's tale than is really there. Eighteenth-century novelists are not usually thought of as dredging up subconscious sexual images, or writing dream fantasies, or fictionalizing psychological ideas. Yet what we know of the late eighteenth century and of Walpole himself provides evidence to support these possibilities.[10] All Walpole remembered of his dream was the giant hand on the stair rail, but his own feeling that he wrote the novel under the pressure of that dream indicates that he was able to release his imagination and allow the story to well up in his mind, rather than starting with an idea and a conscious plan.[11] That he should have chosen a medieval setting for it was, he said, natural to a mind afloat in the Gothic atmosphere of Strawberry Hill, and, indeed, he was just the person to invent the device of the identification of the villain and his castle, regarding his own house, as he did, as an expression of his personality, an indulgence of his fancy.[12] At the same time, the sort of personal expression this suggests was quite naturally welded in Walpole's work with the fictionalization of ideas. His interests lay with the antiquarianism that was part of the Sentimentalist movement of the day, a movement that, in its many aspects, was bent on exploring the emotions. In literature, Sentimentalism was embodying ideas about human nature, and Walpole was part of that movement.

Thus, personal reasons account for Walpole's having been the one to produce the tale that began the whole tradition, while the age he lived in accounts for the genre's having appeared when it did. No such work, after all, appeared from the pens of authors under similar personal pressures in earlier times. The late eighteenth century was an era of interested inquiry into the nature of the human mind and of an interest in the inner self that was also manifested in other new genres appearing at the time which probe and reveal the psyche.[13]

Although Walpole and his contemporaries cannot have known his work would establish a literary convention, they were aware of the nature of the work itself. We can already see in the preface to the second edition of *Otranto* what Walpole saw himself as having achieved in the novel. He states explicitly that when he blended "the two kinds of romance, the ancient and the modern," the ancient, which was fantasy, freed his imagination, while the modern, reflecting the real world, lent reality to his characters.[14] The characters are not very convincingly real, of course, but they are recognizably eighteenth-century figures embodying current ideas about the human mind. By placing them in the world of dreams and fairy tales, Walpole was able to present his age's concept of human evil—pride, hatred, violence, cruelty, incest—as part of man's psychology. The one kind of romance enabled him to delve into his own subconscious, the other helped him to relate what he found there to the human condition in general.

He was able to use the by-now traditional Gothic "claptrap" symbolically because, like later Gothic authors and their readers, he did not believe in the supernatural happenings that activate his tale. Regarding the Middle Ages as a benighted and superstitious time, these authors could use its superstitions to create their fictions. The "editor's" claim in the preface, for instance, that the tale is probably written by an "artful priest" to reinforce his readers' superstitions establishes Walpole's use of its supernatural elements for purely literary purposes. We find the same attitude in Ann Radcliffe's essay on "The Supernatural in Poetry" and Nathan Drake's *Literary Hours,* as well as in scholarly eighteenth-century studies of medieval and renaissance romance, such as Hurd's and Percy's. Hurd, for instance, says of criticism of the marvelous: "This criticism . . . supposes that the poets . . . expect to have their lyes believed. Surely they are not so unreasonable. They think it enough, if they can but bring you to *imagine* the possibility of them. . . . [But the reader] is best pleased when he is made to conceive (he minds not by what magic) the existence of such things as his reason tells him did not, and were never likely to exist."[15] Scott says the same thing in his life of Walpole: "The reader who is required to admit the belief of supernatural interference understands precisely what is demanded of him; and, if he be a gentle reader, throws his mind into the attitude best adopted to humor the deceit . . . and grants, for the time of perusal, the premises on which the fable depends."[16] Hurd, like Walpole later, regrets the loss of imaginative power in an age, as he sees it, bound by the fetters of rationalism. The "growth of Reason which dawned in Elizabethan times has routed imagination," he says, complaining that, in the eighteenth century: "What we have gotten by this revolution, . . . is a great deal of common sense. What we have lost, is a world of fine fabling."[17] Walpole, in seeking to restore the world of the imagination, of fantasy, by drawing imagery from his own subconscious mind, showed his readers, as in a mirror, their minds and the place of evil in them. The approval that greeted the tale suggests that it spoke to a widespread interest in Walpole's time.

Walpole's scornful rejection of Clara Reeve's attempt to minimize the supernatural further shows that he understood how the symbolism of his novel worked, as did Ann Radcliffe when she put similar symbolic devices to use. The very fact that Ann Radcliffe first presents her supernatural phenomena and then supplies explanations for them shows that she was using them for aesthetic reasons, to evoke the sublime and thus arouse pity and terror in the reader. In reawakening the imaginative world within himself by setting the tale in the dark, irrational past, Walpole started an enduring tradition. The inevitable doubts that arise about applying a complex psychological interpretation to his work seem to be far less bothersome when recognized in others.

For example, Poe's tales, which have received an abundance of symbolic analysis, have much in common with Walpole's novel. Poe's "The Fall of the House of Usher" shows remarkable resemblances to *Otranto* in both theme and device, which seem not to be either mere coincidence or simple imitation on Poe's part.

Manfred's castle in *Otranto* and Poe's House of Usher fall apart in an identical defiance of physical laws and in direct correspondence to the owner's collapse. In both tales, building and owner are one and the same. Poe says so explicitly, and we can see in the affinity of the two works that Walpole's fantasy, too, strikes deep into psychological paradigms of the mind. Poe's narrator has told us at the very beginning that the inbreeding of the Usher family has caused "the perfect keeping of the character of the people." The "deficiency . . . of collateral issue, and the consequent undeviating transmission, from sire to son, of the patrimony with the name. . . . had, at length, so identified the two as to merge the original title of the estate in the quaint and equivocal appellation of the 'House of Usher'—an appellation which seemed to include, in the minds of the peasantry who used it, both the family and the family mansion."[18] The house is then further specifically identified with Roger Usher. When Roger disintegrates, the House, meaning the family, of Usher collapses into ruin, and the house, the building, in which that family has lived splits apart and falls into the tarn.

Poe's tale of degeneracy and incest contains no comic resolution and its horror displays little of Walpole's optimistic view of the place of good and evil in the mind. But Poe uses devices similar to Walpole's (collapsing house and master; subterranean passages; indirect, mediated narration; romance characters, one of them wraith-like; an uncanny painting and a premonitory storm), and he uses them in a way that seems an urgently personal expression, indicating that he, too, has brought together his own psyche and prevailing psychological ideas, and is using the convention Walpole had established for the same purposes as Walpole did, while giving it a twist peculiar to himself. This is the way a convention works.

Otranto is just the first of many a fictional plunge into the subconscious mind. Some later Gothic novels owe their origins, as it does, to actual dreams. Others result from their authors' conscious dredging up of dream symbols from their own minds. The later authors added new devices to fit their particular needs, but all these works are set up as revelations of horror. They present as psychological evil a sexual obsession, overwhelming guilt, or pride that defies the limits God has set for man, and they seek to arouse fear and sickening horror in the reader. These tales may see evil as an aberration in man or as an inherent part of his nature, they may question the value judgments placed on the phenomena they are symbolizing, but they all show the world its own dreams, drawing the reader into their closed worlds, playing on his emotions, and preventing him from denying that what he experiences in the novel may also be within himself.

It seems almost paradoxical that this depiction of man's nightmares should have grown out of the gentle tenets of Benevolism and the Sentimentalist movement.[19] Yet the works of the first Gothic authors are based on the Benevolist view of man.[20] The central belief of that view is that man, though fallen indeed, still has the potential for Good. An infinitely benevolent Creator has not abandoned his creature to inevitable depravity; man is born, not inherently evil, but with a nature that, if he is properly nurtured, enables him to live the virtuous life and so be happy. These ideas, held by the Sentimentalists, have been traced back to the Cambridge Platonists, a group of theologians at Cambridge University in the late seventeenth century. Their followers, the Latitudinarians, were active in both Church and State during and after the Restoration period, preaching religious tolerance and an active charity, and were highly influential. With help from Shaftesbury and the deists, they were primarily responsible for the widespread acceptance of Benevolism, as Louis Bredvold, among others, has shown. The Platonists, as Bredvold notes, were explicit about man's natural goodness. He quotes Henry More as saying, "Virtue . . . is the health of the soul, its natural state of well-being," and Benjamin Whichcote as writing: "Nothing is more certainly true than that all Vice is unnatural and contrary to the nature of Man. . . . A depraved and vicious Mind is as really the Sickness and Deformity thereof, as any foul and loathsome disease is to the body. . . . The good Man is an Instrument in Tune."[21]

If he lives in conformity with the nature with which God has endowed him, man will be in harmony with Nature, the natural order, and so be happy.[22] To accomplish this he must nurture and cultivate his innate good feelings. Social virtue springs from love of one's fellow man which must be fostered by developing the good feelings of the heart.[23] The Sentimental movement that grew out of these ideas is thus a system of thought that makes "virtue" manifest in "good feelings," in pleasurable inward sensations. The protagonists of the Sentimental novels, the man and woman of feeling, are repositories of such virtuous feelings and the inner content that goes with them. Demonstrating, through the emotions they express and through their occasional actions, a natural benevolence uncorrupted by a faulty upbringing, they are oversimplified as characters. Objections were made, in the eighteenth century, as they are today, to the self-indulgent effusions and apparent smugness of these characters. Even those who admired Sentimental literature did so for the "fine feelings" to which it gave expression. Yet those heroes and heroines who exclaim about their own feelings and, in fact, do little else but emote, reflect the Benevolists' replacement of the traditional faith in Reason as the foundation stone of morality with the concept of feeling (Sentiment) as man's moral arbiter. All men are endowed by their Creator with a Moral Sense, the innate power that enables them to tell right from wrong instantaneously. Properly cultivated sensibilities keep people sensitive to this monitor and enable them to "sympathize," to feel with and for others. It was the didactic duty of literature to direct the "passions" toward the good ends for which God implanted them in man by drawing models of refined sensibility.[24] The Sentimental novel educates the reader's emotions by embodying in these characters correctly cultivated feeling, which the reader shares as he reads.

Evil, in this system of thought, is that which mars the harmony of the universe. It is the twisting and distortion of the potentially good feelings into destructive impulses that render the individual unhappy by setting him at war with God's harmony within and outside himself. Both good and evil are inner states of man's mind and, since beauty lies in God's order, the good and the beautiful are one, and evil is monstrous.[25] These equations of goodness with beauty and wrongdoing with ugliness, which by mid-century were appearing in the writings of Adam Smith and others, were put to use by the authors of Sentimental and Gothic literature.[26] They made their good characters physically lovely and gave the evil ones twisted bodies and ugly faces. The Gothic novel, in making monstrosity the outward show of the terrible inner distortion of man's innate good nature into evil, is thus an expression of the other side of the benevolist ideas reflected in the Sentimental novel. It forms a variant of the Sentimental genre, with related structures, forms, and devices. Sentimental novels reflect an ideal that, coming from God, is possibly realizable; the Gothic represents the distortion of that ideal.

Sentimental and Gothic literature is, as a result, highly paradigmatic. The characters are more nearly representations of the general human state than depictions of individual human beings. They are not personifications of good and evil nor yet either type characters or highly individualized portrayals. Occupying the hazy no-man's land between the abstraction of allegory and the "reality" of social and comic novels, they are manifestations of the semi-abstract, semi-real area occupied by concepts of the place of good and evil in the human mind. These characters are not realistically drawn because, to represent what all men are like, they must be drawn without strongly individual quirks; yet they are also not allegorical figures, because they do represent people, however simplified. They are strictly limited portrayals and their reference beyond themselves to the ideas they embody makes their outlines fuzzy. Plot, setting, structure in this literature are also determined by such outside reference to Sentimentalist concepts, lending an insubstantiality to the whole work that is desirable because it is conducive to evocation of the sublime, and so a prime means for catching the reader up in the work.[27] These characteristics bring about the special kind of symbolism found in Gothic tales, which, directed to the reader's feelings, put him in touch with intuitively known aspects of his own nature. To understand Gothic fiction, then, it is necessary to open up Sentimental fiction to interpretation not unlike that which Gothic fiction demands.

In the past, this has not been done because, although Sentimentalism itself has been well and thoroughly delineated by modern critics, the Sentimental novels embodying its ideas have been, like Gothic tales, read for the surface fiction only. For the most part, they have met with critical treatment even rougher than that meted out to Gothic fiction. If Gothic tales are said to instill horror for its own sake, Sentimental novels are said to evoke feeling in the reader that reciprocates the characters' tearful, exclamatory expression of emotion for emotion's sake and to provide an opportunity for self-indulgence in pity and self-pity.[28]

While it is true that the reader is intended to reciprocate the characters' feelings, these novels are not meant to provide an opportunity for pleasurable weeping only. The eighteenth-century ideas of man's nature, which Sentimental literature makes manifest, guaranteed a correspondence between the feelings portrayed in the characters of literature and those to be aroused in the reader. As Adam Smith puts it: "Whatever is the passion which arises from any object in the person principally concerned, an analogous emotion springs up, at the thought of his situation, in the breast of every attentive spectator. Our joy for the deliverance of those heroes of tragedy or romance who interest us, is as sincere as our grief for their distress, and our fellow-feeling with their misery is not more real than that with their happiness . . . In every passion of which the mind of man is susceptible, the emotions of the by-stander always correspond to what, by bringing the case home to himself, he imagines, should be the sentiments of the sufferer."[29] When characters express feelings of compassion, describing their free-flowing tears and the warmth that envelops their hearts at the words of gratitude of some "poor, good people" they have helped (often materially), they appeal to reciprocal feelings in the reader. They do so with the intention of refining those feelings. But, because a first-person account is frequently used, characters, readers, and authors alike have been accused of self-righteousness bred of congratulating themselves on laudable sentiments which remain untranslated into action. Above all, these novels are criticized for their unconvincing portrayal of character. The condemnation is then sealed once and for all by the frequently expressed opinion that this was a literature "for women by women," which means, either implicitly or explicitly, that it was for and by a silly and unliterary social group.[30] Yet, in fact, the Sentimental authors were sophisticated people, both men and women, interested in a new formulation of morality, a rather optimistic idealism. They preached that happiness could be derived from a simple life lived close to nature, and celebrated virtuous love in marriage as idyllic.

The Sentimental novels make the reader weep with and for the afflicted characters and the Gothic tales inspire pity and terror, similarly experienced by both reader and characters, to transport the reader beyond himself into the world of the mind. The reader's natural compassion is aroused and his sensibility refined through the sympathy which he and the protagonists share in viewing the Sentimental scene.[31] The Sentimental novelists thus seek to cultivate the reader's finer feelings by appealing to his Moral Sense and engaging his sympathy. They invite the reader to "admire fine feelings" in this way because the emotions expressed are neither a means of characterization nor a way of creating atmosphere, but themselves the subject matter of the novel. Setting and characterization take on a special quality that gives them that air of unreality so frequently criticized. It is, nevertheless, a "sentimental journey," a journey through the emotions, on which these novelists first send their readers. They were very serious about their task, and their works found acceptance in literary circles.

Henry Mackenzie, for instance, was a dignified Scots lawyer with serious literary aims, whose novels were admired by the literati of his time.[32] He can no more be supposed to have written his Sentimental novels as circulating-library fare than Horace Walpole can be imagined to have wrought the first Gothic tale to meet the tastes of a newly book-hungry audience of merchant-class women. The novels of sentiment of Frances Sheridan were admired by Johnson and Boswell alike; *Evelina* launched Fanny Burney into Society. The *Vicar of Wakefield* enchanted Goethe; *Tristram Shandy* achieved lionization for Sterne in London and Paris. There is thus abundant evidence that the Sentimental novel was not just a temporary aberration or a sop for a fatuous audience. There were, of course, circulating libraries and a plenitude of romances; the reading public had grown in numbers; and more women than previously both could read and had the leisure to do so; but these facts do not alter the seriousness of the initial movement or the value of some of the works. The Sentimental and Gothic novels simply were not written and read only by women and were not only pulp fare. Both types enjoyed a vogue that resulted in the production, even in the eighteenth century, of both serious works and formulaic imitations.

Sentimental literature has fared even worse than Gothic, mainly because its central concern is to portray virtue, while the Gothic highlights vice. The Sentimental consequently tends to be unexciting and unreal without being fantasy. In serious literature only its heroines survived into the nineteenth century, as pale and untarnished female protagonists of many a Victorian novel, although some male figures—the more schematic of Dickens' heroes and a central character like Thackeray's Pendennis—retain the earmarks of Sentimentalism. Whatever the ultimate literary value of the Sentimental novels, however, they merit discussion on their own terms. They sought only to a very limited extent to portray "real people" in "real" social situations.[33] Didactic novels, portraying in their characters innate goodness unwarped by the corruptions of civilization; appealing, by showing finely developed sensibility through the Moral Sense, to their readers' own innate goodness, encourage their readers to develop their Sensibility and to avoid corruption. The Sentimentalists did not deny that the world was an evil place. They were well aware and, indeed, frequently asserted that a virtuous Sentimental character was a *rara avis,* and they set the ordinary wicked world in opposition to their virtuous protagonists. They did so, however, to put these good characters in relief. It was with the virtuous protagonists and the fine honing of their sensibility that they had to do. In portraying them they did not delineate the nature of virtue but the virtuous nature. They demonstrated how mankind might be virtuous.

The history of the Sentimental novel has already been chronicled.[34] The variety of its forms, however, merits discussion, for it indicates how widespread Sentimentalist ideas were and shows how they were related to concepts of society as well as ideas about the nature of the human mind and of human virtue. There are comic and social Sentimental novels and others that have a symbolic structure that the Gothic borrowed. These novels are many in number but a few examples and the models on which they are based sufficiently demonstrate the different types.

There is no doubt that the novels of Marivaux, appearing between 1730 and 1740 and quickly translated into English, influenced English authors as did Rousseau's *Julie, ou La Nouvelle Héloïse* (1761). Richardson and Fielding were also primary influences on the Sentimental novelists, as on so many others. They themselves give expression to such benevolist concepts as that virtue is the only happiness; that virtue is its own reward; and that it may receive that reward in this world. But it is technique, above all, that the Sentimentalists derive from them. Richardson's epistolary mode was a truly innovative means of portraying character by allowing the reader to view the fictional world of a work through the eyes of the protagonist. The authors of serious Sentimental novels adapted it to their purposes, while those who used comic techniques followed Fielding. *David Simple* (1744) by Fielding's sister Sarah, with its good and bad brothers, while foreshadowing the "education novel" of a later day, is Fieldingesque, organized, picaresque style, as a journey through life in which society is constantly measured against the virtuous Sentimentalist ideas of David. Fielding himself refers to the work as "a Romance" and "a comic Epic Poem," like *Joseph Andrews,* patterned on the *Odyssey.* His preface to the second edition contains several remarks that mark the novel as Sentimental. "The Merit of this Work," he writes, "consists in a vast Penetration into human Nature, a deep and profound Discernment of all the Mazes, Windings and Labyrinths, which perplex the Heart of Man." It is necessary to point out these features to the general reader, he says, because only a profound genius may realize that they are what the novel reveals. In answer to critics who thought Sarah Fielding too young and inexperienced (she was thirty-seven when the novel appeared!) to have written it, he notes that it takes very little knowledge of the world to know its evil, and that "a short Communication with her own Heart, will leave the Author of this Book very little to seek abroad of all the Good which is to be found in Human Nature."[35]

This is more than just a compliment to his sister; the heart, if not corrupt, is the source of knowledge of "Human Nature" and Sarah Fielding's hero, David Simple, is such a heart. Not very gripping as a character, he is useful in showing the follies of the world and the value of friendship. Unconvincing though David is, the fact that Sarah Fielding chose to cast her novel in the form of an eighteenth-century *Odyssey* shows that she shared her brother's belief that such goodness is inherent in human nature and so possible in the world and "probable" in literature. Neither is likely to have thought that a paragon of virtue was an everyday phenomenon. This is why Fielding writes that "this Fable hath in it these three difficult Ingredients, which will be found on Consideration to be always necessary to Works of this kind, viz. that the main End or Scope be at once amiable, ridiculous and natural."[36] It is the middle quality ("ridiculous") that makes it possible to integrate the ideal of human potential in a portrait of the real world. Fielding's own Parson Adams is, like Don Quixote, an idealist not an ideal and is made ridiculous to make him acceptable to the reader.

The same is true of Goldsmith's vicar in *The Vicar of Wakefield* (1766, written circa 1762), which is strongly influenced by Fielding's work, and less directly of Sterne's Yorick, particularly in *A Sentimental Journey* (1768), and Uncle Toby. Parson Adams and the vicar are laughable in their vanity and this is what catches the reader's sympathy—vanity leads them into many a clash with a world more vicious than they and, though they may lose the immediate battle, they are shown to be true to their ideals, unlike those who oppose them. The ideal is thus shown to be desirable as an ideal.

Such a scheme is adapted at some risk in other Sentimental novels by retaining the caricature of the worldly characters, making the central Sentimental character ridiculous only in his innocence, which causes him to fail to see the most blatant wickedness, and including tableaux in which the Sentimental character views scenes of pathos and the reader, seeing them over his shoulder, shares his distress. In this manner the reader's own sensibilities were to be educated. The most famous British Sentimental novel, Mackenzie's *The Man of Feeling* (1771), is organized on this scheme. Its opening page and its typographical vagaries utilize Sterne's comic techniques, but, in the opening section, Mackenzie establishes the hero as a serious portrayal of a man of sensibility. He then sends him on a journey that puts him in contact with the corrupt outside world. The "action" of this section of the novel is largely a record of the man of feeling's reactions to the situations he observes. In this way he is kept free from the moral taint that involvement in action inevitably brings, and the reader is invited to share his feelings, while admiring his elevated sensibility.

The events of the world and the lightly satiric tone with which Mackenzie's narrator presents the hero, Harley, force the reader to vacillate between serious and comic in a way that endangers the serious mood. Light though the comic element is, it is probably mainly responsible for the derision that the scenes of heavy pathos, particularly that of Harley's death, have frequently met. The problem occurs greatly aggravated in Smollett's *Humphrey Clinker,* which appeared in the same year as *The Man of Feeling*, and still more so in Fanny Burney's *Evelina* (1778). Both combine the journey structure of Fielding's novels with Richardson's epistolary technique. In both, Sentimental characters live and act alongside comic, Fieldingesque caricatures. The resultant incongruity is greater in *Evelina* than in Smollett's novel, in part because Smollett uses multiple correspondents. Jerry's affectionate comments on his uncle's behavior, for instance, balance any tendency in the reader to see Matt Bramble as only ridiculous. The reader is nevertheless forced into some rapid switching. While it is possible to imagine Tabitha sharing the same comic universe as Matt Bramble, Jerry and his sister are portrayed more seriously as denizens of the ordinary world. At the other extreme, Lishmahago almost seems to belong to that realm presented by the techniques of the grotesque. As a result, the tone is constantly in danger of breaking.

The extremes in *Evelina* are greater still. If we are inclined to go along with the compassionate Sentimental views of Evelina's guardian, we may balk at the grotesquerie with which the cruel treatment of her grandmother is described. Evelina's account of such incidents may seem inconsistent with the Sentimentalist characterization of her as a beautiful innocent brought up in the countryside.[37] If, on the other hand, such antics of Captain Mirvan and the beaux of Bath as the race between the two old women or the introduction of the monkey strike us as effective satirizations of society, we may take the effusions of Evelina's reconciliation with her father or the love scenes with Orville as also ludicrous exaggerations. Such is the danger of mixing Sentimentalism with the comic in order to show it in operation in the social world.

Other Sentimentalists are really concerned with the inner world and it is for this reason that they draw so heavily on Richardson's devices. Through the epistolary method he showed the world as seen through a character's eyes and by this means delineated the character psychologically. It is clear from his novels that Richardson fully understood what he had discovered, as an example from *Pamela* shows. When Pamela describes breathlessly how two bulls frightened her into retreating from her attempt to escape from Mr. B.'s house, until she saw that they were only cows of which she need not have been afraid, she tells us that she saw in the bulls the spirits of Mr. B. and Mrs. Jewkes, keeping her prisoner. Here, and in other instances, Richardson shows that it is Pamela's view that we have been given and, through it, the understanding of what it feels like to be a "poor maiden beset," a sixteen-year-old in the hands of a libertine master.[38]

This is a psychologizing technique, and it was useful to the Sentimentalists, seeking to present their characters' feelings and thoughts more than their actions, although it also has serious drawbacks. A letter writer who is sitting recording what has happened can be a part of or an observer of the action itself and naturally comments upon it as well. For Richardson, the epistolary method gave a sense of his characters "writing to the moment," that is, he used it to create suspense, but the same technique has a different effect in the Sentimental novel. Nothing could be less suspenseful than the first-person Sentimental novel in letters. A narration at one remove with a running comment on the action is, if the letter writer is also a Sentimental heroine, very slow moving and it is also a very limited method of characterization. Richardson had, in fact, hit upon a technique for creating suspense—the account in which the characters do not know the future, as opposed to the first-person account told with hindsight—but the Sentimental novels are so far from building up to a climactic action that their use of it does not create suspense. The epistolary technique is also the cause of the central character's appearing smug and seeming to luxuriate in feeling that has no consequences, that does not give rise to deeds.

A novel in letters does, nevertheless, keep the work centered in the letter writer's mind, as can be seen in Frances Brooke's *Emily Montague* (1769). An important part of this "the first American novel" is set in Canada and the account of that far-away place holds its own interest. Emily describes life among settlers in a vast and empty land virtually cut off in the winter from communication with the outside world. Life in Quebec, Montreal, and the surrounding countryside, however, forms only a rather sketchy background to the central love affair of Emily and Rivers, two decidedly one-sided, noble Sentimental characters. The movement between Canada and England sets up a variant of the city-country contrast that places innocence in symbolic opposition to venality throughout the eighteenth-century novel. *Emily Montague* is much more a portrait of its heroine's sensibility than a Canadian landscape.

The city-country contrast is particularly useful to those Sentimental novels that embody the ideas of Sentimentalism in their characters through a symbolic structure that isolates the letter writer from the everyday world. When the letters are sent out to a world that is in some sense equivalent to the reader's own, the world from which they are written appears remote and strange. Because it is set up as different from the reader's, that world can be made to delineate "the naked soul" of sensibility, especially when the letter writer dwells on feelings and sufferings. The supreme example of this type is Goethe's *The Sorrows of Young Werther* (1774). By having Werther write to his friend and emphasize his isolation, which is voluntary, Goethe evokes in the reader a sense that the village in the countryside is a closed world shut off from the outside. The tableau-like scenes (the village maiden at the well, the two children on the green) and Werther as observer and commentator as much as participant in them; the symbolic parallels (the stories of the young man and of the widow and the young man driven mad by love); the correspondences of season and weather with moods—all these make the events of Werther's short remainder of life utlimately the events of an inner world, the contours of a state of being.

Mackenzie's *Julia de Rubigné* (1777) uses the same method but, on the model of *Clarissa,* has pairs of letter writers to provide multiple points-of-view. This allows Mackenzie to introduce a decidedly Gothic element. The letters from the closed world are sent to two separate recipients, from the heroine, Julia, on the one hand, and, on the other, from a character portrayed as the villains in Gothic literature are portrayed. The closed world with its correspondence to an inner state reveals the nature of Good in

Julia and the nature of evil in the villain she marries. Mackenzie's novel thus stands like a demonstration of the connection between Sentimental and Gothic fiction, the same technique having been used to body forth the ideas of Sentimentalism and the corollaries of these that give rise to the Gothic tales.

In much the same way, we can see a commonality of purpose in Bernardin de St. Pierre's *Paul and Virginia* (1787), a Sentimental novel, and some later novels in the Gothic tradition. The narrative structure of *Paul and Virginia* is built on the same principle as an epistolary novel like *Werther* but it is not in letter form. Instead, it uses a system of multiple narration—the narrator who appears in the frame of the novel relays to us the story that an old man tells him of people and events that have left hardly any trace. Because the world in which Paul and Virginia grow up is thus presented as remote, we accept it as an idyll and its inhabitants as true children of Nature. They are representatives of mankind as it might be, free from the corruptions of civilization. They are not, however, Noble Savages. Rather, they are fairy-tale figures of pure sensibility and so, ultimately, portraits of man's unsullied inner nature. The idyllic life in nature appears again in Gothic fiction, where it is invaded and destroyed by a dark, albeit ambiguous, force. This is a major theme in *Frankenstein* (1818), *Wuthering Heights* (1847), and *The Turn of the Screw* (1898), and each of these has a similar system of mediated narration. It is an enabling device, establishing the work as fantasy and laying the groundwork for symbolic interpretation.

The device of the discovered manuscript, which Walpole had used in *Otranto* to achieve a sense of remoteness, is also used by Mackenzie with the same purpose in both *The Man of Feeling* and *Julia de Rubigné*. Mackenzie, indeed, plays with the device, presenting us with a damaged manuscript, as Clara Reeve does in the *Old English Baron*. This relates these works to another genre, the fragment, which from Nevile's *The Isle of Pines* (1668) through Fielding's

Journey from This World to the Next (1743) to Sterne's *A Sentimental Journey* (1768) adds a sense of the transitoriness of life and the fragility of evidence. In Sentimental and Gothic fiction the remoteness of the world portrayed is increased by this sense of its frailty. The fragmentary manuscript suggests a world of beings so delicate that they were in danger of vanishing without leaving a trace. We would never have heard of Paul and Virginia, the narrator would have us believe, if he, who could record their story, had not happened on the old man, the last who could tell it. Structural devices and methods of narration thus correspond to characterization. The world in which the characters are found is as delicate as they because ultimately the two are one. Delicacy, a proneness to weep and to faint, these are the outward signs of sensibility. The characters who display them, however, are not depictions of mawkish human beings any more than Gothic villains are realistic portraits of human predators. Rather, both they and the correspondent settings make manifest the fragility of virtue and the torments of evil.

Sentimental and Gothic tales have their own rules and methods. They share common methods of characterization, structural and narrative systems, devices and images, and a common aesthetic because they share underlying ideas and pursue a common purpose—to present representations of the human mind in a fiction directed at its reader's feelings. The aesthetic principles on which they are written developed parallel to the development in thought expressed in Sentimental and Gothic fiction. The Sentimental and Gothic novels are very *au courant* in putting into practice the theories of their day and accord with the new ideas both in subject matter and form. If they are effusive, it is part of the new emotionalism; if they are melodramatic, melodrama was the coming thing. They put the sublime and the picturesque to special uses, and these were very much the modes of the time.

As with the Sentimental novel, the reputation of Gothic

fiction as the product of romance-writing women is quite simply contrary to the facts. The Gothic authors were not women striving to satisfy the longing for excitement in their home-bound sisters of little education. They were of both sexes and had interests parallel to those of their contemporaries who were busy learnedly unearthing old ballads, the Nordic myths, and other phenomena of the "Dark Ages," or those who invented their own versions, as Macpherson and Chatterton did. In search of symbolic constructs for their fictional worlds of the mind these authors exhibited the same affinities as their archaizing contemporaries. Both Ann Radcliffe and Clara Reeve, moreover, were educated women who wrote about the literary theory on which their novels were based, and the novels themselves were appreciated by an audience far distant from the frequenters of lending libraries. Such learned and literary types as Gray, Warburton, and Joseph Warton had high praise for *The Castle of Otranto* and *The Mysteries of Udolpho.*[39] Scott admired and wrote about all the principal Gothic authors and numbered Matthew Lewis among his literary friends, as did Byron, who was also a great admirer of *Otranto.*[40]

The Gothic authors, writing a new type of romance that would free the imagination of the author and engage the emotions of the reader, consciously wrote fantasy in the face of the rising taste for the social novel. The actual terms "romance" and "novel" were unstable at the time, as can be seen from Clara Reeve's effort to "fix" them in her *Progress of Romance.*[41] They were at times used interchangeably, as they can be today, and at others to differentiate the two kinds. The kinds themselves, however, were consistently seen as separate, the one "fabulous" and the other a "picture of real life."[42] As Walpole and Clara Reeve claimed, the Gothic was a new type combining techniques of the new novel writing with the fantasy of the "old" romance. It thus put the ordinary world in touch with the mysterious. This linking of the techniques of "new" and "old" romance (or "novel" and "romance") reflects the increasingly inductive study of the human mind. The fictional form would educate the reader by manifesting the connection between abstract concepts and general human reality. Through the isolated world, ostensibly remote in space or time, the Gothic novels explore the dark aspects of the mind and, through their characters, they locate that world within everyday experience. The paradigmatic, eighteenth-century European types who people Gothic fiction are frightened almost witless by the impingement of supernatural horrors and diabolical cruelty on their neat, virtuous, and orderly lives. They are thus half figures of the imagination, half representations of ordinary people.

The Gothic authors used their devices to make manifest the effects and sometimes the cause of evil in the mind of a creature (man) with a potential to be free of it. The Fall of man was still the cause of his evil—this is why the problem is abysmal and the abyss itself used as a metaphor throughout the tradition—but since the Fall had not resulted in inevitable depravity and evil was unnatural, a fresh delineation of the psychology of good was needed, which, in turn, inevitably meant a new formulation of the psychology of evil.[43] These authors wished to show their readers the "myself am Hell" of Milton's Satan and the "paradise within thee, happier far" of his new Man.[44] The attempts to portray the "Good" inevitably opened up the problem of the nature of human evil. Indeed, among the early Gothic novels, there are two kinds: those that use the Gothic supernatural to "ravish" and "transport" their readers by opposing the virtuous of Sentimentalism to Gothic evil and then conclude with a Sentimental resolution; and those that, using the Sentimental characters as contrast, focus their attention on the villain and conclude with the disaster that overwhelms him.

Contemporary aesthetic theory, itself an aspect of the Sentimentalist movement, shows that both authors and readers were aware of the questions these works raise. In a series of essays John and Anna Aikin defend "romances" for their didactic value and examine the psychological effects they have on the reader.[45] In the process, they discuss most of the problems that the Sentimental and the early Gothic novels presented for the eighteenth century and still present today. They also attempt to pin down the reasons for the appeal this literature has. In discussing "objects of pity," they wonder why the pain caused by a pitiable scene is nonetheless pleasurable and consequently pleasing to readers. They explain that it is so because "the view of human afflictions" calls forth "our benevolent feelings," which are, of course, pleasurable, as a result of "that relation between the moral and natural system of man, which has connected a degree of satisfaction with every action or emotion productive of the general welfare."[46] Another essay qualifies this idea: "The view or relation of mere misery can never be pleasing," because the strong sympathy it arouses in us is "a feeling of pure unmixed pain . . . and never produces that melting sorrow, that thrill of tenderness, to which we give the name of pity."[47] If the pain caused by sympathy for suffering is to produce "the sweet emotion of pity," it must be mixed with "love, esteem, the complacency we take in the contemplation of beauty, of mental or moral excellence, called forth and rendered more interesting, by circumstances of pain and danger. Tenderness is much more properly than sorrow, the spring of tears. . . . No distress which produces tears is wholly without a mixture of pleasure."[48] Thus, when the Sentimental hero witnesses the distress of a worthy, virtuous individual or family in a tableau-like scene, it arouses in him, and reciprocally in the reader, the pleasurable pain of sympathy and benevolence. Because the feeling is pleasurable the reader will not only keep reading but will also be taught the value of sensibility.

Hence, the heroes and heroines weep as well as the reader. Their outer persons conform to their inner beings, because "deformity is always disgusting" and "the poet and romance writer" are justified "in giving a larger share of beauty to their principal figures than is usually met in common life."[49] Characters must not be too perfect, however. To hold the reader's sympathy "virtue must be mixed with something of helplessness or imperfection, with an excessive sensibility, or a simplicity bordering on weakness." This is probably the reason for the frequent but puzzling defeat of the Sentimental protagonists who so often die after passively enduring a great many vicissitudes.

Other contemporary writings, as well as those of the Aikins, show why authors set about terrifying their readers with their Gothic novels. Even Sentimental fiction draws the reader out of himself through his sympathy for the characters and it does so in order to put him in touch with his own nature. The Gothic novelists go a step further and evoke the sublime. To make manifest the evil within they present it in a "sublime" character, which will raise a "pleasing terror" in the reader and again draw him out of himself.

The sublime was an important aesthetic concept throughout the eighteenth century as Samuel Monk shows in his study of the subject.[50] He quotes critics of the time who list certain physical phenomena or human actions that are the means of creating a sublime effect—tall cliffs, vast seas, dire chasms, noble deeds. Sights and sounds of great magnitude fill the mind with wonder and amazement. If an idea of danger is involved, the result will be a terror that is pleasing because the viewer knows he is himself safe.[51]

It at first seems strange that eighteenth-century critics should have suggested the sublime could be evoked automatically in this way, but their views are more complex than is immediately apparent. There is a gradual transfer, as Monk notes, from the view of the sublime as "residing in objects" to "the exploration of the subject rather than the description of the object."[52] Nathan Drake, discussing descriptive poetry, makes a great deal of the evocative power of natural scenery and transfers this power intact to descriptions of such scenery. Tranquil evenings and moonlit nights will produce a pleasing contemplative mood and so can be used in literature as directly corresponding to the mood of the characters or as sharply contrasting with it. It should be noted, however, that the characters arrive in the landscape with the mood already upon them; it is the reader's emotions that, already in tune with the characters', will be enhanced by the description.[53] And it is also true that, however sublime or beautiful a landscape, it will tire the eye and the mind if there are no figures in it. "The mind is soon satisfied with the view of rock, of wood and water, but if the peasant, the shepherd, or the fisherman be seen, or, if still more engaging, a group of figures be thrown into some important action, the heart as well as the imagination is affected."[54] Furthermore, Drake writes in another essay, painters and writers who place figures like Rosa's banditti in their landscapes effect "an impression of the utmost power, and not otherwise procurable than through the medium of a combination of this kind."[55] Having established the idea that the reader shares the feelings of the characters, however, eighteenth-century critics wonder why readers should submit to the "pain of terror" instead of avoiding it by putting down the book. This was a difficult question to resolve.

The Aikins grapple with it directly, if not very satisfactorily. The "relation between the moral and natural system of man" that makes pity pleasurable because it is socially useful, does not explain the taste for frightening stories: "The apparent delights with which we dwell upon objects of pure terror, where our moral feelings are not in the least concerned, and no passion seems to be excited but the depressing one of fear, is a paradox of the heart, much more difficult of solution."[56] Yet there is a great deal of evidence that this taste for terror exists. Among others, "the old Gothic romance and the Eastern tale, . . . however a refined critic may censure them as absurd and extravagant, will ever retain a most powerful influence on the mind, and interest the reader independently of all peculiarity of taste." The rather inadequate answer offered for this puzzle is that our pleasure derives from "the excitement of surprise from new and wonderful objects. A strange and unexpected event awakens the mind, and keeps it on the stretch; and where the agency of invisible beings is introduced . . . our imagination, darting forth, explores with rapture the new world which is laid open to its view, and rejoices in the expansion of its powers. Passion and fancy co-operating elevate the soul to its highest pitch; and the pain of terror is lost in amazement."[57] In effect, the Aikins are once again offering the effect of the sublime here as an explanation. If the sublime explains the taste for Gothic fiction, however, it also raises a new problem. The reader seeking the "rapture" and "amazement" of the sublime might cease to look to literature for the moral it was supposed to impart. From the beginning critics saw that the devices used in both Sentimental and Gothic novels were a possible threat to the didacticism of which they were supposed to be the instrument. In the literature of feeling, the danger lay in the passivity of the characters that was necessary to display their great sensitivity. The Aikins declare, in another essay, that the distress aroused by fiction, though it always "afford[s] an exquisite pleasure to persons of taste and sensibility," does not necessarily improve morals since it does not lead to action.[58]

In *The Progress of Romance* Clara Reeve reveals the controversy this question aroused. A writer in *The Monthly Review* had declared that novels like Frances Sheridan's *Sidney Biddulph* "are by no means calculated to encourage or promote virtue" since they "draw tears from the reader by distressing innocence and virtue as much as possible."[59] Another, in the *Critical Review* had said that the same novel seeks to show that "neither prudence, foresight, nor even the best disposition the human heart is capable of" can "defend us from the inevitable evils" of life. This reviewer declared, however, that he could not even consider whether the novel was effective didactically for he was "so interested in the distress of *Sidney Biddulph,* and so absorbed in the events of her life, that in short, every arrow of Criticism was unpointed."[60] Clara Reeve's three characters, Sophronia, Hortensius, and Euphrasia, conclude that the effect is to make the whole seem real and Sidney "a well known and beloved friend." Although in other places they worry about the moral purpose of literature, here they say that "there is not a better Criterion of the merit of a book, than our losing sight of the Author."[61]

This apparent adoption of realism as a criterion should be seen in relation to its time. "Losing sight of the Author" inhibits the direct expression of his didactic purpose, but it is the sympathy of the reader, his distress, that has distracted him from the moral of the tale. He reacts to the novel as if it were "a true history" because his feelings have been aroused, not because the character has been drawn with the meticulous detail of the nineteenth-century realists. He is so wrapped up in the character that his judgment is suspended. The question was whether the appeal to his feelings would serve the purposes of didacticism or defeat them.

The sublime character presented an even greater problem than the distractions of Sentiment. In one of his essays, James Beattie, the poet, declares that ideal characters as well as villains can be sublime. He remarks that "sympathy as the means of conveying certain feelings from one breast to another, might be made a powerful instrument of moral discipline, if poets, and other writers of fable, were careful to call forth our sensibility towards those emotions only that favour virtue, and invigorate the human mind." These virtuous emotions respond to the sublime and the reader's mind is elevated. Thus, Beattie says in another essay: "Our taste for the sublime, cherished into a habit, and directed to proper objects, may, by preserving us from vice, which is the vilest of all things, and by recommending virtue for its intrinsick dignity, be useful in promoting our moral improvement."[62]

The sublime, however, is the means, not the end: "A

character may be sublime, which is not completely good, nay, which is upon the whole very bad. For the test of sublimity is not moral approbation, but that pleasurable astonishment wherewith certain things strike the beholder."[63] Thus, sublimity in itself is morally neutral and may be dangerous if it arouses admiration for an evil character. Beattie seems to threaten the reading public with a perpetual and unappetizing diet of honor and virtue in his insistence on limiting the use of the sublime. Yet, in advocating such restrictions, he showed that he understood how the sublime might erode didacticism. The features of the Gothic villain, which, to the eighteenth century, made him a sublime character, result in the compounding of good and evil in him, the creation of a mixed character, and a frightening vision of a world of relative moral values.[64]

Just because the Gothic villain is "sublimely" wicked, the terror he arouses fills the reader with "pleasurable astonishment" and causes him to feel with the villain. Consequently, the reader cannot condemn him entirely. The sublime in Gothic novels "calls forth our sensibility" toward emotions that do not "favour virtue," as Beattie warned it would. In attempting to set forth the nature of human good and evil, the Gothic novelists are like Victor Frankenstein in Mary Shelley's novel. They create monsters, which force an unwilling recognition of the dread blend of good and bad to be found in themselves and the rest of mankind. The reader, sharing the characters' feelings, partially suspends his moral judgment of the villain and, thereby, an understanding of the evil in him is opened up. Willy-nilly, authors and readers alike are faced with the fact that they have accepted imaginatively an unexpected moral relativity, an unlooked-for consequence of the adage that "to understand is to forgive."[65] That is, having imaginatively inhabited the tortured mind of the evil character, they see the potential for such evil in all minds, and experiencing compassion for it through an understanding of its psychological causes, they can no longer look on good and evil as absolute or as forces outside the human psyche.

As a consequence of such understanding the villains of later authors are given more ordinary human dimensions than those of their predecessors, for, however wicked their deeds, they still embody the human condition, as we all do in real life. The Hell within, to the extent that it engages the reader's sympathy shows him the benighted and paradoxical condition of man. Consequently, he cannot apply absolute moral judgments. Gothic fiction makes him constantly aware of human frailty and suffering, and this awareness, by facing him with the paradox and agony of the human condition, inevitably modifies condemnation or praise of the characters and so of the psychological conditions which those characters make manifest.

From his reading the reader receives the literary satisfaction of a resolution on an emotional level something like the catharsis of tragedy, as the Gothic novelists and their admirers were always quick to claim.[66] But beyond this, his fear puts him in touch with his own murky nature. The imagery of Gothic fiction is a symbolism of spiritual states, in which the highest spiritual aspirations bring with them the greatest evils. It shows within the outwardly everyday figures of ordinary people, strange, frightening, half-understood, but dramatically-sensed impulses. As Northrop Frye notes of "literature as process, pity and fear become states of mind without objects, moods which are common to the work of art and the reader, and which bind them together psychologically instead of separating them aesthetically."[67]

Walpole claimed that the "modern romance" (that is, the eighteenth-century social novel) limited and deadened "the great resources of fancy . . . by a strict adherence to common life."[68] To set the imagination free to explore the mysterious, the dark and unknowable, the Gothic novelists avoided the lighted streets and firelit domesticity of such novels and resorted to exotic worlds, the weird, and the monstrous.

The tradition they set up has definite and recognizable features for which they drew on the antiquarian aspect of Sentimentalism. As Nathan Drake notes in an essay on

"Gothic superstition," by which he means the beliefs and myths of ancient Europe: "the most enlightened mind free from all taint of superstition involuntarily acknowledges the power of Gothic agency." Consequently, "it is here only as furnishing fit materials for poetical composition that a wish for preserving such a source of imagery is expressed." Because it is necessarily "to us altogether unknown," the supernatural "furnishes, if not the probable, at least the possible," and so sends "a grateful astonishment, a welcome sensation of fear" through all men, "the Sage and the Savage." Celtic and Gothic superstition have "the same happy facility of blending [their] ideas with the common apprehensions of mankind. . . . Founded chiefly on the casual interference of immaterial beings, and therefore easily combining with the common feelings of humanity, they may yet with propriety decorate the pages of the poet."[69]

Drake's ideas about primitive man indicate how these poetically useful materials come to affect "the Sage and the Savage" alike. Early man, according to Drake, was an isolated being always defending himself or hunting for food. In this state, "unacquainted . . . with any rational system of religion, he calls into being . . . the wanderings of a terrified imagination." And thus, he imagines storms, mists, meteors, mountain torrents to be populated with supernatural beings. Drake goes on from these general remarks to a description of the "superstitions" of Scotland. Since he is dependent on Macpherson and *Ossian* for much of his information he must not be given much credit as an anthropologist. His discussion does indicate, however, the importance to Gothic fiction of landscape and weather corresponding to mood. He says of the "inhabitants of Morven" that "they imagined that . . . the merciful and the wise enjoyed their earthly pursuits in the region of the clouds . . . and that they frequently visited their native hills and former friends, to whom they were propitious and lovely in their appearance, whilst the cowardly and the vicious were the sport of all the winds of heaven, appeared only in marshy vallies, and amid scenes of gloom and desolation, were full of ill omen to those who saw them, and of terrible and ghastly form."[70] These spirits were evil and to be feared. Since Macpherson himself embued the Scots legends with his eighteenth-century sensibility, it is not surprising that these "superstitions" should turn out to be just what was needed to supply Gothic fiction with imagery for an internalized concept of evil.[71]

Drake's society had not yet dreamt of Freud and did not have the term "symbolism." Consequently, his is as clear a statement as was possible of the idea that this imagery was useful to the poet because of its direct correspondence with emotions all men experience whether they hold the "superstitions" or not. Drake seems to be saying in his own way that the images evoke fear because they enable the reader to recognize his own emotions in Gothic "claptrap," since his own mind is stocked with such symbolism.

Like the Aikins, Drake worried about the danger of producing pure pain instead of pleasurable terror. The supernatural, being an unknown agency, necessarily has qualities of the sublime. But "excited by the interference of simple material causation . . . terror requires no small degree of skill and arrangement to prevent its operating more fear than pleasure." Indeed, it may produce horror and disgust unless "picturesque description or sublime and pathetic sentiment" is introduced, or curiosity is stimulated "by the artful texture of the fable, or by the uncertain and suspended fate of an interesting personage."[72] These elements, the authors of Gothic fiction supply in abundance.

Setting out to explore the place of evil in the mind, the Gothic novelists found that their expedition into unknown territory uncovered the dream landscape of a closed world separated from that of everyday. The setting of the first Gothic novels in a remote historical time seems in itself an almost symbolic reenactment of the need to go back from the concealing refinements of civilization to the fundamentals of human nature. It is part of the late eighteenth century's general turning away from the two classical periods, gilded or silvered over (as the eighteenth century saw them) by rational light, to the "barbaric" and "Gothic" myths. To uncover the symbolic manifestations that *are* the country of the mind, the heirs of the enlightenment brought back out of the wilderness, the bogs and mountain fastnesses, the most emotion-laden images they knew, symbolic figures and landscapes from the dark, irrational past.

Their characters are not natural inhabitants of the settings in which they are placed because the very purpose of the setting—itself derived from literature and painting, not from nature—is to create an isolated environment in which to show eighteenth-century readers figures they can recognize as familiar and accept as showing what they and all mankind are like.[73] Authentically medieval characters would not fulfill this purpose because they would delineate the local, differentiating features of the denizens of the middle ages.

The medieval setting was soon abandoned for a contemporaneous one, however, as if to bring home the depicted evil to the reader's own time. When the tale is no longer set in the distant past, a system of "nested," concentric narration maintains the illusion of a strange world, isolating a symbolic landscape within the ordinary "world." In these settings, the inner spiritual state of the characters retains its physical manifestation. Their souls shine or glare from their eyes, revealing peace or torment, which, in correspondence to the concept of the Moral Sense, is instantly recognizable as the consequence of virtue or vice. The heroes and heroines continue to be portrayed as beautiful. The villains, being mixed characters, vary in appearance, and the split-off doubles are ugly.

The omnipresent old house or castle is one of the most stable characteristics of the Gothic. A dire and threatening place, it remains more than a dwelling. It starts out as a stone representation of the dark, tortured windings in the mind of those eminently civilized, and therefore "unnatural" vices, ambition and cruelty; it bears the whole weight of the ages of man's drift away from an ideal state; and it becomes a lasting representation of the torments of the subconscious pressing upon the conscious mind and making a prison of the self. The landscape it stands in also remains part of the weeping and storming Nature of the pathetic fallacy. The heavens rent by terrible storms contrive to express human torment and rage; sunshine and singing birds convey spiritual peace. And at the most intense moment of moral danger, there still appears in this landscape the terrible abyss of damnation.

The characters in this literature find themselves teetering with terrifying vertigo on the edge of this abyss or they leave the craggy moral landscape to grope through dank subterranean corridors of evil into which only an occasional ray of the sunlight of virtue can filter. And these characters are, on the one hand, sensitive, tearful, one-sided depictions of man's virtuous potential transported whole from the Sentimental novel and, on the other, towering villains caught in the fearful psychomachia of evil. Weeping and shuddering in weird surroundings quite foreign to their well-ordered personalities, the Sentimental protagonists contend by the sheer force of their virtue with the storms set up by the violent struggle in the villain between his Moral Sense and natural goodness and the evil within which contorts him into madness.[74]

The Gothic villains have an interesting potential for ambiguous, suggested meanings. When provided with the necessary sublime setting, these villains of the early Gothic are paradoxically more nearly recognizable as depictions of human beings than the good Sentimental characters who are their victims. Derided though they have been as bugbears too exaggerated to frighten adults, they have elicited greater critical admiration than the Sentimental characters. Neither type, however, should be measured as nearer or farther from human "reality." The depiction of the human potential for goodness in the heroes and heroines and of that goodness in a struggle to the death with its own evil in the villain are special and highly symbolic forms of characterization. The first produces heroines whose veins are filled not with blood but with water that continually overflows at their eyes, and who have no spirit; heroes who weep unmanly tears and are extravagantly noble, too ethereal to sweat. The second draws an exaggerated villain deliberately made larger than life, a towering storm of torment, whose evil is as great as his crippled potential for good was large.

The implications of such portrayals were quickly picked up by later authors, who made them explicit in rather different characters. Since the villain, representing the place of evil in the mind gone wrong, is caught in his interesting, soul-searing conflict and unable to obliterate consciousness of the lost possibility of virtue, he always has a certain pathos. Consequently, he is quickly transformed from a giant figure to a man-sized one, corresponding to the realization that his condition and the human condition are analogous: man born good and driven half mad by the torture of the evil into which he has been twisted. The depiction of an ordinary man suffering the torments of evil in place of the towering Gothic villain, however, produced a new and special aesthetic problem. How could the reader be made to feel the pathos of a character whose crimes were to be presented as horrible and bloody and were supposed to fill the reader with horror? The solution to this problem is just one example of the way the entire tradition has undergone a gradual modification while remaining, in its essence, unchanged. Since the reader was to sympathize with the tormented man who replaced the villain and who was a victim of his own evil, the device was formed of projecting the evil in him out onto a separate character. The figure of the double was thus born from the split and warring factions of the personality of the Gothic villain. The doubles figure showed that it was the nature of every man that the good in him must struggle in unending battle against the distortions of evil. It did so in a way that would make the reader accept the terrible certainty that this was true of himself, for it not only prevented him from rejecting the central character as evil; but, to the extent that he sympathized with that character, the double became a potential mirror image of himself as well.

The nineteenth-century works of this literature have not met with the same reluctance to interpret them as their eighteenth-century forebears, but they have not been treated as belonging to a single convention. They have not been clearly seen as descending in a direct line from the eighteenth-century works, because the origins of Gothic literature in eighteenth-century ideas have not been adequately shown and its tradition and meaning as a convention have found little recognition. Readers, for instance, who see Walpole's walking portrait as just "machinery," have little trouble ascribing symbolic significance to the strange behavior of the portrait of Dorian Gray, which behaves as no ordinary painting would. They find Edgar Allan Poe's Ligeia more acceptable than Matilda in Lewis' *The Monk,* although Ligeia does not more closely represent an ordinary flesh and blood woman; indeed, she is the more fantastic of the two. Robert Louis Stevenson's Mr. Hyde is nerve-racking, even though no reader believes an English doctor can transform himself into his own hairy, evil counterpart; and Hyde is less not more "real" than, say, Lewis' Ambrosio. If these later works seem to be more acceptable today than the early Gothic novels, it is probably because what they symbolize is nearer to the modern reader's own time and thought. The fact that they are symbolic is more easily seen because they are more closely representative of the underlying "myths" of today's culture and so more directly available to modern imaginations and feelings. The methods of the later authors, nonetheless, are demonstrably the same as those of the early writers of Gothic fiction. Evil is still ugliness in Wilde's tale, as it is in *Frankenstein; The Turn of the Screw* sets forth repressed sexuality through ghosts, as *The Monk* does through demons. Throughout the nineteenth century, however, the referent level of the symbolism becomes increasingly specific, until, finally, in the 1890s, a character within a work, Dr. Jekyll, himself provides an explicit "scientific" explanation for everything that, up to that point in the tale, has been manifested symbolically.

In a series of developments parallel to the invention of the double, other characteristics of the Gothic novel were modified as the tradition continued through its unending hall of mirrors in which the reflections, however weird, continued to be images of man. The process is one of gradual discovery, an expanding awareness modifying what has previously been intuitively known. It is a fresh formulation of ancient nightmares in the light of developing ideas. The Gothic moon, like any other celestial body, shines on nothing new. Man is as he has been, committing acts of greater or lesser nastiness, which he himself then dubs evil or otherwise with varying degrees of absoluteness. That moon, nevertheless, makes the world look different; having appeared in the second half of the eighteenth century, it has been casting strange shadows ever since.

CHAPTER TWO

CHARACTERS—THE REFLECTED SELF

Whatever flames upon the night
Man's own resinous heart has fed.
W. B. Yeats, "Two Songs from a Play"

ETWEEN the 1760s and the 1890s, the characters in Gothic fiction underwent some major changes. Principally, some bizarre new types—such as doubles and monsters were added. The villains of the eighteenth century were also considerably modified in the nineteenth. The virtuous heroes and heroines did not change much, however. Instead, they tended to fade gradually away. When good and evil became more and more closely intertwined and the moral outlook of Gothic fiction became increasingly relative, there was less place for the beautiful characters representing the Good. They, nevertheless, did not vanish entirely. As late as Bram Stoker's *Dracula* (1897) a heroine appears whose sole function is to be beautifully and passively innocent.

Lucy in *Dracula* and her predecessors appear at first to be rather silly embodiments of an inhibited, puritanical notion of female virtue, and the heroes seem no better. They, in fact, play a fairly complex role in Sentimental and Gothic fiction. As bearers of ideas, moral, psychological, and mythic, they are necessarily simplified figures of humanity. They are sensitive, passive, and interestingly pale. Their eyes shine with a sense of honor or are lighted by the lambent flame of loving kindness and virtue. They are frequently defeated in the course of the plot to demonstrate that virtue is its own reward. Thus far, they are characters who bid fair to irritate the reader and, because they prate a great deal and act very little, to bore him too. In other respects, however, they are fairy-tale, mythic figures. They have a child-like quality and often stand in a quasi-incestuous relationship to one another. The heroines, in particular, are also frequently equated with Nature as earth-mother figures, and they embody a dilemma which is important in Gothic fiction: the question of what true innocence is and how it can be guarded.

As early as Lewis' *The Monk* (1795), these characters become highly ambiguous. The Sentimental hero and the Gothic villain begin to merge into one character torn by terrible conflict, while the gentle earth-mother figure may reappear as a wicked witch. These changes barely increase their mimetic qualities but, because they are ambiguous, mixed figures, they are more acceptable as characters. A myth-bearing figure need not, indeed must not, display great individual complexity, for the more nearly a character is made to represent an individual human being such as we meet in everyday life, the less it will, in fact, appear mythic.

The most famous of English Sentimental novels, Mackenzie's *The Man of Feeling* is a good place to look at the hero and heroine in their least complex form. Harley and Miss Walton in that novel are ethereal creatures, sensitive and delicate to a fault, and not much more.

Characterization of Harley, the man of feeling himself, is strictly limited. He feels, he observes, he is moved. He does very little. The first thing we are told about him is that he showed that sort of "bashfulness" which is "a consciousness, which the most delicate feelings produce, and the most extensive knowledge cannot always remove."[1] Having received his first education at a country school and then studied on his own with a little help from the parson and the excise man, he is not uneducated. Rather, he has managed to acquire an education without adopting with it the corruptions of civilization—pride, envy, ambition. The description of his upbringing, in a chapter entitled "Of Worldly Interests," shows him to be lacking in worldliness and unwilling to pursue his "interests," in ironic contrast to his guardians.

Through this contrast Mackenzie gives Harley a tinge of the quixotic, a slightly comic air, which is conveyed through the mildly satiric tone of the narrator. This hint of the comic, which Mackenzie no doubt derived from Sterne and Fielding, works to the detriment of the novel. It pushes the characterization of Harley toward the mimetic. That, however, only makes him seem exasperatingly ineffective, if one does not conclude he is drawn by an author too sentimental to face up to reality. When Sentimentalist set pieces and their paradigmatic characters are viewed with an amused air from inside the novel by the narrator, the reader tends not to laugh sympathetically over the weaknesses of a lovable comic character as he does over Fielding's, Sterne's, or Goldsmith's characters. Instead the novel itself appears ridiculous, because a reader tends to take the narrator's point-of-view while he is reading. We can see that Mackenzie's point has been lost when a critic writes quite typically, for example: "And when . . . Harley and Miss Walton collapse in a heap of expired sensibility upon his declaration of his love for her, we are apt to be more amused than moved."[2] Such a judgment results from accepting the narrator's view. Harley's ridiculousness, however, should be seen as absurd only in the eyes of the world. That is, he and the narrator should reflect ironically on each other. In this way, the ideal of virtue as its own reward is enhanced by his pursuit of it oblivious to the world's laughter, while his vulnerability is admitted.

Sentimental characters stand at the paradoxical point where the human condition in the here and now clashes with the hypothetical state of human beings as the Almighty created them to be. Love in Harley and his beloved, whose first name we never learn, is integrated among the virtuous feelings. It has grown out of their reciprocal recognition of each other's beauteous virtue. They love each other because they are like each other, virtue loving virtue, loving itself reflected in another. It is the concept of virtue as "natural," as the harmony that is Man's ideal state, which leads other Sentimental novelists to give this self-reflecting love considerable mythic significance. Mackenzie, however, does hardly more than integrate it into his characters.

Harley loves Miss Walton as Virtue personified and she loves him reciprocally. In the benevolist view, however, the "passions" must not be repressed but directed wisely, so Mackenzie's pair are not devoid of sexual attraction for each other or incapable of physical love. Miss Walton's virtue is enhanced for Harley by her beauty and the delicacy of her response to him. In her, we are told, "the most delicate consciousness of propriety often kindled that blush which marred the performance of it: this raised his [Harley's] esteem something above what the most sanguine descriptions of her goodness had been able to do; for certain it is that notwithstanding the laboured definitions which very wise men have given us of the inherent beauty of virtue, we are always inclined to think her handsomest when she condescends to smile upon ourselves." The "easy gradation from esteem to love" in Harley causes him to act ludicrously in the eyes of his friends "who often laughed very heartily at the aukward blunders of the real Harley, when the different faculties, which should have prevented them, were entirely occupied by the ideal. In some of these paroxisms of fancy, Miss Walton did not fail to be introduced; and the picture which had been drawn amidst the surrounding objects of unnoticed levity, was now singled out to be viewed through the medium of romantic imagination."[3]

Miss Walton plays a very small part in the novel. Her sole function is to be perfect and to be loved in silent anguish by Harley. Most of the space devoted to her is used in description, indicating that it is her function to be, not to act—to be an embodiment of humanity at its natural best; to show that what is virtuous is also what is lovable; and that men when they are not corrupt have a propensity to love virtue. She is intelligent, modest, quiet, charitable, and demure, her soul visible in eyes that shine with the subdued light of virtue. The following are only extracts from the description of her, a description so conventionalized that it is virtually interchangeable with those of other Sentimental heroines:

> A blush, a phrase of affability to an inferior, a tear at a moving tale, were to [Harley] . . . unequalled in conferring beauty. For all these Miss Walton was remarkable. . . .
>
> Her complexion was mellowed into a paleness, which certainly took from her beauty; but agreed, at least Harley used to say so, with the pensive softness of her mind. Her eyes were of that gentle hazel-colour which is rather mild than piercing; and, except when they were lighted up by good-humour, which was frequently the case, were supposed by the fine gentlemen to want fire. [This is an example of the narrator's mildly ironic tone.] Her air and manner were elegant in the highest degree, and were as sure of commanding respect, as their mistress was far from demanding it. Her voice was inexpressibly soft. . . .
>
> Her conversation was always cheerful, but rarely witty; and without the smallest affectation of learning, had . . . much sentiment in it. (pp. 14–16)

The interesting pallor, the mild eyes, and the inexpressibly soft voice might, of course, have given way to flushes, sparks, and sharp tones if Mackenzie had not kept Miss Walton free, as far as possible, of action or involvement in society.

Since this is a novel about sensibility, her virtue is born in her heart not her head: "Her beneficence was unbounded; indeed the natural tenderness of her heart might have been argued, by the frigidity of a casuist, as detracting from her virtue in this respect, for her humanity was a feeling, not a principle: but minds like Harley's are not very apt to make this distinction, and generally give our virtue credit for all that benevolence which is instinctive in our nature" (p. 16).[4] Despite the narrator's tone, this passage expresses the benevolist belief that the path of virtue is not thorny. The virtuous life is happy because it is natural, that is, the fulfillment of human nature which alone fits man into the harmony of God's order.

This is why the Sentimental novels make extensive use of the country/city contrast, which is a staple image in the eighteenth-century novel in general. The virtuous characters are found in the remote countryside where they grow up uncorrupted by civilization. There they live happy, well-ordered lives, often still in a child-parent relationship. A daughter, for instance, devotes her life to a beloved parent or parents who have withdrawn, much bruised and impoverished, from a wicked world. The conflict of the novel usually arises because even in such idyllic surroundings the natural and perfect love of the hero and heroine cannot be consummated in marriage—usually he is too poor and so, with a very eighteenth-century sense of propriety and prudence, refrains from declaring his love out of a sense of "unworthiness." Mackenzie's Harley and his Savillon in *Julia de Rubigné,* for instance, both follow this pattern. Since the heroine cannot speak if the hero dare not, both are paralyzed in this situation, for neither ever envisages improper action or even a breach of social decorum. Consequently, little happens. The idyllic existence is marred by unfulfilled love and the Sentimental characters go down to defeat, fading away in gentle sorrow without having put up much resistance to their plight. With the inevitable weakness of their kind they suffer and are victimized, but nothing in these novels is allowed to suggest that the alternatives to this fate are desirable. There is no poetic justice. Mackenzie's Julia and Harley and more subtle Sentimental characters like Paul and Virginia and Young Werther go down to defeat so that the reader may see that virtue is its own reward and the only source of happiness. It is not death that is evil but human corruption and the unhappiness and torment it brings with it. The characters of sensibility suffer and die, but suffering imposed from outside cannot destroy their inner peace.

The portrayal of "good" characters is a problem in all types of literature. Mackenzie himself noted, however, a special danger for the Sentimentalists. They may make the characters in their novels choose a rare virtue over a more ordinary and practical one. If they do, they may foster a mistaken and pernicious system of morality by contrasting "one virtue or excellence" with another and so bring about "that war of duties which is to be found . . . particularly in . . . the *Sentimental.*" Defending novels as promoting "a certain refinement of mind," Mackenzie nevertheless attacks "refined sentimentalists" who talk of virtue rather than practicing it. A too great sensibility, he says, fosters pride in superior delicacy and contempt for the ordinary. Like Beattie, however, he sees the greatest danger to the didactic purposes of the novel in the "character of mingled virtue and vice," since "the application to ourselves in which the moral tendency of all imaginary characters must be supposed to consist" may result in "a very common kind of self-deception, by which men are apt to balance their faults by the consideration of their good qualities."[5]

As a consequence, Sentimental novels tend to confine themselves and their "teachings" to inner states. They are more concerned with psychology than society.[6] They draw ideal figures, virtuous characters with, as the Aikins suggest, some slight weakness to make them believable. These characters are designed to appeal to the reader's moral sense and to refine it. They portray the inner self as in a mirror through which the reader may recognize and develop his own best feelings. It is perhaps this psychologizing impulse that leads the Sentimental novelists into the realm of myth, where their most interesting themes are found.

The reflection of the virtuous self in the equally virtuous beloved has the same sort of symbolic function as other features, such as setting in these novels. Because the virtuous love virtue positively, they also love the virtuous. But they are each also made to see their own virtue reflected in the other because to look at the mind in general—as opposed to examining the pecularities of a particular, individual mind—one must look in upon oneself. Just as Theodore in *Otranto* is truly and exactly reflected in the statue of Alfonso, so the mutual reflection of Sentimental characters is also a true image. The reflection of evil characters on the other hand is seen in a distorting mirror, as in the evil doubles figures, because evil is seen as a distortion, a monstrousness abhorrent to the virtuous mind.

When the mutually reflecting Sentimental characters appear in a remote and idyllic setting, they are true children of Nature. It is here that they appear in a quasi-incestuous relationship. They are children who have grown up together like brother and sister, although they are not related by blood. Then, when they reach a suitable age, their feeling for each other develops into sexual love—naturally, it is said—and they wish to marry. This pattern is to be found in Mackenzie's *Julia de Rubigné* (1777), in Bernadin de St. Pierre's *Paul and Virginia* (1787), and in Chateaubriand's *Atala* (1801).

Mackenzie's *Julia de Rubigné* is set in a quiet village where Julia and her parents, upper-class but unpretentious, live away from the social scramble of the city. They are attended by a few loyal retainers and render happy by their care the peasants who dance under the trees after their satisfying day's work. Julia and Savillon are young adults but they are presented as children throughout. They have grown up together in the house of Julia's parents. They have shared the same wet-nurse, who speaks of them as her children. Their shared sensibility creates a perfect understanding between them, making their love natural and inevitable when it changes from childhood attachment to adult passion. It is the world that parts them and introduces the misunderstandings that lead to Julia's marrying Montauban and to the disaster that marriage brings with it. In sharp contrast to Julia and Savillon, Montauban appears as an adult. He comes to the house as a friend of Julia's father and with his haughty pride and inflated sense of honor he is unchildlike. Indeed, he is a torn, tormented, isolated figure closely resembling the earliest Gothic villains. He is the shadow against which the light of virtue shines brightest. Although these characterizations make this a novel of ideas embodied in a fiction, the relationship between Julia and Savillon is still presented as part of social life. In Bernadin de St. Pierre's *Paul and Virginia,* which closely follows the same pattern, we find a fairy-tale fantasy that makes the symbolic quality clearer.

Paul and Virginia grow up side by side in a beautiful, isolated valley in exotic Mauritius where Nature is bounteous. Instead of the village life in the countryside found in *Julia,* there are wild forest and plantations worked by slaves. The relationship between Paul and Virginia, however, is again a childhood attachment turned into quasi-incestuous adult love. Each is an entire small world to the other and their relationship forms the core of the novel's meaning. They have child-like qualities of innocence and a spontaneous brotherly love, which is displayed in the incident with the runaway slave. Children of Nature, their innocence, goodness, and instinctive mutual understanding are natural and true, in contrast to the falsity of civilization whenever it appears in the novel. As children together they sense each other's needs, as twins in literature are often said to do. Their relationship is epitomized in the description of Virginia, a tiny earth mother, sitting under their favorite tree by the stream, while Paul gathers fruit which he brings to lay before her. For Paul she is Nature and when he loses her Nature itself becomes empty for him and he can no longer live.

Paul is persuaded to let her leave the island to go to France to be "finished." Like Mackenzie's heroes, Harley and Savillon, he is guided by reasons of prudence and consents against his true feelings in order not to deprive her of those things the world thinks necessary to happiness. Virginia's name is significant here. The merest touch of civilization becomes a loss of innocence. Because the smallest compromise is impossible in the figure of virtue, the mere fact of that contact is sufficient to spell ruin. When Virginia returns to the island in her worldly attire she is inevitably lost, and Paul with her. Hence her strange death which can be understood only symbolically. As the returning ship founders on the rocks and she, standing on the stern, refuses to shed the dress with its many skirts that will drag her beneath the surface of the water, her decision is explained as an uncompromising modesty. It is, however, a symbolic inability to cast off the trappings of civilization she has acquired. Back in the world of Nature, she drowns and Paul also dies. The Nature he loved in her has become meaningless. He cannot breathe in the natural surroundings when she, his very means of life, is missing from them.

In *Paul and Virginia* Bernadin de St. Pierre makes manifest not the conflicts of the human psyche but its innate potential for good. In reflecting each other, Paul and Virginia see their own goodness—the source of moral satisfaction and so of happiness—in each other. There is a tone of narcissicism in this kind of mutual feeling. It has the same relationship to real narcissicism, however, as does the quasi-incest to the real thing. Love in the ordinary sense is not the subject of this love story. Virginia is not a girl growing up but a young goddess and Paul is her priest. Theirs is an abstract, ideal love, which, because it is presented symbolically and as a part of Nature, remains triumphant although they are destroyed.

Chateaubriand's René and Atala are as romantic as the fairy-tale pastoral figures of Paul and Virginia. *Atala,* published in 1801 but written in the last years of the eighteenth century, is a hybrid of Sentimentalism and traditional Christianity, the result of Chateaubriand's return to the religion of his fathers.[7] *Atala* has the narrative structure of a story within a story, which is a characteristic of Sentimental and

Gothic novels. It sets out in direct narrative, describing the beauties of the American wilderness and relating in summary the events that have brought together René, a Frenchman, and old Chactas, the symbolically blind Indian leader. The older man relates his earlier experiences (the story of Atala) to the younger. René has adopted the life of the wilderness, but it is a strange, closed-off world into which he has penetrated. He needs Chactas to explain to him the story of Chactas' love for Atala.

The story is thus mediated through Chactas to René and finally to the reader when, in the epilogue, the narrator of the whole reveals himself: "I, a wanderer in faraway lands, have faithfully reported what Indians have told to me."[8] Thus, the reader has the tale at fourth-hand at least. As similar devices do in Mackenzie's novels and in *Paul and Virginia,* this technique enhances the sense of remoteness, of the ephemeral nature of those lives which might have gone altogether unrecorded. At the same time, here, it gives them a legendary flavor. In the other works, the narrator emphasizes the element of chance in his finding the tale at all. Here it has been preserved in memory and passed on by word of mouth.

As in other Sentimental novels, civiization in *Atala* is a corrupting force compared unfavorably to the simple life of the forest. The natural men, however, the Indians, are not naturally virtuous—they are savage because they are pagans. The tale concludes that man is depraved, but that the combination of Christianity and the simple life (which is still an unhappy one) can bring salvation.

In attempting to reconcile Sentimentalism with Christianity *Atala* loosens the very cornerstone of Benevolism, the belief in man's essential goodness. Yet, the novel still has the earmarks of Sentimental fiction, including the quasi-incestuous relationship between Chactas and Atala. Already in love, the two have wandered for days through the forest, burning with unfulfilled passion for each other. Then they discover they are "brother and sister." In the course of conversation Atala reveals that she is the daughter of Philip Lopez, a man who had adopted Chactas as his son. The revelation takes place in the midst of a raging storm. The corresponding storm in Chactas' breast is one of joy, not dismay, at finding that his beloved is his "sister." Describing the moment when he learns of her parentage, he says: "Pressing Atala to my heart, sobbing, I cried, 'O my sister! O daughter of Lopez! Daughter of my benefactor!' " And when Atala understands what Chactas is saying, "She was seized too with confusion and joy." Chactas goes on to say that "this fraternal friendship which had come to visit us and to join its love with ours was too much for our hearts."[9] The internal and external storms abate with the appearance of the Christian missionary, Father Aubry. The love of Chactas and Atala, however, is complete. They continue to call each other brother and sister and yet to consider themselves destined for each other. They are parted only by death, the result of a mistaken vow.

The "innocent incest" here has the same purpose of conveying a self-reflecting natural virtue as it does in other Sentimental novels. It contrasts sharply with the treatment of real incest in Chateaubriand's *René.* There the effect of the narrative convention used in *Atala* is adroitly reversed. Now the story is related by René to Chactas and Father Souël. The reader is led to expect that it will reveal a horror of civilization almost too strange to comprehend as these two old men wonder aloud what can possibly have driven a wealthy young man like René to leave it and bury himself with them in the wilderness. René then tells them of the source of his sorrow, which turns out to be his sister Amelia's incestuous passion for him. While the quasi-incestuous relationship is treated lyrically in *Atala,* the mere thought of real incest in René arouses the utmost horror, indicating the completely different literary purposes for which they are used.

The blood relationship between René and Amelia is of brother and sister, but emotionally it also is a mother-son bond. In other novels, when the link to Nature makes the Sentimental heroine also an earth-mother figure, the symbolically incestuous relationship again casts her in the role of mother with the hero as son. This is the relationship of Lotte and Werther in Goethe's *The Sorrows of Young Werther* (1774).

Lotte is first introduced as a beautiful young earth mother giving bread, the staff of life, to the children with her own fair hand. Despite premonitory storms and admonitory human warnings that she belongs to another, Werther allows himself to love and court her. He invests in her all the meaningfulness that he has been searching for in the natural surroundings of the countryside. His love is typically Sentimental and narcissistic. "And how precious I have become to myself," he writes, when it appears that Lotte loves him. . . . "How I worship at my own altar since I know that she loves me!" Then, when he is unhappy over her, he exclaims: "When we are robbed of ourselves, we are robbed of everything!"[10] Werther's love for Lotte is passionate and physical, but he puts himself in a childlike relationship to her. He believes that his love will bear him above the mundane and that he will be able to transcend jealousy of Albert, whom she marries. With them he is like a child with its parents. He plays with the children, Lotte's younger brothers and sisters, rolling on the floor with them and glorying in his ability to forsake his adult dignity and frolic on their level.

He also behaves childishly toward Lotte and Albert and after he goes away, in his one attempt to be sensible, he returns to them sulkily and obstinately like a child to rejecting parents. On his journey back he takes a detour to visit his real childhood home, which is now empty for him. This visit, which brings back to his mind the childhood that is now lost, emphasizes the futility of his return to Lotte and Albert, just as Werther's coldness toward his real mother casts doubt on his attitude toward Lotte. Werther, having first tried to lose himself in Nature, has then tried to do so in the human figure of Nature, Lotte. His earlier experience of love has shown the same combination of attachment to a mother figure and identification of her with Nature. "With her," Werther writes of the "sweetheart" of his youth, "I could fully develop that wonderful feeling with which my heart embraces nature. . . . Alas, the years she was my senior took her to her grave before me."[11]

He finds, however, that he cannot love Lotte on an exalted Platonic plane, and Nature, and life with it, grow empty and meaningless for him. It is, perhaps, because Goethe is critical of the Sentimental ideal as divorced from reality that the quasi-incest of his novel takes the mother-son form, reproducing in Werther's relation to Mother Nature something of the relation of all sons to their mothers. Werther, unlike Bernadin de St. Pierre's Paul, is a trangressor, though an "innocent" one, and so he does not simply expire as Paul does, but destroys himself—and it is Lotte, in effect, who hands him the gun. In a subtle twist, Goethe makes the quasi-incestuous theme bring about a penalty feared for real incest. Werther is brought to destruction for trying to live out a fantasy.

Werther has the troubling qualities of a conventional theme handled by a great master. It displays all the attractiveness of Sentimentalism, its idealism, its gentleness, its delicacy. It presents along with them, however, its pitfalls and the inevitable destruction, not just by the worldly but by themselves, of those who live in its fantasy, becoming self-indulgent, refusing to come to terms with the world, refusing in fact the compromises called "growing up."[12] These qualities are not set against each other but are shown as part and parcel of each other in a sustained paradox, an ambiguity that reflects the human condition. Few Sentimental novels attain such complexity of awareness, but Werther's famous malaise, which grows out of a desire to transcend the human condition, and the pathos of his self-destruction make this a pure example of the genre, nevertheless. It also shows the connection between Sentimental and Gothic fiction. In the mad scientists and the wizards of the Gothic tales, the same aspiration to break through the limits of one's humanity reappears in evil form.

These brother-sister, parent-child relationships strangely transformed into adult sexual love indicate an at least intuitive understanding of basic patterns of development that authors transpose into their fictions, putting them to the service of their particular ideas. The childhood companionship that turns into adult love is a means of showing these kindred delicate souls as uncorrupted figures in a harsh and wicked world. It emphasizes the delicacy of their feelings by first showing their childhood love as a pure emotion unclouded by adult passion. Thus, when evil is introduced into the picture, the sense of it as the corruption of human nature and therefore unnatural is increased. This quasi-incest is only peripherally connected with real incest and, in expressing the idea of evil as unnatural, it takes on a mythic quality related to what Northrop Frye describes as "the Romantic redemption myth."[13] In both Sentimental and Gothic literature the relationship of the hero and heroine brings this myth down to earth to convey psychological concepts. In Sentimental novels, the relationship is combined with the equation of the protagonists with Nature and their oneness with the natural setting to which they belong. This adds up to a vision of man's natural state as an inner one which, ideally, is harmonious within the individual and makes him a part of Nature's harmony as well. The Gothic uses the same theme to express its concern with aberration and the absence of harmony.

The failure of the Sentimental characters to achieve complete spiritual union with one like themselves is as inherently a part of novels of sensibility as their initial attempt to achieve such a union. Mackenzie's Harley goes into a "decline" and dies. His Julia de Rubigné is poisoned. Virginia is drowned. Werther shoots himself. Such chronic failure, however, does not detract from the ideal itself. These novels affirm the Sentimental concept of virtue by showing that to know oneself virtuous, to develop one's sensibility to the full, is more important than worldly "success" and even than life. As the figure of the heroine demonstrates that perfect virtue is a delicate flower, so the disastrous endings of these novels reflect its evanescence and vulnerability. As R. F. Brissenden has pointed out, the term "sensibility" often reflected "the fear that . . . to be endowed with a delicate sensibility was to be cast inevitably into the role of victim."[14] Such a natural tendency to be victims makes the delicate characters of Sentimentalism suitable to be transported bodily into the cloudy world of Gothic fiction. There a malign set of villains assaults them with a ferocity disproportionate to their frailty.

The close relationship of Sentimental and Gothic tales can be seen in these characters. They are not just "borrowed" from the Sentimental novel by Gothic authors. They appear in both types of novel because Gothic fiction is a necessary corollary of Sentimentalism. Building on the premises of Sentimentalism and positing a concept of evil as the unnatural corruption of man's fundamentally good nature, it uses the same paired Sentimental characters to embody that good nature uncorrupted. What happens to them then, however, is different. For the most part, the heroes and heroines of the Sentimental novels are defeated by the mere vanity of society, although *Julia de Rubigné* with the sinister Montauban is an exception in this. In the Gothic novel they become victims of the giant figure of the villain. They are contrasted with him, also, in being a pair, while he is an isolated figure, dark, corrupt, and unchildlike. In the Gothic novels the quasi-incestuous brother-sister relationship between the hero and heroine again appears. It is sometimes used to present a central male character as good-gone-bad rather than an absolute, unexplained evil. Such characters are highly ambiguous figures of relative evil.

There is an interesting difference between those works that use the brother-sister relationship and those that do not. In Beckford's *Vathek* (1786), Lewis' *The Monk* (1795), and Mary Shelley's *Frankenstein* we find variations of the theme. In *The Castle of Otranto* (1764), Clara Reeve's *The Old English Baron* (1777) and Ann Radcliffe's *The Mysteries of Udolpho* (1794) and *The Italian* (1797) it does not appear.

In *The Castle of Otranto* the relationships, as we have seen, are all of parents and children—the dire effect on the children when parents are evil and the beneficial effects when they are good. The threat of real incest is the precipitating force for the action. The twin heroines are both paragons of virtue as a result of their Sentimental upbringing. Matilda, having grown up in the shelter of her mother, Hippolyta (also a paragon), is perfection itself. She is also, however, a victim of her father's evil. Isabella and Matilda presage a long line of paired female figures in the Victorian novel.[15] There, they are usually contrasted, one dark, lively, willing to risk action, the other a blonde descendant of the Sentimental heroine, very passive and very "good."

In Walpole's novel both are Sentimental heroines and there is only the slightest shade of difference between them. Isbella is more worldly than Matilda but only to the extent that she wishes to live in the world and to marry. She represents the strength Manfred hopes to infuse into his line. Matilda is a saint, not of this world. In her relationship to Theodore, she is a clear example of the self-reflecting virtue embodied in these characters. She first sets eyes on Theodore as Manfred is condemning him to death, and she instantly recognizes in him the living image of Alfonso, before whose statue she habitually offers her most fervent prayers. She falls in love at first sight with this image of the figure of goodness before which she has always prayed, and he with her. When the evil in her own father, whom she loves, threatens to overwhelm this goodness, she cries out and faints. In later releasing Theodore from his prison she is freeing the goodness that is no longer a representation, the statue, but a living, moving force in the world. She frees it to do its work. When finally she is immolated at the foot of Alfonso's statue, it is this evil act that brings about the final restitution of justice and the triumph of virtue. Matilda dies, but virtue and order are restored.

When, in the final sentence of the novel, Walpole's chronicler avers that Isabella will marry Theodore and share with him the sorrowful memory of Matilda, his dead love and her erstwhile companion, we may see Matilda as a feminine ideal, the spirit of virtue itself, which raises love to a higher plane. She then becomes an idealization of love that could not live in this world but that ennobles Theodore and Isabella, who are virtuous but human.

In *The Old English Baron* the hero Edmund is, like Theodore, a scion of nobility disguised as a simple lad. He, too, is reflected in a work of art—this time a portrait. He is a typical Sentimental hero. He weeps, trembles, sighs. Acting in accord with his sense of honor and virtue he will not try to marry Emma until he is "worthy" of her in "degree." Emma in turn recognizes his innate nobility when others scorn him for his outward lack of social standing. Edmund and Emma have grown up together, but Emma appears very little in the novel and nothing is made of the "incest" theme. Like Walpole, Clara Reeve stays close to romance tradition.

In the 1790s, with the appearance of Ann Radcliffe's novels, the ideas of virtue embodied in these characters are employed in the development of character. The heroines are the central characters in *The Mysteries of Udolpho* (1794) and *The Italian* (1797) and consequently have more substance than Walpole's or Clara Reeve's heroines. The villain's assault on them is more sustained and they do more moving about, voluntary and involuntary, take decisions, right and wrong, and generally are more mimetically portrayed. The beauty of virtue is still personified in their beauteous forms and the heroes fall instantly in love with them. These heroes are important to the novels, of course, and they fit the Sentimental pattern. As characters, however, they are secondary to the heroines. In accord with the old romance tradition hero and heroine are separated by cruel fate and the machinations of the worldly.[16] Before they are reunited, the heroine must conduct a single stuggle with only her intrinsic virtue to set against a wicked and rapacious villain. In the course of the novel she must learn the wisdom to wed virtue to life in this world. Thus, in Walpole and Clara Reeve, the Sentimental characters are a virtuous contrast to villainy; in Ann Radcliffe, they are the same with the added feature of some character development in the heroines as a result of their experience of evil.

In none of these novels would a childhood attachment have suited the presentation of these characters. An early love between Theodore and either Isabella or Matilda would have diminished Isabella's role as a figure of strength brought in to fulfill first a false role through the projected marriages to Conrad and Manfred, then a true one in marrying the true heir. In Clara Reeve's novel it would have interfered with the gradual revelation of Edmund's true nobility. And in the case of Ann Radcliffe's heroines, a childhood love would diminish our sense of the lonely struggle through which they must learn and mature.

When the quasi-incestuous relationship does reappear in Gothic fiction the results are strange and wonderful. It introduces a major theme: the quality of innocence that is based on ignorance of the world and the paradoxical involvement of virtuous characters in the causes of evil. In William Beckford's *Vathek* (1786) the little princess and her cousin, Nouronihar and Gulchenrouz, are another Paul and Virginia except that they are actually children and are related by blood. The identity between them is almost complete: "The two brothers [the fathers of the children] had mutually engaged their children to each other; and Nouronihar loved her cousin more than her own beautiful eyes. Both had the same tastes and amusements; the same long, languishing looks; the same tresses; the same fair complexions; and, when Gulchenrouz appeared in the dress of his cousin, he seemed to be more feminine than even herself."[17] The description of Gulchenrouz here as a mirrored reflection of Nouronihar points up her narcissism. This in turn explains her desertion of her cousin. It is her childhood self she is leaving. Here, Sentimental narcissism takes on a darker tone, just as there is a hint of real incest. For Nouronihar does not mature. She simply plunges headlong into the path of evil.

The girl, again, is the stronger of the two sentimental figures. Gulchenrouz follows her lead in everything as they play and romp and nestle together in a childhood idyll that is interrupted by the arrival of the caliph Vathek. A jaded sensualist, Vathek is enchanted by the innocent naturalness of Nouronihar. And she is fascinated by him. Gulchenrouz is abandoned and Nouronihar joins Vathek. But it is not love that has caused her to desert her cousin. She sees Vathek as the way to forbidden knowledge. Urged on by his mother, the witch Carathis, he is on a journey in search of the halls of Eblis, the Moslem name for Satan. To his mother's disgust, sensuality has diverted Vathek from this quest and he is content to dally with Nouronihar in the beautiful valley. It is Nouronihar who persuades him to take up the journey again. She is thus, beneath her Sentimental heroine's exterior, a little witch figure seducing the lumbering Caliph into the abyss. Her interest is identical with Carathis', although in everything else they appear to be contrasted. Eventually all three attain their goal and find themselves among the damned, whose hearts burn in their chests.

Gulchenrouz, on the other hand, remains an eternal child, living in a roc's nest "remote from the inquietudes of the world, the impertinence of harems, the brutality of eunuchs, and the inconstancy of women." He is cared for by a "genius" who "instead of burdening his pupils with perishable riches and vain sciences, conferred upon them the boon of perpetual childhood." This unearthly childhood is contrasted with the equally unearthly torments of Hell where "unrestrained passions and atrocious deeds" are punished: "Such shall be the chastisement of that blind curiosity, which would transgress those bounds the wisdom of the Creator has prescribed to human knowledge; and such the dreadful disappointment of that restless ambition, which, aiming at discoveries reserved for beings of a supernatural order, perceives not through its infatuated pride, that the condition of man upon earth is to be—humble and ignorant."[18]

Thus, Beckford's Eastern tale introduces a second major theme that appears again and again in nineteenth-century Gothic novels—the Faustian pursuit of forbidden knowledge foreshadowed in Werther's push beyond the limitations of feeling. The equation between the "humble and ignorant" condition man should be content with and the eternal childhood free of "vain sciences" of Gulchenrouz indicate again that the innocent, childlike characteristics are symbolic of man's natural virtue. The choice in *Vathek* between the roc's nest and Hell can, of course, only be read symbolically. The novel introduces the recurring exploration, in Gothic fiction, of the dilemma of innocence that relies on ignorance and also establishes the use of such startlingly symbolic imagery as the burning hearts of the damned. *Vathek* suggests the innocence of man's natural state, the vanity and danger of his pursuit of knowledge, and, especially in the Episodes, the corruptions of civilization—the sexual transgressions and worldly crimes of ambition and the misuse of power, which bring men to a Hell that is a spiritual state.

Although Vathek is the central figure, these themes are first manifested in the Sentimental relationshp of Nouronihar and Gulchenrouz and her later desertion of it. Matthew Lewis in *The Monk* (1795) joins the ignorance/innocence theme to that of real incest between brother and sister, integrating the figures of the Sentimental hero and heroine, the Gothic villain, and the witch. His novel has two self-reflecting Sentimental pairs—Lorenzo and Antonia, and Raymond and Agnes. In both cases love occurs at first sight; the men are all goodness and nobility, the women sweetness and virtue. Agnes, it is true, trangresses sexual propriety, but Antonia is a carefully guarded innocent who knows nothing of the world. Both couples undergo extravagant Gothic horrors. The interesting development that Lewis adds, however, is another pair. Ambrosio, the monk of the title, is Antonia's brother and their likeness to each other is emphatic. Like his sister, he has started out innocent, but he has been betrayed by pride into extending the human limits of virtue. In setting himself up as a chaste adherent of all Christian virtues, he first behaves with a lack of compassion when faced with human weakness and then succumbs to a lust as fierce as his chastity was severe. Matilda is a witch figure who turns out to be an agent of the devil. Once she has seduced him from his strait and narrow path, his instantaneous passion for Antonia (he does not know she is his sister) is an evil desire for self-gratification that knows no bounds, stops at nothing, and entirely lacks that delicate feeling for the beloved that makes the Sentimental hero incapable of doing her the smallest harm. By making Ambrosio and Antonia brother and sister and making them alike in their innocence, Lewis presents their total ignorance of the world as a trap. She remains pure to the last, but she is victimized and destroyed. He becomes a maelstrom of evil desires and actions that are worse in proportion to the stringent virtuousness from which they arise. Thus, Ambrosio and Antonia, a horrifying parody of the quasi-incestuous Sentimental characters, embody the idea of evil as the distortion and destruction of natural goodness.

Ambrosio and his crimes are as glaring and strident as everything else in Lewis' novel, but Victor Frankenstein in Mary Shelley's *Frankenstein* (1818) is a more ordinary human figure. Here the quasi-incestuous childhood relationship appears again.[19] It is used to throw a subtle light on Victor as "villain." He is no longer really a villain but, rather, a complex character. Consequently, the reader, as much as the characters in the novel, is prevented from making clear and absolute moral judgments concerning him, the very "danger" Mackenzie and Beattie had foreseen when they inveighed against mixed characters. Victor Frankenstein looks both forward to the later nineteenth-century tradition and backward to the early Gothic novels. In his occult dabbling in medieval science his ancestry in Vathek and Carathis and in figures like Ambrosio and Matilda in *The Monk* is evident. A guilt-ridden character like Manfred in *Otranto* is also one of his forebears, while Hawthorne's Rappaccini and Aylmer (of "The Birthmark") are among his progeny. He has a "good" descendant, too, in the first of the detectives, Poe's all-seeing deductive genius, Dupin, in "The Murders in the Rue Morgue."

Frankenstein is a noble figure gone tragically wrong, one of the Romantics' Faustian characters who have crossed the border of legitimate inquiry into the realm of forbidden knowledge. The appearance of this particular theme in the scientists of later Gothic novels reveals the underside of scientific Utopianism much as earlier Gothic fiction shows the underside of Sentimentalism. As man came to be seen as able, through science and education, to make himself and his society whatever he wanted them to be, the dangers as well as the power and value of knowledge must have become abruptly vivid. Frankenstein, a Sentimental character lured into Faustian wrongdoing, is an exemplification of the link between the two lines of thought.

In this respect, *Frankenstein* is more interesting than its contemporary *Melmoth the Wanderer* (1820). Melmoth is condemned to walk the earth because he, too, has transgressed the bounds of forbidden knowledge and Maturin's novel is full of allusions to the Garden of Eden and the fruit of the Tree. The transgression, however, puts Melmoth beyond the pale of ordinary humanity. He is handsome, but the fire of Hell burns in his eyes and his laugh is demonic. He certainly is not delicate. He is a damned spirit intent on enticing another to take his place. As such he is an embodiment of the internalized Hell of Gothic literature, a preternatural creature, no longer an ordinary human being. He is set in stark and simple contrast to Immalee, the pure child of nature. Alone on her island, she has no childhood companion. She has grown up completely innocent—and completely ignorant. Consequently, she cannot recognize Melmoth's evil until it is too late. Her devotion is so great that she declares she will follow him to Hell itself, an error committed only by Nouronihar among other Sentimental heroines. She and Melmoth appear in a realm of pure fantasy where the good and evil aspects of human nature are starkly and separately portrayed in beings who slide beyond the realm of the human, he as a damned soul, she as goddess of Nature. The worlds within worlds of *Melmoth* circle by degrees to the center of the soul. The novel, however, leaves the reader at this center, contemplating his nature in the abstract. *Frankenstein,* on the other hand, combines the themes, the devices, including reflecting characters, and the ideas of Sentimental and Gothic fiction in order to portray Victor as a tormented, living man.

Frankenstein is a character with whom the reader sympathizes even as he recoils from his deed—the creation of the monster. Sentimentalism and its Gothic underside are thus set up in contrast to each other, with science, the forbidden knowledge that brings evil in its train, as the link between them. The Sentimental heroine, Elizabeth, is seen through Frankenstein's eyes and it is true that the preface warns that all Frankenstein says cannot be taken as expressing the author's views. No ironic counterview of Elizabeth is provided, however, to offset Frankenstein's account. No alternatives are given, such as are provided by Henry Clerval and Elizabeth to Frankenstein's view of his scientific investigations, and such as Frankenstein himself gives us in telling of his friends' mounting distress and his own persistence in the downward path. It can be assumed, then, that a corrective to Frankenstein's view of Elizabeth would have been provided if such were needed. It is not needed—for literary rather than human reasons. The very limitation of the characterization gives Elizabeth the same quality of character-as-device seen in other Sentimental heroines. The flat, Sentimental portrait counteracts implicitly the notion of man as inherently degenerate—Elizabeth is what man should be and, later, the monster's tale specifically outlines man's natural state as benevolent.

Elizabeth, like others of her kind, has been brought up in seclusion by Frankenstein's benevolent and gentle parents. The marriage of the parents themselves is based on virtue. "There was a sense of justice in my father's upright mind," Frankenstein recalls, "which rendered it necessary that he should approve highly to love strongly."[20] Here again, we find virtue loving virtue. When the parents first set eyes on Elizabeth, they recognize her at once as an angel-child of a quality quite different from the cloddish little peasants with whom she lives. In true Romance fashion, her golden hair, blue eyes, and delicate features, which even at four years old are "expressive of sensibility and sweetness," turn out to be her inheritance from her father, a Milanese nobleman. In this respect, Elizabeth is like Theodore in *Otranto.* First presented as physical manifestations of nobility and refinement, they and others like them are found to be of noble birth as well. This convention is found in early novels of all types. No more than the princes in fairy tales should the noble characters in these novels be taken as primarily expressing class consciousness in the author. Nobility in rank corresponds to nobility of soul, just as a yawning chasm corresponds to the spiritual abyss, and that true nobility is, in turn, manifested in delicacy and physical beauty. There are enough dark, wicked, forbidding-looking noblemen to show that we are not asked to take such correspondences at face value, but rather to see them as literary, symbolic representations.

Elizabeth is described in extravagant terms and allowed very little action in the novel because action would make her too "real" and detract from her function. She is Frankenstein's "more than sister—the beautiful and adored companion of all my occupations and my pleasures." She is, in life and death, the same sort of inspiration as Walpole's Matilda is in death. Frankenstein says of her: "The saintly soul of Elizabeth shone like a shrine-dedicated lamp in our peaceful home. Her sympathy was ours; her smile, her soft voice, the sweet glance of her celestial eyes, were ever there to bless and animate us. She was the living spirit of love to soften and attract; I might have become sullen in my study, rough through the ardour of my nature, but that she was there to subdue me to a semblance of her own gentleness. And Clerval—could aught ill entrench on the noble spirit of Clerval? Yet he might not have been so perfectly humane, so thoughtful in his generosity, so full of kindness and tenderness amidst his passion for adventurous exploit, had she not unfolded to him the real loveliness of beneficence and made the doing good the end and aim of his soaring ambition."[21]

The novel thus presents the ideas of nature and nurture that the Sentimental novels posit and that are the center of "education" novels. The seeds of goodness, if properly nourished and sheltered, flower forth in human beings of true sensibility. Brought up in "considerable seclusion" by actively benevolent foster parents, Elizabeth remains angelic and herself enhances the good effects of such a childhood in Henry and Victor, for Victor, too, grows up with "bright visions of extensive usefulness." It is true that both boys seem to have an innate personality that is not all virtue and gentleness. But the Sentimentalists, as Beattie's remarks on sublime characters show, did not deny the existence of other human qualities. They claimed that the strong aspects of a virtuous person's personality would enhance the effect of his goodness in the world; an evil man's corruption would have consequences the more dire as his abilities were great. Henry, the son of an unimaginative merchant, loves "enterprize, hardship, and even danger for its own sake." Victor's "temper was sometimes violent, and my passions vehement." The adventurousness of the one and the passionate temperament of the other have the power to propel them into great virtue. Both, under Elizabeth's influence, wish to dedicate their lives to the good of mankind. Victor's degeneration from this state is carefully accounted for and is reflected in his monster. Our sense of the cause and nature of his evil is conveyed by the initial establishment of his character as one of Sentimentalist virtue in a setting far removed from "civilization."

The remote and idyllic setting is nevertheless brought forward in time and space to contemporary Switzerland and Germany so that the reader is faced with the dilemma of mixed good and evil in the novel as one of pressing immediacy in his own world and his own mind. The road from the simplified idyll of the Sentimental embodiments of man's potential good to an ambiguous treatment of good and evil like Mary Shelley's is beaten out by the feet of the Gothic villains. The basic devices keep recurring, used and re-used to present ideas about psychological aberration. As the Gothic novels explore the nature of evil, their villains follow a line of development. At first they are isolated and tormented giants at war with themselves. But then they are combined with the Sentimental characters and become men of more ordinary, less villainous stature. As the human in them is stressed, their inner conflicts split them in two. Then, in the doubles figures, two separate characters appear, an ordinary but basically good man who is confronted with his own evil self, a physical copy who is a spiritual contrast. With this development the characters of the Gothic grow more complicated, but they are hardly more realistically portrayed. It is Victor Frankenstein's affinity to his monster that makes him interesting. The changes in characterization reflect a deepening confusion over moral absolutes in their application in human nature and a growing awareness of the depth and complexities of the human psyche.

CHAPTER THREE

CHARACTERS— THE SPLIT PERSONALITY

To wicked spirits are horrid shapes assign'd,
This beauteous form assures a pitious mind.
John Donne, Holy Sonnets IX [Gardner]

THE Gothic villain is a mythic, symbolic figure. He is presented through techniques that show, not frail humans, but the nature of human frailty. These villains are symbolically, not literally, diabolical, and they appear along with ghosts and monsters to reproduce evil, madness, and torment located in the human mind. Their vices are presented as distortions of human nature and as essentially unnatural. Their monstrosity lies in their being embodiments of spiritually misshapen humanity with the unfulfilled potential to have shared natural grace and beauty. Their sense of this lack in themselves and the struggle between their good nature and their evil propensities is what awakens echoes of real nightmare in the reader, however extravagantly the manifestation of evil is portrayed.

Villains fall into three principal types. Villain/heroes, whose madness and evil derive from the conflict within them, have a close affinity with the Sentimental hero, and give rise to the doubles figures. Manfred, Ambrosio, and Frankenstein belong to this type. Manfred is a reluctant villain, Ambrosio a shrinking villain, and Frankenstein so much the hero that his villainy appears in a separate character. In contrast, a second type has little of the Sentimental hero about him because it is his function to be the darkness opposing light. Ann Radcliffe's Montoni in *The Mysteries of Udolpho* and Schedoni in *The Italian* are among these. Finally, the villain as a figure of the grotesque is demonic, confronting the reader with unrelenting evil. Such are Vathek and Melmoth the Wanderer. These categories overlap, of course. Manfred, as an ancestor of them all, shows only a little of Ambrosio's torment. Frankenstein is portrayed sympathetically, but the evil he causes is as dire as the depradations of Manfred and Ambrosio. And his monster is a grotesque as well as a doubles figure. Montoni and Schedoni by their very impenetrability veer toward the grotesque at the same time that the Sentimental premises of Ann Radliffe's novels contradict this view of them. These premises imply that her villains must "really" have started out good of heart and assert that the diabolical features are illusory. Vathek, because he is weak and less intent upon evil than his mother, is not entirely a grotesque. And the portrayal of Melmoth vacillates between the demonic and the human. Both consequently are drawn back from grotesquerie toward the same sort of characterization as the other villains. Thus, the three types are variants giving different emphasis to the common ideas they portray.

They are densely packed with characteristics that symbolize the varied implications of Sentimentalism regarding evil. And their enigmatic personalities often express the confusing dilemmas of moral relativism. The Gothic villains have twisted natures and are full of unnatural lusts and passions. They suffer the torments of the damned while committing their nefarious deeds because they must battle with themselves to commit them and must often also repress their own feelings. Yet, the reader is invited to feel with and for them in the rending conflicts from which they suffer.

The attempt to arouse the reader's sympathy is adapted from the Sentimental novels. Since those works seek to show that no amount of suffering through lacerated sensibility is as intolerable as the spiritual emptiness of worldly vanity, they invite the reader to have compassion for misguided worldly characters. Unfeeling and incapable of the deep joys of virtuous conduct, the worldly gain nothing in opposing the hero and heroine and they destroy their own happiness.[1] The Gothic villain, too, is ultimately more to be pitied than his victims.

At first sight he seems a more substantial figure than they, just as the worldly characters of the Sentimental novel are more mimetic than the heroes and heroines, because they are less idealized. A gloomy adult glowering out of his isolation, the Gothic villain is a complex battleground where evil makes war with Nature. He is consequently less passive than the heroes and heroines. Necessarily, he is the aggressor, the oppressor of his innocent victim, and can be involved in action without detracting from the structure of the novel as a reflection of the mind. He is the storm that breaks over the calm world of virtue.

As a consequence of this kind of complexity, Gothic novels occupy a middle ground where concepts of general human psychology can be portrayed.[2] Their characters fall between the abstract and the concrete, between the transcendental and the everyday, between the allegorical and the mimetic. As Walpole put it, they "think, speak and act, as it might be supposed mere men and women would do in extraordinary positions."[3] Real toads, in fact, in imaginary gardens. Or, alternatively, imaginary toads in real gardens. They emit conflicting signals to the reader. On the one hand, they tend to resemble the mimetic characters of the realistic social novel. On the other, they are mythic characters of fantasy. The features that make them resemble mimetic characters are designed to elicit sympathy and understanding, while those that differentiate them give them their symbolic power.[4]

The characters yield their full meaning only when they are analyzed in relation to the special narrative structures set up for them. Their place in their own craggy, mist-filled settings, however, is elucidated by an anatomy of the characters themselves. The characterization of the Gothic villain has clear demarcations. The action he takes is the expression of the violent emotions that sweep through him and he must be kept clear of minor, everyday doings. If he eats and drinks at all, he carouses; if he rides a horse, he leaps on to one already saddled. He must not be caught shaving or chatting at the hearthside or his effect will be lost.[5]

Even Montauban in *Julia de Rubigné* is a dark, brooding, undomesticated character. His sense of honor is so confounded with pride that it has become false and twisted. When he realizes it has blinded him to true honor such as Julia's he is rent in two and kills himself in despair. In *Otranto* the even more stormy Manfred also finally recognizes the extent of his own evil but with that realization the evil is stripped from him. He has been broken under its weight but he does not go further and destroy himself. Because now he is no longer at war with himself, he can retire in sorrow but no longer in anguish to the contemplative monastic life. His former exasperation came from inner conflict, driving him to commit an impressive list of misdeeds. He is not only a usurper, he is also cruel to his wife. He tries to make an incestuous marriage and finally commits a wanton murder in killing his own daughter. Nevertheless, to do these things he has constantly to war against his own nature and the more his conscience smarts the worse he behaves. We are told that "ashamed . . . of his inhuman treatment of a princess [Hippolyta], who returned every injury with new marks of tenderness . . . but not less ashamed of feeling remorse towards one, against whom he was inwardly meditating a yet more bitter outrage, he curbed the yearnings of his heart, and did not dare to lean even towards pity. The next transition of his soul was to exquisite villainy."[6]

The first characteristic of such a villain is his isolation. He who cuts himself off from virtue divides himself from his fellow man. The evil in him, moreover, by also cutting him off from his own "nature," causes him to suffer a continual psychomachia. Perhaps it is for this very reason that incest associated with violence is such a persistent motif. Just as the quasi-incestuous relationhip of the Sentimental characters was a reflecting device, so real incest, an assault against a daughter or sister seems to epitomize the self-destructive struggle within the evil mind.

The incest motif fits with precision into the central theme of *Otranto*—that the sins of the fathers will be visited on the children. Manfred's psychological agony grows out of the burden of guilt and crime he has inherited with the castle. Though his "temper" is "naturally humane" he is obsessed with the need to continue the usurpation. It is in dire conflict with himself that he tries to put aside his wife and marry Isabella, who, because she was originally intended for Manfred's son Conrad, stands in the relationship of a daughter to him. All the characters in the novel react in horror to this design because it is incest.

In the time of retribution that constitutes the action of the novel Manfred's two children suffer death. Conrad, crushed because he is too delicate to take over the burden of the guilty usurpation, is little more than a representation of degeneracy in Manfred. Matilda, killed in a rage by her father who thinks he is stabbing Isabella, depicts the virtue which viciousness attempts to annihilate. The distortion of Manfred's nature prevents the natural continuation of his line, leads him toward the unnatural crime of father-daughter incest, and directly from there to the murder of a daughter.

The theme of children suffering for their fathers' sins is played out in Manfred. He himself carries the burden of crime and guilt. And his sins are "visited upon" Conrad and Matilda in that they suffer death through him. The murder of a child is also the final step into the morass of unnatural crime, bringing about the reassertion of the virtuous life. And, finally, the stabbing is sexually symbolic. Manfred thinks he has come upon a love scene between Theodore and Isabella and in his jealousy "stabs" her (actually Matilda) to prevent Theodore from possessing her. The setting for this incestuous murder in the sanctuary before the statue measures with dramatic irony the extent to which crime and passion have blurred Manfred's perceptions so that he completely misinterprets the situation; the crime he commits is perpetrated blindly. In this act he symbolically commits the incest he has planned.

Earlier in the novel there is a suggestion that Manfred is unknowingly, even unwillingly, tempted to incest. When he rejects Matilda's gentle effort to comfort him in his rage and frustration because Isabella has escaped from him, his inexplicable ferocity toward her suggests he is desperately spurning a temptation that she represents. He spurns this daughter and his wife as fearsomely as he claims his son's betrothed. At the end of the novel the full realization of all that has happened brings collapse of the castle and the translation of the giant figure of Alfonso to Heaven. Retribution is thus completed by the destruction not of Manfred but of the wicked and forbidding manifestation of Manfred's evil mind—the castle. Manfred, broken but purged of the evil, retires to a pious life of renunciation in the convent.

In contrast, Lewis' *The Monk* ends in total disaster for Ambrosio. All his life he has been imprisoned in the monastery. And he finally finds himself in the prison of the Inquisition. These buildings do not collapse like Manfred's castle because they represent the prison of the self. Ambrosio has spent his life locked up and, to the end, he is unable to free himself. His break-out into a life of lust and crime is only more enslaving than the life of piety. And his pact with Lucifer does not release him as he thought it would. Lucifer effects his escape from the prison only to destroy him. In *Otranto* the Spirit of Alfonso soars up into Heaven. In *The Monk* Ambrosio is carried up into the sky alive to be pitilessly dropped in a physical fall to earth, and to despair and death.

The combination of the quasi- and real incest themes produce an interesting amalgam in Ambrosio of awareness and unconsciousness of what he is doing. To an even greater extent than Manfred he is exasperated into greater evil by his knowledge that he has betrayed and brought to nought his own high standards of purity. It is surely the beauty of that purity that he loves in Antonia but, driven on by lust aroused by the she-devil Matilda, he first tries to destroy Antonia's goodness by seducing her, then, when frustrated, destroys her. Incestuous rape, fratricide, and matricide—Lewis' choice of crimes emphasizes the unnaturalness of evil. Since these the crimes are incestuous, moreover, the sense of self-destructivenes is enhanced.[7] In his plunge into crime, Ambrosio loses all control over himself. He watches in agony his own descent into evil. In making him ignorant of the worst of it—that Antonia and Elvira are his sister and his mother—however, Lewis also symbolizes the idea of sexual repression. Ambrosio's violation and murder of Antonia is also set in symbolic opposition to the self-denying and life-giving love of Lorenzo and Antonia. Ambrosio's violent imposition of himself allows Lewis to combine the theme of isolation with the device of the self-reflecting characters. Ambrosio can never attain the satisfactions available to his almost identical sister.

In Ambrosio a number of characteristics of the Gothic villain are adumbrated. He is an embodiment of virtue, purity, and sensibility such as makes the perfect Sentimental hero, until pride pushes him to exceed the human limits of his nature, a trait found in the Faustian scientists among his successors. This inability to accept human limitation is an aberration. Eighteen-century optimism saw the bounds set for humans as a happy state. The view that Man when true to his own nature was in harmony with all Nature meant that he could find self-fulfillment along the *via media.* In

Sentimental and Gothic tales, the characters who transgress, from the gentle Werther through the frantic Ambrosio and ferocious Melmoth and many a scientist right down to Dr. Jekyll, all pay for their refusal to accept limitation as the price of happiness.

Lewis' portrayal of Ambrosio as sexually repressed, although it at first seems surprisingly "modern," is also typical. It was certainly a factor in the shock the novel caused when it first appeared,[8] but sexual crimes caused by a distortion of natural drives is a major Gothic theme. Lewis is quite explicit about the repression itself, about the sexual dreams that torment Ambrosio once Matilda has aroused his desires, and his hungry addiction to physical gratification once the barriers are broken down. Ambrosio is monstrously guilty of sexual crimes as a direct consequence of his repression of his natural sexuality. He thus reflects the Benevolist view that all man's faculties, endowments, and feelings, including his sexual feelings, are God-given and so should neither be denied nor over-indulged. This can be seen in what we are told of Ambrosio's upbringing.

Both he and Antonia have attained adulthood in a state of innocence because they have been brought up ignorant of the world. She grows up like other Sentimental heroines in the countryside, isolated from the corruptions of civilization and in harmony with external and internal nature. He, with essentially the same powers of sensibility, is confined to the forbidding imprisonment of the monastery. He is isolated from the world's corruptions but also from Nature. As a result, he first denies his own nature, and then drives his natural impulses to unnatural extremes.

By making Ambrosio and Antonia brother and sister by blood and making them unaware of it, Lewis is able to present the situations in his novel with typical Gothic symbolism and irony. Antonia is physically a true Sentimental heroine. She is first described as seen through the eyes of Lorenzo: "What a seraph's head presented itself to [Lorenzo's] admiration! Yet it was rather bewitching than beautiful; it was not so lovely from regularity of features, as from sweetness and sensibility of countenance. . . . Her mild blue eyes seemed an heaven of sweetness."[9] The occasion is that important moment in Ambrosio's life when he first preaches in public, exposing himself for the first time to contacts outside the monastery and their concomitant temptations. A complex of parallel relationships is set up in this scene. Lorenzo typically falls in love with Antonia at first sight. Ambrosio captures Antonia's innocent heart as she listens to him preach, and Matilda's, too, or so we are led to believe. When Matilda later turns out to be an agent of Lucifer, we have to adjust our understanding of her earlier claims.[10] Later on, Ambrosio will be overwhelmed with desire for Antonia in the same instantaneous fashion. In between, however, he goes through his temptation and fall, seduced by Matilda who first presents herself to him disguised as the young novice Rosario.

The Sentimental convention of hero and heroine each instantly recognizing a mirror image of sensibility in the other is played upon in these parallel attractions: Lorenzo/Antonia, Antonia/Ambrosio, Matilda/Ambrosio. Thereby, Ambrosio's marred, distorted, unnatural passion for Antonia is shown to be an aberrant mangling of the ideal of Sentimental love. When their blood relationship is finally revealed, the "unnatural" passion of incest reinforces this idea in the reader's emotions.

In general, the novel is directed at the reader's feelings. The scene of Ambrosio's first preaching, for instance, concludes with Lorenzo's dream foreshadowing Ambrosio's final fall from the devil's claws into the abyss. In the dream a human monster breathing fire, with "Pride! Lust! Inhumanity!" stamped on his forehead, tries to drag Antonia down to Hell with him. In effect, the dream warns that Ambrosio in pride, lust, and cruelty will kill Antonia, damning himself in the process, while she flies from his arms to heaven. At the time, however, Lorenzo has seen Antonia only once and neither he nor the reader is in a position to understand the warning. Thus, the purpose of the dream appears to be to create a tone and atmosphere early in the novel that anticipates the lurid intensity of its conclusion. Much of the sensationalism of the novel, which is probably ascribed correctly to the extravagance of Lewis' youthful imagination, furthers this assault on the reader's feelings. The macabre scene of rape and murder in the crypt of the convent, where Ambrosio and Antonia are surrounded by the mouldering remains of the dead, for instance, underlines the idea of its unnaturalness by its very disgustingness.

That such a monster as Ambrosio should make any bid for the reader's sympathy is surprising. Yet, everything in Lewis' way of presenting the character makes such an appeal. Entirely chaste and virgin at the age of thirty, Ambrosio thinks that, unlike other men, he can overcome any temptation. In reality, the opposite is true. His resistance is particularly weak because of his purity, just as Antonia is especially prone to deception because she is so innocent. The price of purity is lack of experience and the inexperienced are the most easily misled. Antonia, however, is misled about others, whereas Ambrosio is self-deceived, entirely out of touch with his own motives and feelings.

At the beginning of the novel, his repressed sexual feelings are sublimated into adoration of the virgin. Like Matilda in *Otranto,* praying before the statue of Alfonso, Ambrosio prays in his cell before the portrait of the Madonna. Lewis is crudely explicit about his psychological state. Gazing at the painting, Ambrosio exclaims in his confusion: "Oh! if such a creature existed. . . . Should I not barter for a single embrace the reward of my sufferings for thirty years?" He immediately dismisses such sacrilegious thoughts, but this is another foreshadowing device. Barter his soul is exactly what he does. The portrait is in fact, in itself, sacrilegious, being not of the Virgin but of the flesh-and-blood Matilda, who introduced it secretly into his cell.

Matilda, a witch-demon figure, twice finds her way into

Ambrosio's unsuspecting heart before he realizes she is a woman—and her female form is also a deception. She is an agent of Lucifer, and not a human being at all. Ambrosio is first transported—in religious adoration, as he supposes—by the beauty of the painting. Then he is further seduced into a love he thinks innocent and protective when Matilda, disguised as the young novice Rosario, enters the convent and attaches her/himself to him.

This very girlish young novice with "his" sweet voice and docility of manner, who brings flowers to the abbot's room, is hardly convincing, but the disguise does take one step further the idea of the danger of Ambrosio's unconsciousness of his sexual desires and motives. Here, his affection for Rosario renders him incapable of resisting his/her entreaties when he turns out to be a woman, Matilda, who declares she is in love with him. Thus, Matilda's seduction of Ambrosio is brought about by her first appearing to him as a young man. In a parallel development his later and much worse descent into sin is effected by a male figure. When Ambrosio damns his soul by allowing Matilda to call up Lucifer, the devil appears in the form of a beautiful, naked young man, a fallen angel with the cast of sadness which is the shadow of Hell across his handsome features.[11] Ambrosio's complete confusion and the agonized eagerness with which he rushes to his destruction convey a sense that his desires have a violent grip on him because he cannot understand either their origin or their object.

All this suggests that, because of his repressed human nature, Ambrosio is more, not less, liable to sin than others. The impulse to sin, though unnatural, is buried deep in his subconscious mind where he cannot control it. At first himself seduced into abandoning his chastity, he is then swept by lust into attempted seduction and from there into murder, rape, and another murder. But this abrupt slide into crime has taken him into depths of evil beyond what he knows. By making him unaware that his victims are his mother and his sister Lewis emphasizes the moral morass which is the paradox of sensibility: Ambrosio's blindness symbolizes the inability of his native "goodness" to recognize evil.

Everything in Lewis' novel is like a distortion of the devices of the Sentimental novel. Ambrosio's unnatural upbringing travesties the natural upbringing of the Sentimental heroes and heroines. His lust for his sister ending in rape and murder travesties the natural love of Sentimental characters. The beauty of Matilda as the Virgin in the portrait and as the novice Rosario, instead of reflecting her spiritual state, is a cruel disguise to bring Ambrosio down. Lucifer's appearance as a beautiful young man is also a deception. When he carries Ambrosio away at the end of the novel and literally hurls him into the abyss, he appears in all his ugly ferocity. Even the subplot of Raymond and Agnes is a travesty of the Sentimental. Its heroine's trials and tribulations are luridly exaggerated and its hero's adventures, with dark forests and bandits, pure fairy tale. There is little reason to suppose, though, that the work is parody. Rather, these distortions indicate the belief that evil in the human mind makes a travesty of what that mind should be in its natural beauty.

Ambrosio's fall from virtue is equated with the original Fall in Eden and his self-abandonment to sin is portrayed as the selling of his soul. Early on, when Matilda first throws off her novice's disguise and reveals herself to be a woman, Lewis uses symbolic foreshadowing to equate the sexual seduction with the Fall. In the garden scene, when Ambrosio tries to make Matilda leave the monastery, she asks him to pluck her a rose. He does so and is stung by a serpent. The scene suggests the Fall of man through woman and the birth of lust into the world. Similarly, to suggest the loss of spiritual peace, the novel is peopled with real devils. Matilda herself goes from Virgin Mary, to young man, to woman, to witch, to devil. Lucifer appears as fallen angel then as full-blown devil. And there are such incidental figures of the sub-plot as the bleeding nun, who is a ghost, and the Wandering Jew. The symbolic force of these figures depends on our not taking them at face value as the meaningless contents of a grab bag of effects from the *Schauerroman.* They should be examined in relation to one another within the structure of the novel.

Ambrosio is initially depicted as an innocent cut off from reality, especially as he is paralleled by and reflected in the other Sentimental characters: Antonia, Lorenzo, Raymond, and Agnes. As a result, he is later seen as in deadly conflict with himself, his natural goodness poisoned and corrupted. Miseducation in the monastery has made the expression of his nature in true love and normal sexuality impossible. In the older view of man as degenerate by nature, the result would be a struggle with an evil outer force, the busy devil bringing to life in the individual the evil latent in all men. When, however, evil is conceived as internal but not latent, it is not necessarily present. It is an alien presence within the self from which the self naturally shrinks in horror. Paradoxically, such a view brings about the characterization of evil as a separate being external to the self of the villain. In *The Monk* it is the deceptive, self-metamorphosing devils who have Ambrosio in their grip. In later novels it will become the double, a horrifying, misshapen reflection of the distorted self.[12]

That Ann Radcliffe was not as inclined as Lewis to delve into the darker recesses of the mind seems undeniable. That she was therefore a lady too proper to come to terms with her own material seems an unjustified conclusion, however. The connection between her works and Lewis' in itself indicates the contrary. These two very different people, both writing in the mid-90s, have long been known to show a reciprocal influence. *Udolpho* had its effect on *The Monk,* which in turn affected *The Italian.* Yet Lewis is frequently dismissed as a spinner of meaningless fantasy in the same breath that scorns Ann Radcliffe for giving rational explanations for the fantastic in her novels. In fact, they used the same or similar materials to weave stories based on the same set of ideas, but each gave a different emphasis to those ideas. Lewis, like Walpole and Beckford, couched in symbolic form tales that were a fictional manifestation of phychological states. Ann Radcliffe wove stories that come close to being novels of development, a form which itself requires the presentation of the psychological make-up of the central character. Her heroines, of course, are not highly mimetic characters, but they are the central figures of her romances and, dramatic and threatening though her villains are, they are the means through which the heroine attains maturity and wins the hero, not themselves the center of interest. Consequently, when their symbolic usefulness has passed, they are restored to ordinary humanity and the supernatural phenomena are shown in the daylight of common sense to have been projections of the heroine's fears. Thus, while it seems very likely that the novels of Lewis and Ann Radcliffe are expressions of the respective temperaments of each author, the differences between them are mostly important as revealing their different purposes. That in turn makes for different villains.

Ann Radcliffe's Schedoni in *The Italian,* for instance, is said to be inspired by Lewis' Ambrosio. Yet he is different from him in almost every respect and, in some, he is a direct opposite. Schedoni is a man with a criminal past who has taken refuge in the monastic order. Ambrosio was dedicated to God and the monastic life as a child. Schedoni's evil is unexplained and there is no hint of the innocent-turned-evil about him. He is a frightening figure with his cadaverous appearance and his apparent ability to appear and disappear as if he were without the solidity of flesh. He is powerful and self-controlled, not a shuddering sinner like Ambrosio. His crime is associated with incest, however, in that he covets his brother's wife. It, like Ambrosio's, underlines the unnaturalness of his evil. And he comes within inches of murdering his own daughter, like Manfred in *Otranto.* Like Manfred he sets out to stab Ellena, the heroine, to prevent her marriage to the hero, though his motive is not sexual. Like Ambrosio he does not know of his victim's close blood relationship to him. The familiar device of the portrait—this time a locket around Ellena's neck containing a picture of her mother—saves him as he stands on the brink of murder. He also is a tormented soul filled with unquenchable remorse that poisons his very nature. But his consciousness of his sins makes him an exasperated, desperate evildoer like Manfred, not a helpless sinner like Ambrosio.

Furthermore, for all that he is the character in the novel that has aroused the greatest interest, the story is Ellena's not his. Consequently, the Gothic devices of characterization are used mostly to put her into situations which try her courage and her constancy. Certainly, his tortured mental life must arouse some compassion, in order to bring home to the heroine and the reader the usual lesson about the unrewarding nature of evil. It is Ellena's passage through trials and harrowings that is central to the novel, however.

The Mysteries of Udolpho is even more clearly a novel of development of the heroine. In it the world of Montoni is contrasted with the world of sensibility in which Emily has grown up. Like many an eighteenth-century heroine, she has to learn the prudence by which the virtuous are to live in the real world without being corrupted. She learns it by passing through the Gothic world. Even less than Schedoni is Montoni a diabolic figure or a figure of good-gone-wrong. The possibility of taking him either way is undercut when it is revealed that he is not in reality the embodiment of evil that he has seemed to Emily's eyes. The monster that she sees is a mere bandit. He is a wicked bandit but neither as evil as she thinks nor, once all is revealed, a symbolization of psychological aberration. Schedoni and Montoni are bad men of this world, well aware of what they are doing. Because of their different slant *Mysteries* and *The Italian* make their villains part of the characterization of their heroines. Ellena and Emily are not so different from Catherine Moreland in *Northanger Abbey* as has been thought.[13]

A novel of the same period, Godwin's *Caleb Williams* (1794) reflects more directly the Gothic concept of evil. It has always been considered only "borderline" Gothic, but it is of great interest in its development of the idea of the double. It is quite explicit in its treatment of the distorting power of evil weighing on the good soul.

The novel follows the course of the road into evil, rather than mapping the evil mind once formed. It is centered on Caleb and his descent into paranoia. Since he is to a large extent the double of the novel's hero/villain Falkland, however, his paranoia is a distorting reflection of Falkland's own. Falkland is not merely a potentially good man but, in fact, a highly admirable and much respected figure of society. Caleb starts out young, naive, and undeveloped. He is formed in Falkland's image when he joins his household, and Falkland's hold on him lies in Caleb's admiration of his nobility. In this sense, Caleb is the reflection of Falkland's good self.

Like so many others, Falkland's fall is due to pride, pride in his reputation as a good man. His concern for his reputation is not a fault in itself. In the world Godwin portrays reputation is the means by which the world knows a good man and by which he sees himself reflected in the world's eyes. Falkland's reputation is originally the reflection of his true goodness. Before the opening point of the novel, his desire to maintain his reputation is one and the same as his desire to maintain his virtue. Once he has committed a crime, however, he becomes bent on maintaining it for its own sake, to conceal vice, not to portray virtue. Instead of reflecting his goodness, it screens his evil. For Falkland is a murderer, in his own eyes an ignoble, sneaking assassin. The novel traces his total breakdown, brought about because he is tormented by his own spiritual destruction. It is the festering wound of his knowledge of his own hidden evil that destroys him.

Most of the novel is taken up with Caleb, Falkland's reflection. The affinity of spirit between them has developed in Caleb a nobility like Falkland's own. Once Caleb discovers Falkland's secret, however, Falkland becomes an invisible power hounding Caleb from place to place. In this, he is trying symbolically to hound out of sight his own noble self. In wanting to face the secret of his evil, that self (Caleb) has become the source of his mental torment that necessitates the shattering effort to repress his knowledge of himself. Falkland never lets Caleb rest or settle, for fear he may reveal the secret and ruin the noble reputation. The degenerate self thus pursues the good self because it cannot bear the fact that the good self knows of the crime.

The nobility that Caleb has learned from Falkland prevents the younger man from turning on and exposing his tormentor until it is too late. The good self, after trying and failing to escape in a variety of disguises from the evil self, finally turns at bay and brings the evil self to trial. In this Caleb, as double, is many-sided: he is not only a reflection of Falkland's noble younger self; in fleeing Falkland he reflects Falkland's own attempt to flee from the knowledge of what he has done; in turning on Falkland he represents Falkland's reluctant acknowledgment to himself of his own fall; and Caleb's paranoid fear of Falkland parallels Falkland's paranoid fear of discovery.

His feeling at the end that he has destroyed Falkland is true in this sense. The aspect of Falkland that suffered from all the concealment (Caleb) gives the final blow to the repressive other side of him. In the process he makes himself "truly miserable" and reproaches himself because "my reflections perpetually centre upon myself." Once he is dead, Falkland has become pure nobility again. The surviving self can barely live without him. Caleb had gradually become more haunted, more willing to ascribe a supernatural ability to Falkland each time he uncovered another of Caleb's disguises. And finally, driven to desperation, he had turned on him and denounced him. But Falkland had already symbolically turned on and denounced himself. As can be seen from his ghost-like appearance, his own knowledge of his evil had worn his nobility down to a ghostly shadow. He was tortured by the obsessive desire to keep the secret, just as Caleb had become obsessively secretive. The use of the double thus produces a mirror effect. Good and evil are reflected back and forth until their images become confusingly intermingled.

Godwin's novel is subtitled "Things As They Are." It contains some "ungothic" material and its main theme is an indictment of society's hypocrisy. Godwin's view of the causes of such hypocrisy, however, also grows out of benevolist tenets. With its condemnation of prison conditions, his novel is political and social. Nevertheless, it is also an important step in the development of the fantasy doubles figure and it is based on the same premises about the nature and effects of evil in the human mind as the Gothic novels.[14]

By the time of James Hogg's *Confessions of a Justified Sinner* (1824), also considered borderline Gothic, the fantasy double is a fully developed device. Hogg is deliberately confusing about the nature of the sinner's double. In this novel, unnatural self-repression results in ignorance of the self, pruriency, and hypocrisy. The "true" self does not know its other side. The evil impulses are buried in the subconscious and when they surface in evil action the poor Sinner does not know what he is doing, or even whether it is he that is doing it. When the double appears, the Sinner is literally and figuratively beside himself. Set in Presbyterian Scotland, the novel uses the doctrine of grace for literary purposes. The Sinner believes himself to be one of the elect and so he simply cannot see himself as in a state of sin. The first time he meets his double, before any real crime has been committed, he sees him as an exact copy of himself.

On subsequent occasions, however, the double takes on other forms. Sometimes it is the Sinner's brother; eventually it becomes a tormenting devil.

The shifting form of the double reflects the Sinner's bewilderment and his lack of self-awareness. Although Hogg uses the Presbyterian upbringing to account for the Sinner's confusion, the shifting double muddies the question of evil. Whether it comes from within or without remains uncertain, since the double is sometimes seen as separate from the Sinner and at others is a hallucination. By using a system of narrators who tell conflicting versions of the Sinner's story, Hogg shows that society itself is unable to discriminate, to recognize the course of evil, just as Godwin had done in *Caleb.* By the samc method, Hogg also implicates the reader in society's blindness. We are kept expecting that all will become clear as the different accounts of the Sinner's actions are given. Then these expectations are disappointed. The Sinner's complete degeneration into madness and hallucination toward the end of his account makes us more and more sure that the double is his projection of his own evil which he cannot face, despite the old woman's earlier account of having seen two figures. But then the narrator of the whole returns and by his own unsureness prevents us from deciding after all.

Such ambiguous presentations are frequent in later Gothic works and are connected with the use of the doubles figures. Both aim at securing a reaction in the reader that is an amalgam of compassion for and horror of the figure of monstrous evil presented to him. Out of these mixed feelings comes that attitude of moral relativism that is perhaps the most important feature of the Gothic. In accord with the tenets of Sentimentalism, authors directed the didactic force of their works to their readers' feelings. To enhance their readers' sensibility they developed techniques that put the readers in the characters' place, causing them to feel with the characters. From the point of view of absolute moral values, however, it was seen from the beginning that a mixed character or a sublimely evil one was dangerous. If it aroused sympathy, it would subvert didacticism. Presenting the villains as at war with themselves was sufficient to place the reader in a position to have compassion for them. Splitting them into two to form hero/villains bound to self-destruction only increases the reader's involvement. In his struggle with his double the villain becomes a human being in the grip of nightmare. Underlying the perennial fascination of horror stories is this identification on the reader's part; fear is aroused by the murky and incomprehensible that may lurk in the reader's own being. The realization that the work is a fantasy does not diminish this effect. Rather, it makes it possible.[15]

In *Caleb* and *The Sinner,* the implications of the Gothic novels that precede them become clear. By keeping their readers confused about the reality within the work, Godwin and Hogg face them with the frightening puzzle of psychological evil while preventing them from forming moral judgments from an objective detached stance. Both *Caleb* and the *Sinner* are written out of the same general tenets as other Gothic novels and, through the eerie figure of the double, present Gothic psychomachia. They trace the steady degeneration of an individual into madness under social pressures, however, rather than delineating general psychological states. They have consequently been traditionally treated as "borderline" Gothic.

Mary Shelley's *Frankenstein* is the Gothic novel with the greatest claim to fame because it has become a modern myth. It also has a hero/villain, Victor Frankenstein, and makes use of the doubles figure to establish the relativity of moral values with great complexity. Victor is not simply good-gone-bad. Mary Shelley makes him a despairing human being by symbolically projecting the evil in him into the monstrous exterior of his creation. Mary Shelley's use of this device is in itself sufficient to have made *Frankenstein* a myth. Victor Frankenstein is an ordinary man throughout. His charm, his great sensibility, his intellectual brilliance are not presented in images that set him apart. He has neither beetling brows nor piercing eyes, no supernatural powers or malignant diabolical passions. Unlike so many Gothic figures, he is not identified with a house, castle, or any other building that may serve to make such a villain massive, threatening, engulfing. Throughout the terrible story he tells, Victor is an ordinary man in all but the extent of his suffering. His hold on us is inescapable, mythic, because the consequences of his deeds are horrible out of all proportion to his intent in performing them. It is just so that we look on the possibility of evil in ourselves, knowing as we do so many mitigating circumstances, convinced as we are that we are indeed compassionable beings. To the extent that our identification with Frankenstein is close, our fear of the evil that comes from him will be great.

The monster Frankenstein creates is his spiritual mirror image. With its yearnings for love and companionship, it is a Sentimental character hidden within its own monstrous form; just as Victor is a Sentimental hero encrusted over with the evil of false-scientific, Faustian pride. The "man" made in Frankenstein's image is an ugly monster with a Sentimental core as gentle as Frankenstein's own.

Frankenstein's early upbringing is typically that of the Sentimental hero and early in the novel Mary Shelley carefully accounts for his corruption. Victor himself says that "the birth of that passion which afterwards ruled my destiny [arose] . . . from ignoble and almost forgotten sources." He protests that if his father had explained to him the dangerous falsity of renaissance and medieval occultism, "it is even possible that the train of my ideas would never have received the fatal impulse that led to my ruin."[16] The destruction of a tree by lightning leads him to abandon occultism in favor of "mathematics and the branches of study appertaining to that science" and he sees this as "the last effort made by the spirit of preservation to avert the storm that was even then hanging in the stars and ready to envelope me. . . . It was a strong effort of the spirit of good" to save him from "utter and terrible destruction" (pp. 300–1).

Once the original corruption has set in through the

pursuit of the occult, however, it breeds further evil. It has turned Victor's passionate desire to use his science for the benefit of mankind into pride. It makes him twist every opportunity and fly in the face of God. For instance, Professor Waldman, whom Frankenstein meets at the university, is a good man, but his words to Victor concerning the power of "natural philosophy" produce terrible consequences. "As he went on I felt as if my soul were grappling with a palpable enemy; one by one the various keys were touched which formed the mechanism of my being" (pp. 307–8). It may be that Mary Shelley's metaphors are unintentionally mixed here, but they represent the progression of Frankenstein's degeneracy: from a spiritual being, to an instrument played upon, to a machine that is not its own master but must act on impulses supplied from outside.

Once embarked upon his experiment, Frankenstein cuts himself off from everyone, acting on "a resistless and almost frantic impulse" and voluntarily putting himself into the isolation characteristic of Gothic villains. Forgetful of home, blind to the beauty of nature, he pursues his end singlemindedly. Later he sees this very ardor as a symptom of evil: "A human being in perfection ought always to preserve a calm and peaceful mind. . . . If the study to which you apply yourself has a tendency to weaken your affections and to destroy your taste for those simple pleasures . . . then that study is certainly unlawful, . . . not befitting the human mind" (p. 316). Frankenstein tells Walton: "Often did my human nature turn with loathing from my occupation" (p. 315). As he works on his creation he becomes actually feverish and, he says, "I shunned my fellow creatures as if I had been guilty of a crime" (p. 317).

Like his predecessors among the Gothic villains, Frankenstein's self-isolation comes from an inherent and insurmountable sense of guilt that finally becomes insupportable. His crude creation is shaped not out of the clay of the earth like Adam, but from the rotting remains of the charnel house. It is a monstrous being, both literally and figuratively, created by a mock-god, a mere man playing the divine role. Mary Shelley has made it near enough to a man in shape and spirit, however, to make it evident that the eighteenth-century belief in a benevolent human nature was still current. Created full-grown, the monster is aware of the birth of consciousness and the unfolding of its nature. It goes through a foggy period as its senses awaken and its understanding of the outside world increases. It learns language while hidden in the shed attached to the DeLaceys' cottage. With language, it also learns the natural state of man. The feelings that awaken in it with the coming of self-knowledge are all the good social feelings displayed by the virtuous characters in the Sentimental novels. And it knows these to be its nature. It is only when it is rejected by man and sees that it has been abandoned by "god," that is, by Frankenstein, that it turns evil. In this change from good to evil it reflects its creator. Even this blighted creature of a bungling creator may arouse some sympathy in the reader, but it is, nevertheless, a purely symbolic figure of fantasy and not a representation of a man. Mary Shelley's point is that Frankenstein could not create a man, that the attempt was bound to produce only a monster. And, in fact, it is himself that he has made into a monster. The monster is Frankenstein's double, representing not the evil side of Frankenstein only, but his whole, complex spiritual state.[17]

Elizabeth, the heroine of the novel, also reflects Frankenstein. She does so, however, in the Sentimental tradition, as a separate being. She is a character in her own right, not a symbolic embodiment of a part of Frankenstein's personality. She reflects and enhances the good in him, so that, in the beginning of the novel, it holds sway over his passionate character, directing it to good ends. She eventually loses her influence, but it is still her spirit that follows him in his final pursuit of the monster.

In this we have an odd situation: the Sentimental heroine reflects only the good part of Frankenstein, while the double reflects both good and bad. Mary Shelley seems more interested in maintaining the idea of the basic goodness of human nature, than in portraying a split personality. So Frankenstein does not split into good and evil parts. He suffers because he has become a monster. The sensitive, virtuous being that he was remains within him, half aware of its own monstrosity and helpless to change it. He first refuses to face this fact; that is, he flees the monster. Then, when forced to recognize it, when the monster confronts him and tells its tale, he still cannot bear to deal with the consequences. That is, he cannot make the right decision about creating a mate for the monster. With each refusal to recognize his own monstrosity, a fresh disaster occurs. It is only when all that he loves has been destroyed that Frankenstein changes from pursued to pursuer and, at last, urged on by the spirits of Clerval and Elizabeth, tries to track down and destroy the monster. That is, he finally attempts to understand himself and to do away with the evil within. It is as he comes to the end of this journey of self-discovery that he comes upon Walton who, as a scientist with ambitions to benefit mankind, also reflects him. And at this point, he tells his story, explaining, in effect, what he has now understood. He dies still unsure in his advice to Walton. But symbolically, the monster's false god is dead and it reverts to its Sentimentalist self. So we may see Frankenstein, too, as remaining outwardly monstrous because what he has done cannot be undone, but inwardly restored through self-knowledge to his virtuous self.

The monster as a symbolic figure tells us several things. It is only outwardly misshapen until its efforts to win human love and friendship are rejected. When it turns to destructive violence it manifests a complicated concept of the origin of human evil. First, because the virtuous DeLaceys reject it, we see symbolically that Frankenstein's plunge over the border of the permissible makes him a monster that goodness and virtue find entirely inimical—for the DeLaceys see only the monster's exterior, a point that is emphasized by the old man's being blind. This rejection is consonant with the general Sentimentalist idea that virtue cannot love vice and that vice is a distortion of the natural being. It, in turn, makes it possible to interpret the monster's ravages as also symbolic. Frankenstein's family is destroyed by the monster he has created. That creation can be seen to be the monster he has made himself into by pursuing false science and arrogating God's province to himself.[18] Thus, we may say that his pride and self-isolation have cut him off from his own humanity. They have destroyed the fine-tuned relationship of love and sensibility which made his family more than just a group of people related by blood. It is not the descent into crime of an individual that is depicted here. Rather, it is the idea that the human mind that gives way to pride and vanity locks up its finer nature in a monstrous shell. In doing so, it destroys those it loves by cutting itself off from them.

All the benevolist themes of Sentimentalism are epitomized in Frankenstein, who can retain our sympathy throughout since the monster commits all the violent deeds. But they are brought to a despairing conclusion. In the same period, the gloomy view reflected in the use of the grotesque is epitomized in Charles Robert Maturin's *Melmoth the Wanderer* (1820). The grotesque is a way of facing absolute evil. When it is used to characterize a Gothic villain Man's evil comes to seem inherent and inevitable. As in *Vathek,* works in the grotesque tradition often incorporate comic features in their characters. In *Melmoth* and later works, however, it is combined with the tragic Gothic view. Melmoth, a figure who, like the Wandering Jew, cannot die, has sold his soul to the devil. As a demonic character he is different from the villains with split personalities. They enable the Gothic authors to draw man as, in his essence, deserving compassion because his evil is an excrescence on the core of his being. A creature from the abyss like Melmoth works in the opposite direction. The fact of his being a demon makes him other-than-human and he is compassionable only to the extent that he retains something of human nature. His torment lies in his having lost his humanity and with it the ability to die. So he is like the Gothic villains at least in being a victim of remorse that stings him into his lack of compassion and his diabolical cruelty to Immalee. But he is a creature to inspire horror rather than fear, because he is not an example of the goodness and concomitant frailty of human nature.

It can be seen here, perhaps, why the "High Gothic" is seen as reaching its culmination in *Frankenstein* and *Melmoth*. The heroes and heroines of Sentimentalism were defeated and destroyed by the worldly, but for them the world was well lost. Then, in Gothic fiction, such villains as Manfred and Ambrosio were presented as evil distortions of their own good potential. When they went down to defeat, evil itself was shown to be self-destructive, containing the seeds of its own collapse. In Ann Radcliffe's novels, even more optimistically, evil was overcome and sensibility-tempered-with-good-sense restored. In Mary Shelley's novel, however, while the values of Sentimentalism are affirmed, its defeat is almost complete. All the members of Frankenstein's family are killed and he himself dies in his attempt to run down his monster. The only spark of hope lies in the fact that that evil thing, hating itself and still loving its creator, immolates itself. This improbable ending to the novel suggests that if man turns from his own evil and reaffirms his natural goodness, the evil will burn out and a new generation—in this case, Walton who turns back from his scientific quest—will turn away from vain pursuits. This hopeful note, is obscurely sounded, however, and it belongs in the concluding frame. For most of the novel we have lived with a despairing belief in the fragility of goodness and the overwhelming power of evil. Perhaps the pessimism of *Frankenstein* and *Melmoth* have made them appear as the final working out of the questions raised by Gothic literature. They are, in reality, only a step along the way. The remainder of the nineteenth century abounds with Gothic tales that continue to grapple with the problem of evil.

Gothic literature continues to use the doubles figure and other weird and wonderful characters along with the split and tormented hero/villains. Together they indicate a persistent oscillation between optimistic and pessimistic views of human evil. They appear sometimes separately, sometimes combined, but always with a disturbing ambiguity that makes it less and less easy to objectify the horrors portrayed and not to bring them home to ourselves. The Gothic works appearing in the nineteenth century display a great deal of moral confusion and doubt. Throughout the tradition, however, the effectiveness of this literature is dependent on more than the invention and inclusion of ghosts, monsters, and devils, animated portraits, statues, mirrors, and strange buildings. To present this phantasmagoria as the world of the mind, Gothic authors from Walpole to Henry James and beyond, enclose the strange beings they invent in the exotic settings of a world of their own. They achieve the sense of a strange world through systems of narration that amount to structural principles and are perhaps their most important device. It is through the method of telling that Gothic tales reveal their meaning.

CHAPTER FOUR

SETTING AND NARRATIVE STRUCTURE— "FAR OTHER WORLDS AND OTHER SEAS"

The Mind, that Ocean where each kind
Does streight its own resemblance find;
Yet it creates, transcending these,
Far other Worlds, and other Seas
Andrew Marvell, "The Garden"

HERE is a curious "lateral shift" in the techniques of the Gothic. Settings turn out to be part of characterization and methods of narration to be principles of structure. In the same way as the castle is identified with its owner, other aspects of setting convey mood, tone, and emotions. The elements become bearers of anger or fear or tranquility and, as a result, these emotions become general and "the whole world" is filled with them. So that both characters and reader may experience these emotions, the landscapes evoke the sublime, as characters do, through a vagueness of outline and a reaching toward infinity. This treatment of setting is one reason for the limited characterizations in the Gothic. If the villain's anger is expressed as a raging storm breaking over the heads of all and sundry, for instance, the effect of the emotion rather than the fact of it is emphasized. The reader is

imaginatively involved in that effect and the anger rolling through the sky and sending torrents of rain to earth is experienced as having victimizer as well as victim in its grip.

Special means are needed to produce such unusual weather along with the rugged mountains, tranquil plains, seas alternately calm and stormy, and buildings that are prisons or fortresses or havens, all of them expressive of character. They necessitate a structure that makes a closed-off region within an outer world. To create both these worlds, the outer and the closed, within the novel, a special narrative method is used. When, for instance, a narrator returns to tell his hearers about people and events they know nothing of, this narrative method places the reader in the same relation to the world described as the listeners to the tale. Imagery, characterization, and action are made an interpretable whole through the spatial and temporal relations among the narrator, his account, and his audience, which includes the reader. The metaphorical fictive world of the novel becomes a symbolic construct with the reader carefully positioned in relation to it. A sense is created of entering a strange and wonderful place, a closed world within the everyday world. In this, as in all else, Gothic and Sentimental novels are on the same track and use the same devices to lead us into the landscape of the mind. Through their closed, isolated worlds they deal with psychological reality. The mind is turned in on itself. As Werther puts it: "I turn back into myself and I find a world." The closed world is not entirely cut off. Indeed, its effect often depends on the sense of moving in and out of it. Narrators and characters move from one closed world to another, or from the open, everyday world into a closed one or vice versa. Such movements enhance the sense of the static and the strange.

Several devices achieve this effect. The discovered manuscript which tells a tale set in a remote time and/or place, as in *Otranto,* is one. The use of the conventions of a particular type of fantasy, as in *Vathek,* is another. A third, and probably the most important, is the tale within a framework or the closely related tale within a tale. The system of narration is frequently first-person and sometimes also epistolary. Both systems lend themselves easily to these narrative devices and simultaneously produce another effect. They help create confusion and ambiguity. A first-person narrator may be assessed for his reliability if the author supplies the necessary ironic clues. Frequently, Gothic fiction leaves us guessing and thereby greatly increases the sense of groping toward something puzzling and partly known, in this case, the mind. The first-person narrator may be the central character, a major, or a minor one, or one who appears only in the slenderest frame to start the story rolling and sometimes to round it off at the end. Which he is will, of course, determine his effect, but the narrative method is always used to make the world of the novel strange.

Walpole uses an "editor" in *Otranto* to present an ancient manuscript containing a tale from a remote time and exotic place. This prepares the reader to follow his tale according to its own rules. We accept its weirdness and artificiality as a part of it, as a signal telling us how to understand it. Once it has been set up this way, the idea that the castle within the closed world of the novel is a symbolic manifestation of Manfred's mind becomes possible.

Here the "editor" is a sketchy figure and the chronicler a mere shadow in the mists of time. Consequently, when they introduce the exotic setting of the story proper, they demand belief, not literal but figurative, in a world beyond the everyday. This is easily done when everything about that world is unusual. A much more complex sytem is required, however, when the setting is contemporary and also not exotic. This necessarily was the case for the fictional world of the feelings in Sentimental novels. *The Man of Feeling* (1771), Goethe's *Werther* (1774), *Julia de Rubigné* (1777), and *Paul and Virginia* (1787) all have complex narrative structures. These Gothic fiction adopted as soon as it, too, brought the horrors and vagaries of the evil mind from wild and far away regions home to the reader's own hearth. By presenting the reader with a world-within-a-world these quasi-tragic works prevent him from dissociating the mind and feelings portrayed from his own mind. The setting is both contemporaneous and strange to maintain the analogy between the fictional closed world and psychic reality, and also to portray the features of sensibility free from the dinner parties, the inns, the busy traffic of everyday that tell of the external and the individual rather than the internal and the general.

Consequently, the closed world lies within the familiar one. The contrast between country and city is used to set off the world of sensibility from venal society. Frequently, the hero or heroine writes letters from the inner world of the novel to an understanding friend in the "outside" world, thus placing the reader in the same position as the friend—outside, reading a report from inside. In other works, the story is mediated through a narrator, often through two, even three narrators.

The narrator or narrators are at least shadowy figures within the work, providing a sense that the strange story is mediated through someone who belongs to the familiar world. Mackenzie's *The Man of Feeling,* for instance, is presented in the first place by the hunting gentleman who obtains the manuscript from the curate and presents it as a document that he and the reader will find equally strange and interesting. The manuscript itself is torn and incomplete because the curate has been using its pages as gun-wadding. The author of the manuscript is the lonely recluse who has no part in the plot, but who knew Harley and can tell his story. Thus, the story proper comes through this shadowy, nameless being who once flitted vaguely into the field of vision of the stolid curate. The curate is a man of the everyday world, unimaginative and without the curiosity to read what he is gradually putting to a practical (and doubly destructive) use. So, the manuscript passes only accidentally into the hands of the equally nameless "I" and by then, there are only fragments of it left. The result is a feeling that the man portrayed, Harley, is a strange and sensitive being. He might easily have passed all unnoticed through our busy, noisy world, preoccupied as it is with the "business of life" rather than with feeling. The novelist does not portray an unusual person whom the reader will see as very different from himself. Rather, through a man unsullied by the usual compromises and distortions of life in the world, Mackenzie makes his reader recognize that delicate, "good" human nature with which we are all endowed. That nature must be cherished, protected, and cultivated if society is not to distort it. The quiet English village becomes a remote world in which feeling itself is the reality.

A similar effect is achieved by the epistolary novels in which the hero or heroine writes from the closed world to a friend outside it. The story is then relayed to us by the Friend or by an "editor." The most famous instance of this technique is Goethe's *The Sorrows of Young Werther.* Werther himself, writing to his friend in the world he has left, emphasizes the remoteness and isolation of his new world. The reader's sense of this is increased by the friend's mild remonstrances, which suggest an inability to understand either the hero's mental state or the closed world that corresponds to it. And since our measure of the truth of what Werther writes lies in these vaguely implied remonstrances of his friend, Werther is not an entirely reliable narrator. We realize, for instance, that what he is telling the recipient of his letters is not just an account of his life in the closed world but an account of his mental state. Sometimes he exaggerates; sometimes he is mildly hysterical; he sees in Nature, in Lotte, in his situation extraordinary significances that the ordinary person would not attribute to them. This much we can see; we are never able to tell just how unreliable he is, however, and so our sense of ambiguity, of things left undecided is enhanced.

Other epistolary, Sentimental novels that also seek primarily to portray the mind use the same method without ambiguity. In these, the friend in the outside world has previously shared the closed world with the letter writer and so understands it. As a consequence, the account seems sure and reliable because it is confirmed by its recipient. Mackenzie's *Julia de Rubigné* is one of these. Although it is much less known than *The Man of Feeling,* it is a "purer" example of Sentimentalism in the novel for several reasons. It lacks the ironic tinge of the comic. And its character types, the paired, self-reflecting hero and heroine who find themselves in opposition to the world, are typically Sentimental. It also elaborates on the epistolary system by having more than one character send letters out of a closed world, in each case with a slightly different effect. It exhibits remarkable parallels with Bernardin de St. Pierre's more famous *Paul and Virginia,* which appeared ten years later.

As in *The Man of Feeling,* the tale is presented as a manuscript of mysterious origin that has seen the light only by the merest chance after passing through several hands, the intermediary ones oblivious to the world of emotional sensitivity that it reveals. Incomplete and maltreated, it has been given to the "editor" by the son of a Frenchman. He, in his turn, bought it at hazard from a boy in Paris who was trying to sell it to a pastry cook to be used as wrapping paper.

It is a series of letters written by several characters from more than one symbolic, closed world. Julia writes to her friend Maria who is in the outside world, while Julia has returned to the countryside in which they both grew up. Right away, Julia reveals that the letters are to be self-examining musings, not accounts of actions and events. Away from the bustle of society, she tells Maria, she finds "time to settle accounts with myself." She goes on to declare: "I will speak to you on paper when my heart is full, and you will answer me from the sympathy of yours."[1] Savillon is the Sentimental hero. He and Julia having grown up together like brother and sister in the countryside and come to love each other as adults, he has left to seek a "competency" that will make him "worthy" to propose to Julia. He writes from Martinique, a strange country to him, to a friend back in the Paris he has left and which he longs for. Montauban, the mysterious villain of the piece, writes from Julia's closed world in the country to a friend in Spain. Spain, as a result, becomes a contrasted world. The failure of Julia and Montauban to understand each other and the consequent disaster is thus shown as the result of their inhabiting different mental "worlds." Segarva, the Spanish friend, understands Montauban for, from his own point of view, Montauban is writing from the strange outside into the familiar. Their world represents the exaggerated sense of pride and honor in their mental make-up which is inimical to and, indeed, destructive of the world of sensibility so necessary to Julia and Savillon.

Thus, we have three variants of the closed world/everyday world relationship. Julia, Maria, and Savillon belong originally to the closed world of sensibility in which Julia alone is still living and from which she writes. Savillon has left that world, driven from it, in effect, by his poverty and the need to make himself independent. The world he finds in Martinique is neither closed nor exotic—it is a continuation of the insensitive social world in which neither he nor Julia can breathe freely. It is that world exaggerated to naked brutality in its treatment of its black slaves. At this point the interpolated story of Martin is introduced, adding still one more variant. The "editor" proffers ironic "apologies" for the story as being nothing to the purpose, but perhaps interesting in itself—an apology not unlike the ironic manner the "editor" of *Otranto* uses to attract our attention to his theme.

Martin, an Englishman, is the only sympathetic soul Savillon finds. His story is really, of course, very much to the purpose and the "editor's" disavowal highlights that fact. Martin is another character of sensibility and is immediately recognized as a kindred soul by Savillon. He has a perfect marriage but has come to this exotic land to seek his fortune. So painful is separation both to him and his wife that she sets out to join him with their two children. All three are drowned and Martin's life is forever shattered. Like Julia and her parents, the wife and children have been living in simplicity in the countryside, forced there by financial difficulties, but content, indeed happy, except for the pain of separation from Martin. Before setting out the wife writes to Martin that they would have been happy if they had settled down in poverty together. When she and the children are drowned, Martin feels he has destroyed them.

Both Martin's story and Savillon's follow the Sentimental pattern: a perfect love and understanding that comes naturally and an inability to contend with the world that brings disaster but not the defeat of the ideal. Savillon succeeds in making money and returns to propose to Julia. But a character from the outside world, a sea captain, has returned in the meantime to Julia's closed world where he has repeated a false story that Savillon has married. When Savillon arrives, it is too late—Julia is married to Montauban whose hand she has accepted in gratitude for his friendship to her father. Of course, since it is their character to be virtuous, neither Julia nor Savillon dreams for a minute of the possibility of changing the situation. Julia's marriage vows are sacred to both. They have a tearful momentary reunion in the cottage of their "foster mother," their common wet-nurse who regards them as her "children": "[Lasune, the wet-nurse] loved them, said Le Blanc, like her own chilren, and they were like brother and sister to each other."[2] But this reunion is also, for both, a final farewell.

This much of the novel is purely and typically Sentimental, but the presence and actions of Montauban are decidedly Gothic. And his villainy, like the sensibility of Savillon and Julia is shown structurally, through the separate closed worlds he writes from and to. Driven by his pride and overweening sense of honor, he poisons Julia and then himself as well, dying in despair. The sense that this is a development resulting from a distortion in human nature is conveyed by the contrast between the Sentimental country setting and exotic Spain bound by its rigid and mistaken sense of honor. Montauban's twisted nature is revealed through the letters he sends into that world (Spain) which represents the distortion of his character. Julia cannot understand Montauban's nature or even suspect its existence, but he writes to one who inhabits a world where that nature is comprehensible.

Montauban is also given a setting suitable to a Gothic villian. When he visits Julia at home, in her own world, he appears noble and honorable, at least until it is revealed that he has literally bought Julia by taking up and then paying her father's debts. When they are married, however, and he takes her back to his family estate, he is seen differently. This estate represents his own personality, as distinguished from the general codes and customs represented by Spain. Julia, who has no suspicion of him or reason to fear him, describes their approach in this way: "There was a presaging gloom about this mansion which filled my approach with terror; and when Montauban's old domestic opened the coach-door, I looked upon him as a criminal might do on the messenger of death. My dreams ever since have been full of horror; and while I write these lines, the creaking of the pendulum of the great clock in the hall, sounds like the knell of your devoted Julia."[3] Julia experiences the irrational horror of a character of sensibility at the first sight of the villain's house or castle. This reaction symbolizes that immediate, instinctive apprehension of evil that is the counterpart of the instanteous recognition of good in Benevolist theory.[4] And, of course, the house tolling Julia's death knell is once again a representation of its owner, who will bring about her death. In *Julia de Rubigné* the Sentimental novel's presentation of the psychology of good and the Gothic novel's revelation of the distortion of the mind into evil are shown side by side and in balance.

Bernardin de St. Pierre's more famous *Paul and Virginia* is strikingly similar to *Julia* but lacks the Gothic element.

It further emphasizes the common aims and methods of the two types of novel. As in so many Sentimental novels, the ordinary society of worldly France is sufficient to defeat Paul and Virginia, without the assistance of a Gothic villain. The narrative structure, however, has exactly the form used by later authors to bring their Gothic tales into the heart of the familiar world. *Paul and Virginia* also contains in its "Author's Preface" a precise statement of the nature of the Sentimental novel: "I desired to reunite the beauty of tropical nature with the moral beauty of a small society. I proposed to evidence certain great truths, among them: that our happiness consists in living in accordance with nature and virtue."[5] The closed worlds that Sentimental characters inhabit are such "small societies" that display the "moral beauty" of "living in accordance with nature and virtue."

Structurally, the novel depends on a double system of narration. The "Author's Preface" has stated that "the customs of the inhabitants, and even more of the Europeans who live there [in the island of Ile-de-France, that is, Mauritius, where the novel is set], often spoil such landscapes" as he is about to draw. The society of the island is French, bourgeois, and stuffy, and the hero and heroine and their mothers still have to be isolated within it, as Harley, the man of feeling, had to be in England. The narrator of the whole describes his climb to the rock-ridged basin in which Paul and Virginia once lived an idyllic, isolated life. Then their story is related to him by a second narrator, an old man whose "features were noble and of marked frankness." Thus, this island in the Southern sea is not in itself a closed world, even though it is geographically remote. The narrator must still penetrate within it to the plain, now desolate, where Paul and Virginia grew up in solitude. Their sentimental relationship has left no trace and we can know of it only through the venerable old man. Thus the system of narration, like Mackenzie's manuscript fragments, emphasizes the fragility of that relationship.

These narrative structures shared by Gothic and Sentimental novels show variations that would make it possible to sub-categorize them. The unnaturalness of the villain is emphasized by presenting the tale as a manuscript in *The Castle of Otranto* in the same way as the extreme sensibility of the heroes and heroines of Mackenzie's novels is shown. The nature of sensibility is portrayed through the epistolary technique in *Werther* and *Julia.* A sense of the gradual revelation of horror upon horror, or the gradual uncovering of the truth is developed in Clara Reeve's *The Old English Baron,* Maturin's *Melmoth the Wanderer,* and Stevenson's *Dr. Jekyll and Mr. Hyde* through the use of a cumulative technique. At the same time, *The Old English Baron* is also a manuscript, a frgmentary one like *The Man of Feeling,* while *Melmoth* uses interpolated stories and manuscripts, and *Dr. Jekyll and Mr. Hyde* uses written records within the main story. *Frankenstein, The Fall of the House of Usher, Wuthering Heights,* and *The Turn of the Screw,* which is also a manuscript, use the same system of mediated narration as *Paul and Virginia* to suggest worlds within worlds. Related to them, in turn, are the structures of *The Mysteries of Udolpho* and *The Monk.* Ann Radcliffe frames the Gothic section of *Mysteries* with Sentimental sections. Lewis has an extensive interpolated story within his direct-narrative main plot. The main plot is luridly Gothic, the interpolated story basically Sentimental, with an, if possible, more lurid Gothic section within it.

Such complex structures show how these works are to be read. They are variations of a technique for establishing the sense of a fiction that cannot be taken at face value, so that the reader will indeed apprehend the closed world as the isolated world of the self. Rather vaguely, in statements by Walpole, Walter Scott, and Clara Reeve, and quite clearly in an essay of Ann Radcliffe's, we can see this purpose. It is evident, too, that these authors understood what they were doing. When Walpole says in his preface to the second edition of *Otranto* that he was "desirous of leaving the powers of fancy to expatiate through the boundless realms of invention," it is clear that he is thinking of his novel as a fantasy.[6] In a letter years later, when he describes how he let his imagination take over "till I became on fire with the visions and feelings which it excited," he seems to be speaking of a startling new experience of the literary process by which the imagery of his subconscious was brought to the surface of his mind.[7]

Some of Scott's comments on Walpole and his work indicate the purpose of Walpole's techniques. Scott insists that Walpole is not just evoking horror for horror's sake. He provides his supernatural events with a medieval setting to give his tale probability:

> It is doing injustice to Mr. Walpole's memory to allege, that all which he aimed at in The Castle of Otranto was 'the art of exciting surprise and horror;' or, in other words, the appeal to that secret and reserved feeling of love for the marvellous and supernatural, which occupies a hidden corner in almost every one's bosom. Were this all which he had attempted, the means by which he sought to attain his purpose might, with justice, be termed both clumsy and puerile. But Mr. Walpole's purpose was both more difficult of attainment, and more important when attained. It was his object to draw such a picture of domestic life and manners, during the feudal times, as might actually have existed, and to paint it chequered and agitated by the action of supernatural machinery, such as the superstition of the period received as matter of devout credulity.[8]

Historical accuracy is not Walpole's aim here, Scott is saying, but rather, the presentation of a "probable" situation (the medieval setting) in which the supernatural can be used for literary purposes. Walpole's own statement that he had placed "his mere men and women," that is, his eighteenth-century characters, in these "extraordinary positions" (that is, the experience of supernatural happenings) suggests that he is using the exotic and unfamiliar to present unchanging human nature. In other words, he is using it symbolically to gain the reader's assent, not to the medieval belief in ghosts, but to the possibility of his concept of evil as presented in Manfred.[9] Since the castle is

Manfred's mind, the "dark ages" in which the story is set stand for his benighted state, the medieval characters for concepts of honor and valor associated with those times, and the supernatural events for psychological effects of the conflicts set up by clashing emotions and values. Hence, Scott follows his claim for the serious purpose of *Otranto* with the statement that: "The natural parts of the narrative are so contrived, that they associate themselves with the marvellous occurrence; and, by the force of that association, render those *speciosa miracula* striking and impressive, though our cooler reason admits their impossibility. Indeed to produce, in a well-cultivated mind, any portion of that surprise and fear which is founded on supernatural events, the frame and tenor of the whole story must be adjusted in perfect harmony with this main-spring of interest."[10] By portraying that basically unchanging creature man in the costume and setting of a dark age when the supernatural was a matter of real superstitious belief, Walpole makes his supernatural events effective agents of the sublime. In doing so he grips his reader and transports him into sympathy with the villainous character, who is an embodiment of the psychological state of evil.

When Walpole rejected Clara Reeve's attempt to keep the supernatural to a minimum, he probably thought she had failed to understand the reader's willing acceptance of supernatural occurrences as, in Scott's words, "the premises on which the fable depends," which makes apprehension of the symbolic possible.[11] Actually, she may well have understood it and, for that reason, modified Walpole's method to suit the different purpose of her novel. She thought, in any case, that his work was ineffective. In calling *The Old English Baron* the "literary offspring of the Castle of Otranto," she writes that, like Walpole's tale, it combines "the ancient Romance and the Modern Novel." While admitting that the supernatural is a feature of romance necessary "to excite the attention" she charges Walpole with having used it too freely. The result of such extravagance is that his tale "palls upon the mind; . . . the machinery is so violent, that it destroys the effect it is intended to excite. Had the story been kept within the utmost *verge* of probability, the effect had been preserved." She finds Walpole's supernatural so exaggerated that instead of transfixing her, it makes her laugh.[12] Walpole's comment on this was that as a "gothic story . . . but reduced to reason and probability," *The Old English Baron* is altogether lacking in interest.[13] The difference, however, is really one of degree. Both of them, and Scott also, see the supernatural as a device that will direct the reader's attention to the meaning of the tale beyond its frightening effects.

Clara Reeve uses the supernatural more moderately than Walpole because her novel on balance is as much Sentimental as Gothic. In it, for instance, the Good are central to the tale and all ends in an elaborate "comic" resolution with evil conquered, virtue affirmed, and the suitable marriages arranged. *The Castle of Otranto,* on the other hand, ends with the downfall of Manfred. The happy marriage is dealt with in a single sentence, hardly sufficient to constitute a resolution. The difference in tone and emphasis is striking. Clara Reeve presents her unhistorical, sentimentalist view of the Good in a "Gothic tale" to establish the great virtues as timeless and as stemming from the traditional values of Merry England. When she wishes to embody ideas of virtue and honor, vice and the torments of conscience, she uses devices similar to Walpole's. The hero Edmund, for instance, bears his father's face, as Theodore does his grandfather's in *Otranto.* Physical and moral beauty are thus made to correspond, as they do throughout Gothic fiction. The way in which the resemblance is discovered from the portraits of Edmund's parents is again typically Gothic. The ghost, here as elsewhere, symbolizes the unexpiated guilt that lies so heavily on Sir Walter Lovel's conscience. Thus, when she needs the symbolic, Clara Reeve uses it. When the romance tradition by itself is sufficient, she uses that.

Ann Radcliffe, so famous for her after-the-fact rational

explanations of apparently supernatural occurences, is nevertheless quite as clear as Walpole about the aesthetic need to make a flat assertion of the "reality" of such phenomena if they are to achieve their effect. Unlike Clara Reeve, she does not keep them to a minimum. Instead, she gives them dramatic force, delaying her common-sense explanation of the apparently supernatural until it has done its work as a literary device. Some of her ideas are expressed in her essay on "The Supernatural in Poetry," which discusses the use of setting and characterization. A fictional dialogue between "two travelers in Shakespeare's native country, Warwickshire," it was left incomplete at her death. Her characters, Mr. W. and his friend, discuss setting and characterization in Shakespeare and their views were to have been related to the need in the Sentimental and Gothic novels to engage the reader's emotions, to lift him out of himself and into the minds and feelings of the characters. It was, according to the editors of *The New Monthly*, "originally part of an INTRODUCTION to the Romance, or phantasie, which is about to appear," that is, to *Gaston de Blondeville*, also published posthumously and reviewed in the same volume of the journal.[14]

In the essay, she describes at some length the Gothic use of landscape when her characters discuss the way Shakespeare uses setting to affect the reader or audience. Of Shakespeare, Mr. W. says that his was an "undying spirit . . . that could inspire itself with the various characters of this world, and create worlds of its own; to which the proud and the beautiful, the gloomy and the sublime of visible Nature, up-called not only corresponding feelings, but passions; which seemed to perceive a soul in everything; and thus, in the secret workings of its own characters and in the combinations of its incidents, kept the elements and local scenery always in unison with them, heightening their effect." Speaking of the storm scene in *Julius Caesar*, W. says it "was not more terrible to them [the conspirators] than their own passions. . . . How much does the sublimity of these attendant circumstances [the supernatural events accompanying the storm] heighten our idea of the power of Caesar, of the terrific grandeur of his character, and prepare and interest us for his fate. The whole soul is roused and fixed, in the full energy of attention, upon the progress of the conspiracy against him."[15] Mr. W. also discusses the figures of the supernatural. Having spoken of "how much Shakespeare delighted to heighten the effect of his characters and stories by correspondent scenery," he goes on to the witches in *Macbeth.* He asserts categorically his disbelief in witches, stating that "the only real witch [is] the witch of the poet." For this reason, he objects to stage presentations of the witches in Scottish dress and other features that tie them to the everyday world: "The wild attire, the look *not of this earth,* are essential traits of supernatural agents, working evil in the darkness of mystery. Whenever the poet's witch condescends, according to the vulgar notion, to mingle mere ordinary mischief with her malignity, to become familiar, she is ludicrous, and loses her power over the imagination; the illusion vanishes."[16]

Thus, the supernatural must be presented as "real" and as having a reality of its own separate from the concrete and the everyday. The author need only maintain probability. W. believes in ghosts no more than he does in witches. He asserts that the realization that the maker of all things could necessarily also make ghosts possible is enough to make them "probable." The ghost of Hamlet's father is Shakespeare's supreme achievement—supreme because its effect is enhanced by "circumstances [the night on the battlements, the star, the crowing of the cock] which the deepest sensibility only could have suggested. . . . The union of grandeur and obscurity, which Mr. Burke describes as a sort of tranquility tinged with terror, and which causes the sublime, is to be found only in Hamlet [that is, the ghost]; or in scenes where circumstances of the same kind prevail."[17]

Here Ann Radcliffe distinguishes between Terror and

Horror as literary effects. "Terror and Horror," Mr. W. says, "are so far opposite, that the first expands the soul, and awakens the faculties to a high degree of life; the other contracts, freezes, and nearly annihilates them. . . . And where lies the great difference between horror and terror, but in the uncertainty and obscurity, that accompany the first, respecting the dreaded evil?"[18] The distinction recognized here seems to correspond to two attitudes that were to be developed more clearly in nineteenth-century Gothic tales: the optimistic view that continues to see man as good and to regard evil as the consequence of environment, and the pessimistic idea that his evil is inherent and inexplicable. The first is expressed through terror and the sublime, the second through horror and the grotesque.[19]

The distinction does not prevent the two effects from appearing together, however. There are blood-curdling events, for example, in *The Monk* and in *Frankenstein,* which may be seen as using the grotesque to "shrink the soul" with horror. Yet the sublime is also used to make the reader understand the cause and nature of the evil in Ambrosio and Frankenstein. The grotesque elements—Ambrosio and Antonia struggling among rotting corpses; Agnes clutching the worm-eaten body of her dead baby—arouse horror and a sense of absolute evil. Terror and the sublime must predominate over them to draw the reader out of himself and into sympathy for the characters. Unreal though Ambrosio and Frankenstein may be, both are yet seen as potential good turned evil and, to that extent, arouse the reader's "terror," his fear that he might share their case. It is this that gains his sympathy and suspends his moral condemnation.

It was through the "pleasing terror" associated with the sublime that Ann Radcliffe intended to expand her reader's souls and so engage their sympathy. When Emily in *The Mysteries of Udolpho* is elevated by the sublimity of the Pyrenees, the reader can share this feeling with her. When, on the other hand, she is directly threatened by physical danger and in mortal fear, the reader, since he is aware that he is reading a fiction and is himself safe, can still experience the pleasing terror of the sublime. He should be filled with pity and anxiety for Emily and "terrified" by Montoni, who is a sublimely evil character analogous in his effect to a cliff above the abyss. Partly because she does not expect her eighteenth-century readers to accept ghosts and witches, Ann Radcliffe ultimately insists on ordinary, everyday explanations for the supernatural elements. But she knows full well that these explanations must come after the fact and the illusion must be maintained for as long as the effect is needed. In *The Mysteries of Udolpho* Montoni as diabolical character, for instance, is a great deal more fascinating than the Montoni who turns out to be "just a bandit,"[20] and since the first appearance of her work, readers have expressed disappointment over the rational, common-sense view of him they are ultimately asked to accept. But this disappointment corresponds to the development of Emily's character. She, too, must come down from the high Gothic mode to accept dull reality.

In her own time and after, nevertheless, Ann Radcliffe's supreme achievement was seen as her ability to catch her readers up with her effects of terror. The reviewer of *Gaston de Blondeville* in *The New Monthly* could still, in 1826, assert that she remained supreme "over that delicious region of romance." After comparing her favorably with all her successors, including Scott and Jane Austen, he remarks that "she seemed to hold august sway over the springs of terror." Her hold is explained thus: "There was a fine knowledge [in her] of the pulses of curiosity and fear in the human heart. . . . it may be true that her persons are cold and formal; but her readers are the virtual heroes and heroines of her story as they read."[21] Thus a quarter of a century after she wrote, Ann Radcliffe was being praised in the face of the most important developments of the historical and social novel as able to totally involve her readers in her novels and so show them themselves.

It is the involvement of the reader that leads Gothic authors to use the same elaborate narrative methods used in the Sentimental novels. Walpole, Clara Reeve, and Ann Radcliffe along with other Gothic novelists use narrative method to construct the scaffolding for their tales. Like *Otranto,* Clara Reeve's *The Old English Baron* is made remote in time by its claim to be a chronicle. But it is set in England, not in "exotic" Italy and at a precise, not a vague time. A true Sentimentalist, she opposes an ideal yet probable good to the manifestation of evil. To do so, she uses her system of narration to set up a closed world within ordinary, if historical, England. The reader is given a sense of a remote world that is discovered with difficulty and exists unknown to the surrounding land.

It was perhaps to enhance this effect that Clara Reeve changed the method of narration in the second edition by suppressing the claim made in the preface to the first that the tale is from an ancient manuscript written in Old English.[22] Because the manuscript is not mentioned until after the first episode, the reader's first experience of the novel is of direct narration of Sir Philip Harclay's journey toward the castle. In the course of this journey, Sir Philip first loses his servant. Then, continuing on alone, he stops several times to ask his way, finding to his surprise that no one knows of Lord Lovel. Even when he reaches the border of the inner world—when he arrives at the cottage—there is a strange ambivalence in Wyatt's information about the deaths of that Lord and his wife. Thus, Sir Philip penetrates step by step into a world which grows more and more alien. This introductory section is in itself a symbolic rendering of the theme that the old values, which have been suppressed by evil doings and are no longer generally known, still lie at the heart of England.

This principal theme is worked out in the story itself when Clara Reeve brings the supernatural to bear. For the hero Edmund to discover his identity and for virtue to be restored, it is necessary for him to undergo the three-day ordeal in the deserted rooms. There, he finds the rooms closed off, empty and cobwebbed, and the portraits of his parents turned to the wall. He maintains his vigil in these sinister surroundings until the ghost finally manifests itself in the room below. Thus, symbolically, evil (the ghost) is exposed when the Good (Edmund's parents), concealed, locked up, and buried is recovered from death through virtue and courage (Edmund). Edmund, like Theodore in *Otranto,* rises from the bottom to the top of baronial society when his spiritual state has been shown to correspond to his noble birth through his display of patience, integrity, and fortitude.

The central theme, having been introduced through the frame and the device of the manuscript, is elaborated in the body of the novel by another narrative device: a cumulative system of narration that creates the impression of a gradual but steady piecing together of the truth. When Sir Philip completes his journey and enters the closed world the sense of the strange is momentarily allayed, but it is quickly apparent that all is not as it appears, that all is not being told. At first there are hints that the servant Joseph Howell knows who Edmund is, and Sir Philip himself is enigmatic about Edmund's resemblance to "a certain dear friend I once had."[23] At this point, the introductory section ends as Sir Philip returns home. The manuscript is mentioned and the story becomes direct "historical" narrative for a few pages. Then follow several breaks in the manuscript, "effaced by time and damp." They are presented as a device to avoid a long account of the French wars, but, in fact, they increase the sense of mystery by reminding us that the narrative is relayed secondhand and we do not have the whole story. On both of these counts, we become aware that the account is not necessarily reliable, so the sense of incompleteness is further enhanced. Then, within this narrative, other voices begin each to contribute what they know, so that all may be fitted together into a whole. Father Oswald tells Edmund about the ghosts. Then Joseph tells part of his story. Then Margery tells Edmund's story, which she alone knows.

This cumulative technique is well suited to Clara Reeve's shining, optimistic conclusion in which order is restored, just as the pieces of the puzzle are put together. She apparently was aware of this effect, for her final paragraph draws attention to the method: "Sir Philip Harclay caused the papers relating to his son's history to be collected together. The first part of it was written under his own eye in Yorkshire, the subsequent parts by Father Oswald at the Castle of Lovel. All these, when together, furnish a striking lesson to posterity, of the over-ruling hand of Providence, and the certainty of RETRIBUTION."[24]

By using the initial journey into the closed world as well as this cumulative technique, however, Clara Reeve gives us a Gothic world of greater immediacy than Walpole's. She may first lay her ghost, then end her novel with marriage and order restored. Nevertheless, in isolating her Gothic events within the orindary countryside of England, she in effect insists that the terrifying is part of the everyday world, encapsulated within it. The choice of narrative method reveals very directly the novelist's central concern. Clara Reeve wishes to present the stability and lasting power of the ancient virtues. So, through the ancient manuscript and Sir Philip's journey, she evokes a sense of a strange inner world when that world is in the grip of evil. Then, as the testimony of those who know parts of the story (both good and evil parts) accumulates, the evil is recognized and stripped away, leaving Good to reign in its stead.

Beckford's *Vathek* (1786) is at the farthest extreme from Clara Reeve's novel in technique, tone, and meaning, yet it too displays worlds within worlds. It uses the grotesque to evoke horror and a sense of unexplained, inevitable evil. To establish the grotesque convention it adopts the forms of the Eastern tale, opening up its weird world through the devices of the *Arabian Nights.* Beckford's bizarre fictional East has several contrasted worlds. We are first plunged into the nightmare witch's world of Vathek's mother Carathis and the wicked city. Then Vathek travels away from it into the closed, idyllic, pastoral world of Nouronihar and Gulchenrouz, only to draw the little princess out of that Sentimental haven into the caverns of the Underworld itself.

Again it turns out that the narrative technique corresponds to the author's view of the nature of man and of evil.[25] Beckford's presentation of his sinister, but also comic, fairy-tale landscape in direct narrative brings us face to face with his grotesques. Optimism vanishes like the little boys Vathek hurls into the abyss to feed the Giaour. Unlike them, it does not reappear. Beckford seems to have drawn an uncomfortable possible inference from Sentimentalism. As R. F. Brissenden has suggested in discussing de Sade, Man may be seen not as endowed with good sentiments which become twisted into bad, but simply as a repository of feelings of all kinds.[26] Then sensuality, greed for knowledge, or any feeling driven to its extreme may result in grotesque horror.

Beckford alone of the early Gothic novelists gives us this view. His tale, as a consequence, remains in the realm of pure fantasy. The everyday world is excluded entirely and the concluding section portrays eternal suffering set, not above ground at all, but in Hell, the Halls of Eblis. Necessarily the novel cannot end in any kind of resolution. Its affinity to the Sentimental novels and to *Otranto* and *The Old English Baron* is one of cousinage. It uncovers implications and draws inferences about which they would rather not know. It does so through direct narrative use of the grotesque and of the fairy-tale convention to establish a fantasy unmixed with mimetic elements.

Ann Radcliffe's novels belong to the more optimistic strain of Gothic fiction. In fact, like *The Old English Baron,* they lean heavily toward the Sentimental novel. She uses several variations of the devices of indirect narration. *The Romance of the Forest* (1791) claims to be a seventeenth-century record from "the proceedings in the Parliamentary Courts of Paris." *The Mysteries of Udolpho* (1794) is set in the more remote past, in 1584. *The Italian* (1797) purports to be an eighteenth-century Italian manuscript handed to a visiting Englishman to read so that he and the reader may understand an otherwise mysterious situation. Whether set in the past or in Ann Radcliffe's own time, however, her novels rely on exoticism of setting, just as *Otranto* does. Whether the tale is a "chronicle" of ancient times or an eighteenth-century manuscript, the eighteenth-century characters are in some way trapped and imprisoned in massive old castles, or in the prisons of The Inquisition, or in the ruins of such buildings.

Like *The Old English Baron, The Mysteries of Udolpho* comes to an optimistic conclusion. This novel has a tripartite structure with the central Gothic section framed by opening and closing Sentimental sections. Emily starts out in the closed world of her father's country estate. She then moves from it through sublime landscapes to a closed Gothic world. And finally she returns to yet another closed Sentimental world that is contrasted with the worldliness of Paris.

Like the Sentimental heroines, Emily has grown up in the beautiful, benign countryside. She and her parents live in her father's ancestral home in the south of France, to which her father has retired to escape worldly wickedness. Society impinges only in the person of Emily's aunt, an unwise devotee of social vanities who lives in town, in Tholouse (Toulouse). Emily receives the necessary Sentimental education, but her father, full of wise precepts in his knowledge of the world he has rejected, constantly warns her against a too great sensibility, urging prudence and common sense in all things in proper eighteenth-century manner.[27] The lesson Emily learns in the course of the novel is that the Sentimentalist view is indeed ideal, and like all ideals, must be pursued with moderation. The difference between the opening and concluding sections is the difference between Emily's naive Sentimentalism and her father's more balanced view, which she comes to accept at the end as a result of her experience of the nature of evil.

The movement from one section of the novel to the next is also a movement to a different setting. To get from one to the other a journey through mountains is necessary. In each case the landscape has a particular significance as a transitional link. The literary, "picturesque" nature of these scenes, based, as we know, on paintings and descriptions rather than direct observation, is no hindrance to their effect. Indeed, it perhaps enhances it. Readers were not to take them as a reflection of everyday reality but as inspiration for sublime feelings. The division between the first Sentimental section and the Gothic section is marked by the journey through the Pyrenees where the sublimity of nature is impressed upon Emily's mind. On this journey she meets Valancourt, the hero who, fittingly, is at home among these sublime mountains.

The gradual weakening of Emily's father amidst these scenes of God's grandeur brings the St. Auberts and the reader from the mountains into a wood as symbolic of earthly trouble as any in medieval romance. There, in an idyllic village, M. St. Aubert meets his death. The village and the convent in which Emily takes refuge are hidden within the wood, little isolated refuges amidst a surrounding and vaguely threatening tangle of the unknown.

Emily's emergence from this world into the vanity of her aunt's society takes her across the forbidding Alps into the Gothic world of Italy. The social vanities of Venice are themselves more sinister and threatening than those of France. When Emily and her aunt leave that city they pass through the sunlit countryside of happy peasant life—a stock convention of the Sentimental novel—to the sometimes sinister, sometimes beautiful Appenines in the fastnesses of which nestles the castle of Udolpho.

Thus, Emily's travels are symbolic journeys between different worlds that represent different states of mind she must confront and understand, whether they are in herself or in others. The St. Aubert estate represents naive Sentimentalism. The Pyrenees display beneveolent sublimity, drawing the mind out of the self into more spiritual realms. The social milieux of Emily's aunt, first in France, then in Italy, signify worldly vanity. The Alps are a range as sinister in its sublimity as the Pyrenees were benign, and Italy beyond them is a land of contrasts. The happy peasants lead the idyllic life; the worldly Venetians add ferocity to their worldliness. Similarly, the Appenines, which harbor the castle of Udolpho, have sublimity in both its good and evil aspects. It is at Montoni's castle that Emily is to learn what evil is really like, her notions of it being as naive as her understanding of the Sentimental ideal. The landscape throughout is thus used symbolically and reinforces the structural divisions of the novel.

The section in which Emily and her aunt are imprisoned in the castle, the aunt dies, and Emily struggles in terror with inexplicable events recalls the atmosphere of Manfred's castle in *Otranto*. The castle *is* the character of Montoni presented at his most diabolical, and the two women exist within it, engulfed within his sinister personality, much like Hippolyta and Matilda in *Otranto*. This effect is actually increased by the beginnings of Ann Radcliffe's rational explanations of the supernatural and of the real nature of Montoni's evil. Brought up surrounded by goodness and human nature in the full flower of its best potential, Emily the over-sensitive makes out of human wickedness, cruelty, greed, and desperation a nightmare Gothic world of supernatural evil. This Gothic view is hers, not Ann Radcliffe's.[28] Before she can escape, she must first recognize that Montoni is not a human monster but a bandit. The castle is a nest of brigands in a land torn by internecine political strife, not a sinister manifestation of a murderous personality.

Similarly, when she returns to France, she cannot go back to her idyllic childhood or take permanent refuge in the convent. She must find happiness by facing and understanding those illusions created by too absolute an idealism in a fallen world. The basic goodness of human nature is not denied, but the difficulties to its development are shown in the combination of Gothic and Sentimental elements in the Chateau-le-Blanc in Languedoc. The Count De Villefort is a good man who, like Emily's father, is knowledgeable about the world. His castle, its inhabitants, and its surrounding estate reflect the complexity of the view of life with which the newly experienced Emily must replace her former naive outlook. In this concluding section the Countess De Villefort, addicted to Paris, the capital of worldly society, settles into Chateau-le-Blanc unwillingly at the behest of the Count. Thus, worldliness and sensibility-balanced-by-prudence are both centered in the world Emily is about to enter. The estate itself combines all the natural characteristics that have been presented separately in the opening section of the novel. The "ancient mansion" looks to Blanche De Villefort like a Gothic castle, but one out of a medieval romance rather than the supernaturally sinister fastness that Emily saw in Udolpho. Its role as a Gothic castle is still further modified when she finds it is part Gothic, part modern, a suitable representation of the mixture of mental states that will inhabit it. The Chateau and its surrounding estate are "almost secluded from the eye by woods," the same symbolic forest in which are hidden the village where M. St. Aubert died and Emily's convent refuge of the first section of the novel.

The Chateau-le-Blanc stands on a height above the Mediterranean, blue and peaceful most of the time, but also subject to terrible storms. Emily is brought to the Chateau by such a storm, as is fitting since it is the setting for the emotional storm through which she must pass to attain the full measure of virtue balanced by prudence. Extending beyond the woods behind the castle are the idyllic fields and streams of Languedoc. Beyond them the sublime Pyrenees reappear. As a final touch to this symbolic setting, the world of the Chateau, while as closed and self-contained as the others in the novel, is penetrable by the representatives of those other worlds. The Count is returning to the home of his ancestors; the worldly Countess is a reluctant inhabitant of a place she sees as barbarous. Their daugher Blanche, a girl as naive as Emily had once been, sees the Chateau as a joyful alternative to the convent—an important point because here Emily must decide not to seclude herself in a convent.

Into this world come other Parisian representatives of worldly vanity. Into it, also, come Emily and Valancourt, each in different ways scarred, sobered, and matured by their experience of evil. Once within it, Emily learns the secret of her parents. Here, as in *The Italian,* it is a miniature portrait that leads to the discovery that provides the final link in the chain of necessary experience. After this, she can accept Valancourt and reject the cloistered, unreal life of the convent in favor of this world. Sensibility is balanced by prudence and experience makes possible a virtuous life that eschews all extremes.

By structuring the novel in this way, Ann Radcliffe centers it on that recurrent theme of Gothic fiction—the dilemma of innocence and ignorance. Emily has to learn first the danger of a too-idealistic Sentimentalism, then the need to see evil in its ordinary human porportions, and finally, the balance between preserving virtue and accepting the human weaknesses that are a necessary condition of life. Novelistically, though not philosophically, the problem is solved here by the interpolated story of Emily's parents, which she hears from the old housekeeper Dorothée. This character is one of that long line of housekeepers who are so useful as narrators in Gothic tales, particularly when the problem of innocence and ignorance is involved. Dorothée's role, though small, is similar to Nelly Dean's in *Wuthering Heights* or Mrs. Grose's in *The Turn of the Screw.* The old woman who supplies the evidence in the first half of Hogg's *Justified Sinner* has much the same function. As mediating consciousnesses these figures can, in their simplicity, recount events from the past, but they cannot see or understand the spiritual signficance of what they know. Thus, they, too, are ignorant but, at the same time, they are down-to-earth, practical, unidealistic types. They are consequently necessary ballast to the innocent heroine, although they do not understand her. In general, the Gothic novels are replete with retainers who relay vital information that they themselves do not understand. At times they are tediously comic servants, at others they represent the earthy hold on life and the common sense that is a necessary balance to idealism and to all spiritual quests.

As well as hearing Dorothée's long story, Emily must also go through the bitter sorrow of believing she has lost her beloved to "sinfulness" before she can acquire the experience that furnishes wisdom. When she at first rejects Valancourt, the explanation she gives him is an explicit statement of the symbolic significance of the paired figures of sensibility in the Sentimental novels. She does not judge him morally but rejects him because the virtuous cannot love the sinful since to do so is to love sin itself. Valancourt fortunately turns out to have stained his honor temporarily but not to have "fallen" irrevocably and thereby made himself a different order of being.

The novel ends happily with the restoration of rational order. The adventure of the spirit its heroine has undergone leaves us with a picture of the eighteenth-century benevolist's view of human nature. That unspoiled nature that Emily represents grapples with what it at first sees as pure evil, an outside, diabolical force. Then it discovers the evil, Montoni, is of human dimensions after all. A distortion of man's natural bent, his evil is malicious rather than malignant. This lesson learned, the figure of sensibility must then learn how to live in a fallen world by developing prudence: how, through the use of reason as well as sentiment, the good can live on earth. This is the lesson Emily's father had hoped she could learn by precept rather than by painful example.

Ann Radcliffe uses a series of closed worlds and conventional settings and characters in *Mysteries* to bring the ideas of the Sentimental and Gothic novels into an optimistic balance. Matthew Lewis' *The Monk* makes use of those conventions to strike a different emphasis. The main plot of *The Monk* uses direct narration and so, like *Vathek,* relies on extravagance to shock the reader into a sense of its strangeness. It does not make use of convention the way *Vathek* uses the fiary-tale form nor introduce the reader to an alien grotesque world as Beckford does. The wildly melodramatic exaggerations of its lurid scenes, however, create a grotesque effect. They arouse horror on the verge of laughter, as the Absurd universe of the twentieth century does. In this novel, sensibility is betrayed, defeated, and brought to nought without leaving the reader with a sense of a world well lost such as, say, the defeat of Paul and Virginia leaves one.

Antonia's and Ambrosio's innocence and concomitant ignorance are a complete trap leading to utter destruction. It is this pessimistic view that necessitates the use of the grotesque. Unlike Beckford, however, Lewis plays out the battle between Sentimentalism and overwhelming evil in the world. He relies on the exoticism of Spain and the cloister to evoke a world other than the reader's own, and he, too, uses complex, structural narrative devices. Set up in counterpoint to the direct narration of the main plot is Raymond's first-person narration of the interpolated story. His account is, in fact, a sub-plot extensive enough to be played off against the main story.

Set up as an interpolated account by one of the main characters, it is a patience-defying interruption of the story of Ambrosio. Raymond is the narrator, however, of a wonderstruck, horror-filled, after-the-fact account and the sense of the remoteness of the German forest and its castle is consequently enhanced as Raymond recounts his penetration into that weird and benighted world. There are, in fact, two Sentimental and two Gothic stories in *The Monk.* They are contrasted but intertwined to create a fiercesome pull between Sentimental benevolism and Gothic evil. The stories of Lorenzo and Antonia and Raymond and Agnes could easily form the typical double plot of an old-style romance such as Congreve uses in *Incognita.* Here, however, the form of the double plot is rendered chaotic as Sentimental optimism is turned into nightmare.

Lorenzo and Antonia are, of course, part of the story of Ambrosio and so part of another double plot in which one part is a travesty of the other. Matilda's seduction of Ambrosio into lust might in itself be a sufficient contrast to the virtuous love of Lorenzo and Antonia. The contrast becomes entanglement and conflict, however, when Ambrosio intrudes into Antonia's life with his long line of crimes starting with attempted seduction and ending in murder. Thus, in the main plot, Sentimental love is destroyed by Ambrosio, a Sentimental hero perverted into evil and sullying all he touches. Before this plot is played out, however, Raymond tells his story to Lorenzo. His account interrupts the main plot just as the seduction of Ambrosio begins. In this sub-plot, Ambrosio is again the agent of evil, this time because, before his Fall, his ignorance of human frailty caused him to judge Agnes harshly. Thus, both Sentimental plots are perverted into grisly nightmares by the intrusion of Ambrosio, once before and once after his Fall. The "Bleeding Nun" section of Raymond's account is also a story within a story. It and the imprisonment of Agnes and her baby in the dungeon of the convent are Gothic elements encapsulated within the tale of Raymond and Agnes, which has a happy, Sentimental outcome in contrast to the Lorenzo/Antonio/Ambrosio imbroglio, which ends in complete disaster.

Lewis' novel is a deliberate medley of the Sentimental and the Gothic. It also combines the terror of the sublime evoked by the tormented Ambrosio and the horror of the grotesque in the encounter with the bleeding nun or the scene of Agnes cradling her dead and worm-eaten baby. His structures are neither neatly encapsulated one within the other nor juxtaposed in contrast. They seem chaotic and his Gothic devices seem sensationalist, but their very disorder conveys a mixture of hope and despair. Lewis' vision falls somewhere between the neat, optimistic, and common-sensical conclusion of Ann Radcliffe's *Udolpho* and the pessimism of the grotesque in Beckford's *Vathek.* Ambrosio's perversion into evil is complete and he wreaks terrible destruction, yet he might have been good. Every section of Lewis' novel repeats this idea through its structure as well as its events. For this reason, too, Ambrosio is literally bedevilled. The recurrent theme of imprisonment—in cloister, castle, or dungeon—in each plot, subplot, and interpolation, and the repeated transformation of idyll into nightmare say again and again that goodness is locked up inside evil, that innocence is seduced, perverted, but that somehow it might not have been. Ambrosio in the claws of Lucifer is also a victim, a human being of great potential for good betrayed by social forces into a living hell of evil. Later Gothic fiction devises many forms stranger and more subtle than Lewis', but it is perennially preoccupied with the nightmare of uncertainty about the origin and causes of human evil that Lewis expresses in his confusion of victim and villain.

Ann Radcliffe did not reject Lewis' extravagance when she followed his lead, as Clara Reeve had rejected Walpole's. *The Italian* is neither lurid nor sensationalist, but its guilt-ridden monk Schedoni is more diabolical than Montoni in *Udolpho* and the supernatural does not as clearly melt away in the sunlight of common sense and everyday in this novel. Although the tale is brought to a happy ending, the conflict between benign Sentimentalism and Gothic distortions is less neatly concluded, and the difference is reflected in the structure and the narrative method. Given a contemporary, eighteenth-century setting, the novel is presented as a manuscript from the recent past to produce the familiar effect of closing the world portrayed. The Englishman, who is given this manuscript to read by an Italian friend, has already expressed his horror at the idea of sanctuary given to an assassin and been told that such is common practice in Italy. Then, Italy and its customs having been presented as strange and incomprehensible to the English, the manuscript itself turns out to be a record of events strange and terrible even to the Italians. (Ann Radcliffe uses the same irony as Walpole here, claiming that the manuscript shows the defects of composition of an inexperienced writer.)

The whole having been enclosed and made remote through the device of the manuscript, the conflict is set up within the narrative proper by contrasted settings, as in *Udolpho.* Ellena goes from the shelter of her aunt's house into the mountain fastnesses where the convent lies concealed, then to the deserted house on the seashore, and finally back home. These journeys are more perilous than those Emily undertakes in *Udolpho.* Ellena is always either a conducted captive or a pursued fugitive. The theme of imprisonment haunts *The Italian.* Unlike the beautiful estate where Emily grows up, even Ellena's home is a confinement in which she is protected, but also hidden, from the outside world. Both the convent with its wicked abbess and the seaside house are actual prisons for her, as are the dungeons of the Inquisition for Vivaldi, the hero.[29]

Most of the terror in the novel lies in its themes of malignant pursuit and imprisonment. Ellena and Vivaldi are pure and noble Sentimental characters, hunted, hounded, and imprisoned by the worldly and their apparently diabolical agent Schedoni. The conflict is a black-and-white struggle between virtue and worldly evil and, paradoxically, for all its contemporary setting and this-worldly events and characters, *The Italian* is less clear in its Sentimental resolution, less sure that evil can be domesticated than *Udolpho.* Schedoni, for instance, is shown to suffer torments of conscience that exacerbate his already sufficient wickedness, and his devilishness is finally ascribed to the fear-filled imaginations of his victims. Yet, even though he turns out to have no more-than-human ability to penetrate walls, to be in more than one place at a time, or to disappear at will, he remains a figure of unexplained wickedness.[30] Tormented evil-doer rather than devil though he is, there is no trace of the initial exceptional innocence and sensibility seen in Lewis' monk. In picking up the sinister monk as a character, Ann Radcliffe may simply have seen the efficacy of monks, nuns, convents, and the Inquisition as Gothic material. Monastics lend themselves well as examples of the denial of natural, God-given feelings, especially sexual ones. The convent becomes a symbol of self-repression instigated by religion as an institution of civilization. And the Inquisition then fits in as man's inhumanity to man caused by the same self-repression that distorts benign human nature in torturer and tortured. Ann Radcliffe may also have been influenced by Lewis' ideas as well as his devices. The concept of human nature and the relationship between sensibility and human evil is less clear in *The Italian* than in *Udolpho* and the oppressive themes of imprisonment and flight and capture suggest a loss of optimism that is not counterbalanced by a sense of the tragic fall from Grace. In the 1790s a confusing sense of the relativity and ambiguity of evil is already beginning to haunt the Gothic novel.

In this period also the novel in general begins to branch out in many directions. The Gothic becomes one among several streams whose courses can be traced through the nineteenth century. As usual they cannot be kept entirely separate and Gothic techniques appear in other types. We have seen them in Godwin's "borderline" *Caleb Williams,* which appeared in the same year as *Udolpho* and one year before *The Monk.* Aside from its obvious Gothic features, Godwin's novel is also an early move in the direction of the psychological novel, as well as one of a new kind of political novel of the day.[31] It shows traits of all three kinds of novel because the ideas of the time produced them all. The benevolist concepts of the early eighteenth century had become deeply entrenched in men's minds and out of them had developed the doctrine of progress and, with it, new views of the nature of politics and the political nature of man. Comparison of *Caleb* with another political novel, Thomas Holcroft's *Hugh Trevor* (1794–97), indicates the role of Sentimentalist ideas in radical political thought. Holcroft, an associate of Godwin's uses techniques very different from his. He packs his novel with incidents and satirical portraits of social types. It lacks the psychological dimension of *Caleb* and states rather than symbolizes the ideas on which it is based. Those ideas, however, are the same Sentimentalist premises that appear in Godwin and in Gothic fiction: that man is good by nature and becomes evil through bad habits acquired through faulty upbringing; only in Holcroft, these ideas are placed in the characters' mouths.

Godwin, instead of putting these ideas into the mouth of a character, symbolizes them. Consequently, he uses a Gothic narrative structure. *Caleb* is a first-person account with Caleb as narrator, so that, with Caleb's steady descent into paranoia, the reader grows less and less sure of his reliability. As a consequence the reader goes through a process of diminishing certainty of "reality" parallel to Caleb's. With many forewarnings of the terrible things to come, Caleb opens his story with his arrival as an innocent and sensitive young man in Falkland's house. At that point he is confident of his own perceptions; only later does he become unsure of them, increasing the reader's sense of the ambiguities inherent in the whole tale. In the closed world of Falkland's house, Caleb becomes Falkland's shadow, learning not only nobility and right conduct, but also the possibilities of human evil. His flight, his disguises, his conviction that Falkland is a malignant force with supernatural powers of finding out his victim, the theme of imprisonment, and especially the development of the device of the double, make *Caleb* a novel that moves parallel to if not ahead of Gothic fiction. The portrait of Falkland, for instance, contributes to, as well as draws from, the tradition. Falkland, as a study in the effects of evil on a noble mind, descends from Manfred and his successors, but even more clearly he seems to prefigure Frankenstein and to be a direct ancestor of Dorian Gray.

Some of Scott's works could also be called "borderline" Gothic in the same sense that *Caleb* is. In some novels, he bends all his energies toward an illusion of real historical time and in these he avoids Gothic techniques. But in others he mingles legend, Scottish superstition, and "historical" events in a manner that creates at least a Gothic atmosphere. In *The Bride of Lammermoor* (1819), for instance, the eerie, chilling events of the legend instill suspense and fear because they can never quite be dismissed as superstition-shrouded legend of which the "true" historical account is a sensible explanation.

It is no surprise, then, to find in Lucy all the beauty, sensitivity, and tendency to faint of a true Sentimental heroine and to see the struggle in the Master of Ravenswood between his noble nature and the inherited spirit of vengeance, so like the psychomachia of the Gothic villains, not to mention the correspondence between him and his castle, Wolf's Crag, and the suitably timed thunderstorms that break over it. Scott, nevertheless, plays the historical against the legendary in a way that adds a thriller element to a story of "real life" rather than transforming the novel into a symbolic fantasy. In the same way, his method of indirect narration through Peter Pattieson adds to the historicity rather than creating a Gothic world. Because Pattieson as chronicler, here and elsewhere, is just the sort of character who would have difficulty differentiating legend from historical fact, he is not a mediating consciousness conveying a strange tale and the supernatural elements lack the symbolic force of their Gothic equivalents.[32]

The difference can be seen most clearly in a comparison with Mary Shelley's *Frankenstein,* which appeared in 1818. *Frankenstein* presents strange human impulses not as something in the misty past, almost beyond our ken, but much more frighteningly, as part of our own lives. Frankenstein's monster is created in the heart of a German university town in the grubby rooms of a medical student, and the problem of evil it represents thus becomes not the object of hazy intuitions, but something we must face and know.

The narrative structure makes it possible to combine the sense of a real and present question with the usual strangeness of an unknown world. *Frankenstein* is an account sent out of the frozen world of the Arctic by the scientist Walton, who would have found such a story hard to believe if it had not been told to him by a fellow scientist and if he had not seen the monster.[33] He himself only passes on the story told to him. The main body of the novel is told by Frankenstein, and the Monster's own account is included within his. Walton plays a minute part in the novel proper, but the double narration gives the sense that Frankenstein has lived in a nightmare closed world of his own within the civilized world of modern Germany and Switzerland. Walton has ventured within the edge of that nightmare world psychologically as well as physically.[34] As a scientist he is equipped to see its horror and send out an account to his sister in the normal world within the novel, which corresponds to the reader's own world.

Mary Shelley also extends the device of the closed world within Frankenstein's account. At first, Victor's life with his family and Elizabeth is lived in quiet isolation in the Swiss mountains, which at this point represent grandiose but benevolent nature. That life opens up to him the possibilities of the full expansion of the good side of his nature. When he leaves that world for the busy one of scientific study in Germany, he again isolates himself in his own laboratory, this time deliberately, in order to carry out his terrible experiment. When he returns home to Switzerland, he encounters the monster, again in isolation in the mountains, which have now turned sinister.

Then, when the monster tells its tale, it is of another closed world, the cottage with its attached hovel where he observes the DeLacey family through a chink in the wall. The monster's is a little tale of sensibility within the Gothic novel. The family thus isolated are not cottagers but a prominent French family who fled Paris to avoid corruption and imprisonment. They show all the nobility, sensitivity, and passivity of characters of the novel of sensibility and a closed world is again necessary to their tale. Their story is a part of the Monster's own and so the monster serves not only as first-person narrator of its account but also as the frame narrator of their story, like the old man in *Paul and Virginia*. The monster is probably the strangest such narrator yet.

Mary Shelley's novel has a balance of the Sentimental and the Gothic similar to *Udolpho*'s except that, instead of a sinister Gothic section framed by the Sentimental opening and conclusion, the Sentimental story in *Frankenstein* is encapsulated within the Gothic tale. The concentric, nested system of narration leads from the everyday world of Walton's sister to the frozen wasteland of Walton's scientific pursuit to Frankenstein's closed worlds of benign Sentimentalism and tormenting self-isolation, until buried in the very center we come to the strangest world of them all, that of the monster's account. The effect is one of penetrating deeper and deeper into a mystery which at each step turns out to be stranger than one could have imagined. The double, at one point triple, point of view has the effect of focussing a pair of fieldglasses. Rather than presenting several points of view, the novel brings the different views together into a single perspective. The reader sees Frankenstein's evil and his disillusion and despair with Walton's mixture of horror and compassion, but he also sees through Frankenstein's own eyes. And he is actually asked to share the experience of what it feels like to be a monster. Because these views are not kept separate, however, the identity among the three figures is made and Walton and the monster become reflections of Frankenstein. If the reader exercises any imaginative sympathy, he is obliged to suspend moral judgment, to understand and not to condemn Frankenstein. At the same time he shares his overwhelming horror over what has happened. The combination of compassion and regret causes him to bring the tale home to himself. Few have Frankenstein's Faustian aspirations, but the fears he evokes are real just the same, particularly the horrible realization that we may harm those we least want to hurt because of impulses our conscious minds deny absolutely.

The structure of *Frankenstein* provides a sense of gradual clarification. At the end much is still ambiguous and puzzling, but all has been told. Hogg uses structure in his *Justified Sinner* to make the story less and less clear as it progresses. He depends heavily on narrative technique to plunge the reader into the confusion of his character's mind. If this novel is not a "true" Gothic tale, that is because it is centered on its attack against religious "enthusiasm" as creating a penchant to madness in an individual.[35] It portrays the Sinner as driven into hypocrisy by a Presbyterian upbringing that, contrary to benevolist thinking, treats man as depraved by the fall and inevitably sinful. Feeling himself released from all moral restraints when admitted among the elect, the sinner quickly sinks into crime and madness.

The novel consists of a double narrative—first the "documentary" account and then the memoirs—each relating the same events. At first sight, the initial presentation might appear to be designed to provide a measure of the Sinner's madness and to prepare the reader for the distortions of his own account. In fact, it serves the opposite purpose, creating greater and greater confusion. Clearly, especially toward the end, the Sinner is no longer able to tell fact from nightmare delusion, but neither is the reader. The use of the old woman's testimony in the "documentary" section, for instance, works against the otherwise obvious conclusion that the figure who accompanies Colwan in his misdeeds is a figment of his split mind. And to her limited understanding of the story she tells is added the confusion of the narrator whose account is incomplete and unverifiable. In addition, the Sinner's memoirs are written as the action takes place, not after the fact, in contrast to the opening section. The reader is faced with, so to speak, the opposite of an unfolding tale. As the story progresses he finds he is no longer sure of what he thought he knew in the earlier part of the novel. Like the Sinner, he is made to experience a confused mental state in which he can be certain of nothing and in which anything may happen or have already happened without his knowing it. The effect is the reverse of the clarifying cumulative technique of *The Old English Baron* and some later Gothic novels.

Hogg's narrative structure, his direct use of the doubles figure, his portrait of a mind distorted by upbringing, his equation of madness and evil criminality, all continue to be features of nineteenth-century Gothic tales. In the course of the Gothic tradition, whether evil is seen as unnatural to Man or thought to be at the basis of his nature, it is presented as tormenting, maddening.[36] Gothic novels reflect the association of mental illness with violent crime. The idea that evil is madness has as a corollary the idea that madness is evil. The dual view of Man that appears in the Victorian novel must be ascribed to the persistence into a new age of the benevolist view of Man as basically good and of evil as an unnatural aberration. The madman, however withdrawn or hallucinated or violent, is felt to be in the grip of something that is not his true self. One who has committed a hideous crime is still seen as having a sacred central being who is himself and who deserves compassion. Hence the causes of the illness or the criminal behavior are sought in the environment; the madman and the criminal continue to be equated and are also still seen as simultaneously predators and victims. On the other hand, a particularly chilling crime may be presented with a horrified insistence that such things are not merely unnatural, but inhuman, demonic, diabolical, having an origin in something beyond our ken. Although only human beings perpetrate crimes of a grisliness that beggars environmental explanation, the mind still invokes the grotesque, with its images of the otherness of evil, in these circumstances.

In 1824, Melmoth the Wanderer, himself demonic, invokes the first attitude but denies the second. He tries to tempt Stanton, a sane man imprisoned in an asylum by a covetous relative, to change places with him. He tells him that if he goes mad, as he surely will, he will be a damned soul anyway: "Experience must teach you that there can be no crime into which madmen would not, and do not precipitate themselves; mischief is their occupation, malice their habit, murder their sport, and blasphemy their delight." Moreover, not only the mad among humans are capable of hideous crime. When Stanton calls Melmoth a "demon," that lost soul replies: "Demon!—Harsh word!—was it a demon or a human being placed you here?"[37] Melmoth's view of madness and crime is a brutal one, even coming from the damned. It derives, however, from the belief that madness is loss of reason and reason is the manifestation of the Divine in Man.

Gothic fiction was to produce a multitude of demons and criminal madmen before approaching a morally neutral attitude toward aberration. Toward the end of the nineteenth century, the moral relativity that had already become apparent at the beginning of the century begins to resolve itself into an objective stance largely divorced from moral judgment. The anomalies of the human condition have not changed, however, and there is no lessening of nightmare, darkness, and guilt.

PART TWO

THE CONTINUING TRADITION

CHAPTER FIVE

THE VICTORIAN HALL OF MIRRORS

Follow poet, follow right
To the bottom of the night
W. H. Auden, "In Memory of W. B. Yeats"

HE Victorian age is the era of the well-told tale, the mystery story, the detective novel. In the great outpouring of tales, the continuance of the Gothic current is still identifiable. The convention continues to be used by authors interested in portraying human nature and human evil and to be identifiable by the devices it uses and its characteristic symbolism. Some devices become more elaborate, others are continually adapted to particular purposes. The grotesque, for instance, proliferates monsters such as the earlier period, happily for it, had not dreamt of. The successors of Frankenstein continue to make science a Faustian defiance. Above all, the world of the Gothic novel appears as a dream with physical artifacts as well as living beings who are reflections of the self. The features of later Gothic fiction, when examined separately, show the course of the tradition as it winds its way through the century, reflecting an increasing consciousness of the topography of the mind.

Increased understanding, even though it is perhaps often intuitive, works a course of change within the unchanging Gothic tradition. In the period between Walpole's *Otranto* and Mary Shelley's *Frankenstein,* ghosts, the paired Sentimental characters, figures of the grotesque, animated portraits, reflecting statues and the like, "sympathetic" houses, settings, and weather, and Faustian scientists and witches all established themselves in Gothic literature. After Mary Shelley, from Maturin to Henry James, they continue to be the vehicles of tales dealing with the human mind. At the same time, new elements accrue that indicate changing views of the old subject. The pattern of some tales, for instance, takes more clearly and deliberately the shape of a dream, reflecting a greater urgency about the function of dreams in mental life, a conscious effort to give them a fictional manifestation. A proliferation of figures of the grotesque is in part a result of this turn toward dream imagery; in part it shows the erosion of the optimism of the Sentimentalists, which compounded the puzzle of evil and added to the shifting, ambiguous, uncertain atmosphere of Gothic tales.

The Gothic works of the Victorian period seem to suggest that the era's nightmares were more terrible still than the horrific visions that afflicted the late eighteenth and early nineteenth centuries. We are accustomed, of course, to the idea that rigid and repressed Victorians were given to bad habits and worse dreams. But as explanations for the continued appearance of Gothic literature, their inhibitions and strait-lacing are as circular and tautological as the parallel accountings for the appearance of eighteenth-century Gothic tales. The continuance of the tradition (and perhaps Vitorian repression and inhibition themselves) is a primary indication of an increasing awareness of explorations into human psychology. Understanding of the mind was growing in importance. The fact that Gothic elements appear in the mainstream realistic and social novels attests to a general acceptance of an interest that, we must remember, was not a feature of earlier ages. Psychology, which had preoccupied the eighteenth century, was becoming increasingly a subject of general and scientific interest.

This development meant that it became a subject of social concern. In the massive movement toward realism in literature this concern accounts for a seemingly inconsistent adherence to the fantastic. It is interesting to see which of the great social novelists include these incongruous elements in their works. The two prime examples are Dickens and Dostoyevsky, with Balzac as a close runner-up. Unlike, say, Tolstoy, or Flaubert, or George Eliot, these writers include a great deal of the supernatural and the weird in their novels. Dostoyevsky seats a devil of enigmatic reality on Ivan Karamazov's sofa; he splits Stavrogin's personality into a whole gang of conspirators in *The Possessed.* In *The Double* he writes an explicit study of the split personality.[1] The atmosphere of his novels is charged with supernatural causes and symbolic settings and many of his minor characters are caricatures manifesting the combination of the comic and the bizarre that makes a grotesque. Balzac also has many such characters, as does Dickens. Mr. Krook in *Bleak House* is one, as is the old Grandet in *Eugénie Grandet.* Uriah Heep, presented in images of the devil in *David Copperfield,* and Vautrin in *Père Goriot,* with his "expression . . . of a fallen archangel bent on eternal war," are others. Dickens goes further and draws Quilp as a fairy-tale dwarf in *The Old Curiosity Shop,*[2] and he also uses grotesque imagery. People are constantly described as things, and things as people. For instance, Mr. Merdle's dinner guests in *Little Dorrit* are described as houses. Conversely, in *Our Mutual Friend* the silverware in Mr. Podsnap's dining room comes to life and speech. The surrounding circle of acquaintances who are things and the things that come to life reflect on host and owner, satirizing them by showing them to be grotesque in a world that could be sane but is not. Dickens even goes so far as to have a collapsing house in defiance of physical laws as blatant as Walpole's in *Otranto* or Poe's in "The Fall of the House of Usher." In *Little Dorrit* the House of Clennam, the firm, collapses when its owner is forced at last to face the consequences of past hypocrisy. Mrs. Clennam's capitulation is symbolized in the physical collapse and ruin of the house where she has maintained and guarded that hypocrisy for so long.

These elements of fantasy appear because the interest of these authors in society and its workings is based on a primary interest in man as a spiritual being within his society and in the problem of good and evil in his nature. None had much confidence in social theory. Each in his own way believed that the nature of society is determined by the spiritual state of mankind. Consequently, they incorporate the supernatural in their predominantly social novels in order to highlight men's spiritual side. Dostoyevsky portrays his revolutionaries in *The Possessed* as demons to be exorcised from the body of Russia.[3] Balzac visits his characters with the punishments of Hell. Dickens makes his dwarf a symbolic embodiment of malignancy directed against a heroine who is still true to the Sentimentalist tradition.

Many more examples occur in these and other authors. Their appearance in social novels indicates that these concerns, which were important in the thought of the time, were felt to have an immediate effect on social life and the individual. The Gothic works of the same era merely retain their traditional emphasis on Man's mind, largely to the exclusion of society. Throughout the nineteenth century they refract a double image: an alarming view of the world as grotesque and a drifting vision of it as a dream.

In the vision of the grotesque, evil tends to be enigmatic and ambiguous; in the evocation of the dream, the mind turns in on the self and nightmare jostling with compassion makes moral judgment irrelevant. The figures of the grotesque are creatures of the earth and the underworld, frequently drawn from folklore and myth. In symbolizations of the mind, they have many functions but they are usually opposed to the cerebral and the idealistic. Thus, we find stories in which the scientist, the artist, and the intellectual come face to face with these earthy figures. For the most part these characters are male, from Frankenstein and his monster in the second decade of the century to Dr.

Jekyll and Mr. Hyde in the 1880s. Along with them the female figures of Gothic literature are an amalgam of head and heart, of ideal and earthy. They are at times virtuous ideals, at times evil seductresses, and the results of either role are unpredictable and unsettling.

The world of dreams is a hall of mirrors. The devices of reflection, the mainstay of Gothic fiction from the beginning, continue to be its central feature. The heroes and heroines, the doubles, the houses, portraits, statues, and mirrors continue to show images of the self. It is an ingeniously arranged hall. Sometimes a true reflection is thrown back at the viewer, but more often the mirrors are set so that a part of the self suddenly becomes the entire reflection or the mirror image appears at an odd angle that affords a new perspective. Frequently the outlandish reflection stares out at the reader as if it were his own. Sometimes the surface is itself distorted or darkened and the image cannot be relied upon. Most often the sounds of the everyday world are shut out and motion tends to be drifting and non-volitional.

The grotesque and dream worlds are not separate. Together they form Victorian Gothic fiction. The double reflected in a mirror is often a grotesque; the scientist who sees him is the hero who also sees himself reflected in a heroine who is simultaneously an earth mother; the mirror itself may be a house or a portrait. All are one extraordinary kinetic vision. Its components shift and replace each other, and the viewer, instead of standing back on terra firma to watch, finds himself floating among them, unable to wake from another's dream.

FACING THE TERROR AND THE HORROR

The tale of terror really came into its own when it provided characters into whose shoes the reader could step and faced them with doubtful monsters who might be figments of a disordered mind or creatures from the abyss. Even such an obviously fantasy figure as the double can be hair-raising under these circumstances for it is the increased sense of the human possibility of what is symoblized that makes the hair stand on end. Real fear arises, after all, from some sense of danger to ourselves. A tale may make us apprehend the possibility that the nature of the human mind renders the evil portrayed possible. Then the story will be of the type that makes even sensible people afraid of the dark. Effectiveness is not a result of greater "probability" or a move toward realism. On the contrary, Victorian Gothic fiction employs quite blatant fantasy. It is full of the creatures of ancient superstition—vampires, for instance—the universal symbols from dreams, and literary devices like the double and the animated portrait, the obvious "untruth" of shadowy things we fear in ourselves. In fact, it does for us what our private fear so often does anyway—projects its object into a form exterior to ourselves. This is what makes horror literature attractive and what makes it literature.

Ann Radcliffe's distinction between terror and horror is an early attempt to explain how the Gothic tale can be effective as literature. Her idea that the first expands and the second shrinks the soul does not distinguish one type of Gothic novel from another, nor is it a useful description of the effect of Gothic devices on the reader. It does, however, seem to point to the difference between devices in the Gothic that draw the reader into a sympathetic understanding of the evil exhibited and those that face him with incomprehensible malignity. The pleasing terror that ravishes him out of himself produces involvement with the characters. Understanding of them is evoked through use of the dream as device, vehicle, and source of imagery. It is also brought about by persuading him it is himself he sees reflected in the reflecting devices. Soul-shrinking horror in the face of the incomprehensible is conveyed through the devices of the grotesque. When it is combined with sublime terror the result is a fearsome curdling of the blood. The grotesque element greatly increases the ambivalence of a work. It takes it out of the realm of didactic literature and gives an uncertainty to its values and its moral stance, regardless of how definitely they may be stated. Its addition to Gothic fiction suggests a nonplussed uncertainty, as if the Gothic authors themselves had been brought to a stand by the demons they had raised. The Djinn once released would not be persuaded back into its bottle. Nineteenth-century authors needed sharpened wits to make it serve them and not themselves become its slaves.

THE GROTESQUE AND ITS MONSTERS

When good and evil are intermingled they have a slippery tendency to change places and this undermines moral values and makes life seem uncertain and directionless. The grotesque is the literary means of portraying the human condition in such an unsure universe. It is an ancient mode with a long history and life of its own. It has some special characteristics, however, that were put to new and particular use in Gothic fiction. Wolfgang Kayser's study, *The Grotesque in Art and Literature,* shows the grotesque to have been used throughout centuries to show man's place in the world as threatened with meaninglessness. The grotesque asserts that life is haphazard, or may be; that man is a fool of chance; and that the universe is empty of meaning. It does so by looking outward and presenting its strange distorted figures like flat cut-outs against a dark and impenetrable background. Gothic fiction, on the other hand, looks inward at man's mind. It makes use of the grotesque to create a doubtful murky atmosphere. Through it, inner evil is projected outward, but in such a manner that it will ultimately be apprehended as lurking in the shadows within us. It adapts the grotesque's devices, which create a sense of alienation, to symbolize related mental and spiritual states.

Kayser supplies several characteristics of the grotesque that are instantly recognizable as features of Gothic tales.

He writes: "There are certain specific forms and motifs which are predisposed toward certain contents. . . . There is good reason for listing some of the most important themes. Among them belong all 'monsters.' "[4] These monsters tend to be demonic, not of this world, and this is what gives them their incomprehensibility: "Apocalyptic beasts emerge from the abyss; demons intrude upon us. If we were able to name these powers and relate them to the cosmic order, the grotesque would lose its essential quality . . . What intrudes remains incomprehensible, inexplicable, and impersonal. . . . We are unable to orient ourselves in the alienated world, because it is absurd" (p. 183). In the grotesque, "the supernatural world" and the "abysmal realm" must remain outside Man to create "the unity of perspective . . . [that] consists in an unimpassioned view of life on earth as an empty, meaningless puppet play." The images of the grotesque are created "to invoke and subdue the demonic aspects of the world" (pp. 186 and 188).

The grotesque was eminently suited to embody the view of madness as demonic possession: "In the insane person, human nature itself seems to have taken on ominous overtones. Once more it is as if an impersonal force, an alien and inhuman spirit, had entered the soul. The encounter with madness is one of the basic experiences of the grotesque which life forces upon us" (p. 184). The Gothic authors did not, of course, share this view of madness. In seeing evil as a distortion of the natural being, however, they presented it as working like an alien force within the psyche and they portrayed the character suffering such conflict as maddened by it and his unnatural state as madness. Grotesques were consequently well suited to this Gothic theme.

The manifestation of such ideas in figures of the grotesque has the effect of objectifying them without providing a means for dealing with them. It is this that produces the reaction of horror. But horror combined with a sense of helplessness evokes a further reaction—hysteria. Hence the grotesque has two other features. It has a pervasive comic element that seems to arise from and produce that uncomfortable sense of the incongruously horrible that makes the viewer laugh as he inwardly groans. And, to its other monsters, the grotesque adds automata, incongruous beings that can be both horrifying and comic. "The mechanical object," Kayser says, "is alienated by being brought to life, the human being by being deprived of it. Among the most persistent of motifs of the grotesque we find human bodies reduced to puppets, marionettes, automata, and their faces frozen into masks" (p. 185).

The Gothic authors' view of the grotesque is also seen among the Romantics. Kayser shows how Victor Hugo, Friedrich Schlegel, and others modified the traditional concept. Hugo takes the grotesque "to be one pole of a tension whose opposite pole is constituted by the sublime. . . . The true depth of the grotesque is revealed only by its confrontation with its opposite, the sublime. For just as the sublime (in contrast with the beautiful) guides our view toward a loftier, supernatural world, the ridiculously distorted and monstrously horrible ingredients of the grotesque point to an inhuman, nocturnal, and abysmal realm" (p. 58). In Hugo's own words: "The grotesque . . . is everywhere; . . . it creates what is deformed and horrible."[5] Hugo wrote this in 1827, one year after Ann Radcliffe's essay distinguishing the effects of terror and horror was published posthumously. The ideas she voiced were clearly still important in the late 1820s. At the time she was writing her novels Friedrich Schlegel was characterizing the grotesque as producing that mixture of horror and laughter that makes it so uncomfortable. In 1798 he wrote that grotesqueness is "constituted by a clashing contrast between form and content, the unstable mixture of heterogeneous elements, the explosive force of the paradoxical, which is both ridiculous and terrifying."[6]

Jean-Paul Richter, Kayser notes, sees the humor of the grotesque as destructive: "It [the grotesque; he does not use the term itself] is an ingredient of humor . . . namely, its 'annihilating idea.' Reality, the terrestrial, finite world as a whole, is destroyed by humor. . . . The laughter which humor evokes is not detached but contains a certain measure of pain" (p. 54). Kayser thus shows the features of the grotesque that caused the Romantics, among whom he would include the Gothic authors, to adopt it. The single element that makes it suitable for use in Gothic fiction, however, is the natural way its monsters may be made symbolic. In discussing the incubus, Nicholas Kiessling has noted the change that takes place when these many-formed monsters are used symbolically: "Within the Incubus-Succubus tradition, an important alteration of meaning occurs in the Romantic age. The major poets began to use these figures to symbolize both the temptations and aspirations of man in terms of his underlying sense of supernatural fear or wonder at his ability to transcend his condition or transform it. Thus the dark figures in the Romantic period take on more complex meanings." Kiessling connects the new symbolic use of the incubus figure with the ancient mythological one, showing how these monsters were also transferred to Gothic fiction: "More deeply, as his mythological embodiment . . . suggests, the Incubus was a primordial archetype of man's darkest lusts and fears. As such, he became a natural symbol or icon for the Romantic imagination at a time when the springs of imagination were troubled."[7]

It is also true, however, that an absolutely necessary condition for this adoption was a lack of belief, in life, in the supernatural. In this sense, the Gothic novel uses the figures of the grotesque—demons, vampires, ghosts, and the figures of animals, as well as deformed human beings—in a manner opposite to the grotesque's own use of them. The grotesque presents them flatly, asserting their absolute reality, at least within the work. Gothic fiction relies on the reader's active disbelief in them to render them symbolic. Their reality was a matter of dispute during the Romantic era. Shelly noted indignantly in the year when Mary Shelley started to write *Frankenstein* that neither Lewis nor Byron believed in ghosts and that both asserted it was impossible to believe in them and not believe in God.[8] This refusal to give credence to supernatural figures, however, made it possible to use them symbolically. It is through his demons that Lewis suggests that evil is internal, a kind of madness, in Ambrosio. If grotesques represent actual occult forces, then they are demonic powers with a referent in the outside world. When they do not, they have the same symbolic power as a patently unreal creature like Frankenstein's monster.

Possibly the fact that the grotesque was an art form before it was used in literature provided the impetus to adopt it. The grotesque was originally a decorative art. Its monstrous figures appear twisting and twining around friezes that also contain flowers and animal figures. The effect is one of motionless movement. A literary monster is a character taking part in action, but its grimace, its ugliness, its strangeness give, perhaps, an analogous sense of frozen motion. Kayser emphasizes that "a single, isolated figure (such as a dwarf) or object (such as a gargoyle) [cannot] be clearly regarded as grotesque. . . . Only in context, as part of a larger structure or as a vehicle of meaning, does the individual form become expressive and does it belong to the grotesque. Even in the ornamental grotesque the single 'absurd' figure was only a motif within a context that was strongly felt to be dynamic."[9]

Implanted in a Gothic tale, grotesque figures are provided with a context that gives them their ambiguous, symbolic quality. Dwarfs and hunchbacks, for instance, such as Hugo's own Quasimodo in *Notre-Dame de Paris* (1831), who is explicitly described as a grotesque, can be used with typical Gothic symbolism, which equates the crooked figure or limited stature with a mean and distorted personality. Dwarfed and hunchbacked figures, which are traditionally grotesques, appear in Gothic tales and are often also doubles figures symbolizing haunting guilt, paranoia, the split personality, and madness. The earliest of the Gothic novels to use the grotesque, Beckford's *Vathek,* has all its disturbing qualities: the writhing movement, the frozen grimace, the monstrousness, and the disorienting humor that provokes laughter in the midst of horror. The Giaour rolling over the plain like a football is ridiculous, as are Carathis, her attendants, and her camel, and the dwarf wisemen. But they are also monstrous and horrifying. If Beckford really did suffer from a Byronic sense of damnation, it may account for his early use of the grotesque.[10] His novel, however, has successors that make this beginning a part of the tradition.

E. T. A. Hoffmann, writing at approximately the same time as Mary Shelley and Maturin, is harder to classify. He makes great use of the comic grotesque, of monsters, witches, and automata, and his motifs have much in common with those of Gothic fiction. One of the most prevalent themes in his Tales (1814–22) is that of the artist's differentness and his sense of alienation. This relates his stories to the Gothic tales. He uses the grotesque to sketch the nature of the artist's mind in general, rather than in particular, in its conflict with the everyday. The protean witch-apple-woman-nurse figure of "The Golden Flower Pot" (1814) embodies his central theme, the necessary rejection of life as a sacrifice to Art. In his tales, highly ambiguous as they are, he presents the conflict between a life dedicated to art and ordinary social life. Usually the protagonist is torn between love for a young woman and the seductive attractions of strange beings like the little green snake in "The Golden Flower Pot," or the apparent perfection of the mechanical doll Olympia in "The Sandman" (1816). In the first, the seduction leads to happiness, but not of this world; in the second it leads to destruction brought about by that manufacturer of eyes and magical instruments of sight, Coppelius. An automaton is a monstrous creation, suggesting the more horrifying possiblity of human beings worked mechanically, without volition, spirit, heart, or soul. Hoffmann's artist falling in love with the mechanical doll becomes mechanical himself when he chooses to read his poetry to her for the sake of her meaningless response in preference to the human impatience of his former love.

The distorted characters of the Gothic, who suffer from monstrous spiritual states and, indeed, are frequently referred to as monsters, are allied to Hoffmann's automata. Gripped by their own evil, which their "true" nature cannot overcome, they, too, are worked and made to move. They are controlled by an element in their own minds, it is true, but it is alien to their essential beings. The madman, too, is often portrayed as moving without his own volition.

With Maturin's *Melmoth the Wanderer* (1820) we find a grotesque thoroughly integrated into a Gothic novel that is bizarre but hardly comic. The Wanderer is a grotesque, a demonic figure, a man who has made a compact with the devil and cannot die. He has wandered the earth for generations trying to find another human being so desperate that he will change places with him. The novel has a narrative structure that combines the complexities of narration of other Gothic tales and it is Gothic in its interest in human nature. Indeed, the terms "nature," "human nature," and "natural" are opposed on page after page to "unnatural," "diabolic," and "demon." All that is good is natural and, at the very heart of the novel, we find Immalee, an idealized child of nature in an idyllic setting.

At the beginning of the novel, in 1816, John Melmoth, a descendant of the Wanderer, travels from Dublin to the closed world of the family's ancestral home in the Irish countryside. There, he encounters a housekeeper, his old governess, who supplies him with some information much larded with superstition, and a real and rather ordinary Irish witch. Then he sees the Wanderer whose portrait, dated 1646, has preternaturally piercing eyes that make it look alive. It enables the younger Melmoth to recognize the Wanderer himself when he appears momentarily. The younger man then reads an old manuscript, crumbling and fragmentary, which contains the story of Stanton, dated

1676. Stanton, imprisoned in an asylum, is offered his freedom by the Wanderer but chooses to risk insanity. The younger Melmoth next hears the story of the Spaniard Monçada whom he has rescued from shipwreck. This account is also fragmentary, both because at times Monçada is too overcome by emotion to recount certain parts of it and because the written sources of his information within his story are blotched or torn. He, too, was tempted by Melmoth. Within Monçada's story is nested the story of Melmoth and Immalee, contained in a manuscript the Spaniard transcribes. The manuscript, too, has interpolated stories, containing further temptations. "The Tale of Guzman's Family" is told in an inn to Immalee's father. Another, "The Lover's Tale," is told to him by Melmoth. The Spaniard concludes his story after these interpolations. Within each story there are also letters, flashbacks, and minor relations. The Wanderer finally appears and talks with Melmoth and Monçada. He then sleeps and dreams. His dream is a summons from Hell. In the course of the night he is changed physically from an unaging immortal to "the very image of hoary decripitude."[11] Melmoth is released from earthly life, not by man, but by the devil, to whom he owes allegiance.

Thus *Melmoth* is an accumulation of Gothic devices. The cumulative method of narration seen in *The Old English Baron* appears again here. It gives the impression that only the combined efforts of all these story tellers can finally bring together the pieces of this terrible, centuries-long story. At the same time, this technique is combined with the concentric, nested narrative structure used in *Frankenstein* to make the reader feel he is delving deeper and deeper into worlds that are strange and yet more strange. The cumulative technique also allows the novel to range over the countries of Europe and through time, as the Wanderer has done. Since the Wanderer has to wait until a potential victim has been driven to desperation, moreover, he appears only sporadically in much of the novel. The balance of the stories are devoted to human life deliberately devoid of the supernatural. They are filled with the horrors of oppression, imprisonment, and the cruelties of man to man that threaten to drive the victim to madness. Monçada's tale is reminiscent of *The Monk,* though without Ambrosio's lurid sexual transgressions. "Guzman's Family" is a small Sentimental romance; "The Lover's Tale" is a historical romance. All are instances of resistance to diabolical temptation. Since, even when driven to desperation, none will sell his soul to escape the miseries of his human condition, the novel insists ultimately that evil is a product of human beings, among whom only the most benighted—the Wanderer himself—would give up that sacred central core of being that makes him human. The Wanderer, in doing so, has put himself outside the pale of humanity—he is a figure from Hell.

The story of Immalee, the ideal child of Nature, coming at the very center of the novel, corresponds to that soul that is demonstrated in each story to be at the center of Man's nature. Immalee is an unreal embodiment of good human nature just as the demonic Melmoth is of human evil. Ultimately, human beings are presented as a marriage of good and evil, neither of which is a reality in the world by itself. The goodness within, which man so neglects to cultivate, is nevertheless natural like Immalee. The evil is intrusive like Melmoth; when it bears down too heavily, it drives men insane. By including a figure of the grotesque, Maturin is able to make his novel a complex assessment of human nature, showing both the hold Sentimentalist ideas still had and the doubts and fears about the maddening nature of evil that accompanied them. Grotesque though he is, Melmoth is, or was, a man, as he insists to his descendant right at the end of the novel. The view of evil as enigmatic is consequently mitigated.

All grotesque figures have some connection with the human world. A ghost is a spirit from the dead, a vampire is in origin the human victim of another vampire, even an animal figure is rendered grotesque by being given human perceptions and superhuman powers, not simply brute force. Consequently, when figures of the grotesque appear as non-human, supernatural beings, they still make the sense of human evil darker and less optimistic. The ghosts of Sheridan Le Fanu's tales, published in book form between 1851 and 1872, are like this. Their reality as ghosts is flatly asserted and the malignant spirit they represent remains an enigmatic presence in the world. The figure of the vampire is even farther from the human. A grotesque that refuses to yield itself to direct symbolic interpretation, it has a correspondingly greater suggestive power. A polymorphous, protean monster that drains the blood of the innocent, it is an embodiment of evil of special interest in Gothic fiction because of the decidedly sexual nature of its suggestiveness. In a rather primitive example, John Polidori's *The Vampyre* (1819), little is done with this beyond suggesting the personality-splitting consequences of marauding sexuality.[12] Lord Ruthven is at first presented as a corrupt member of fashionable London society, guilty only of seduction. When the novel transports him to the remote Greek countryside, however, his vampire nature appears. By the simple structural device of splitting the novel in two, between the English and Greek settings, the suggestion is made that what appears as ordinary debauchery when dressed up in the trappings of civilization looks different under the revealing sunlight of a primitive landscape. That is, split off from the "civilized" man, Ruthven's sexuality is revealed as predatory and ruthless.

Le Fanu's *Carmilla* (1871) is a vampire tale more overtly and more mysteriously sexual. It is a first-person account by the heroine, Carmilla's near victim, written, the prologue claims, to a doctor in whose collected papers it is to appear. This "scientific" presentation is an authenticating device a bit like the use Bram Stoker makes later of the scientists in *Dracula*. The young heroine wonders whether Carmilla is not a young man in disguise so like love-making is her conversation, and when the horrified father, hidden in the bedroom, watches the amorphous something slither on to the bed and cover his innocent daughter's body the equation of sexuality and evil is compelling. It does not seem so much a question of homosexuality, although in *Carmilla* vampire and victim are of the same sex, as that old Gothic question of innocence and ignorance. The heroine's ignorance, however, is of herself, and in *Carmilla* inner sexual impulses become the center of interest. When the predator is a vampire the sexual assault can no longer be seen as outside the victim, as it can, for instance, in *The Monk,* where Antonia's innocence leaves her a prey to Ambrosio's lust. The shape-changing vampire appears suddenly. It is only slowly recognized even by its victim's guardians and not at all by the victim, who wastes away under its caresses. In *Carmilla,* it thus comes to symbolize the victim's own sexuality, which, at least in her father's sight, is draining her innocence from her. The terrible vengefulness with which the outraged guardians of purity eventually destroy the vampire seems to bear out this interpretation. Here, as elsewhere, Gothic fiction makes telling use of ancient mythic materials. Bram Stoker's *Dracula* (1897) plays on the same theme, with the innocent Lucy unable to understand what afflicts her.

This tale, which like *Frankenstein* has become a modern popular myth, is far more complicated than *Carmilla.* Before the innocent Lucy is assailed in England, Jonathan Harker has penetrated to the vampire's castle itself, where he comes under attack from Dracula, a male figure, and from the female vampires who are Dracula's former victims. The assault is thus first made on a young man who, though virtuous and upright, is able to see the threat. Later the sharp-eyed Minna, contrasted in many respects with Lucy, will similarly be able to face it. In the end all the resources of society and religion have to be mustered to defeat it. All this suggests a strong force, overpowering for those who cannot recognize it, and almost deadly even to those who do see it.

The characteristics of the vampire: the silent, irresistible entry at night, usually through a window; the sleeping victim held in a trance from which he cannot waken; the shifting form, which, often seen outside as a bat, a dog, or a wolf, becomes vague, even amorphous; the way it lies on its victim, pierces and draws blood from the neck; the way, once life is drained, the victim also becomes a vampire as predatory as the victimizer—these together suggest crime, guilt, a distortion of the soul, all bound up with the sex act. The vampire figure has the haunting quality of nightmare and its association with sexuality is an important indication of the direction the exploration of psychological evil was taking. The association of evil with sexuality probably reflects a gradually increasing awareness of the importance of sexuality in man's nature. From the beginning, Gothic fiction is preoccupied with sexual assault. With the vampire it no longer deals only with sexual innocence in the victim and evil in the victimizer. Now sexuality itself is the question and the "innocent" become the "victims" of their own sexual awakening. In Bram Stoker's novel the forces of science and religion combine to destroy the innocent thus awakened—Lucy dies as Dracula drains the life from her. Then she, now a vampire, has a stake driven through her heart to destroy her. The use of a grotesque, the vampire, presents the evil as stark, absolute, and horrifying. The zeal with which it is extirpated appears to be the force of right. Yet, the sexual implications introduce a less sure note. The tale is told in sections written by different characters: Jonathan's and Minna's journals, Lucy's diary, Seward's diary, a record by Van Helsing. The cumulative method would once again seem to add up to the truth revealed—but does it? Do these characters work on one another, perhaps, in a sort of collective hysteria? The very vagueness of the significance of the vampire prevents a final, neat conclusion about the novel.

Grotesque vampires can effectively, if surreptitiously, evoke the feelings of guilt associated with sexuality. Edgar Allan Poe uses other grotesques in a variety of ways. They often also suggest guilt, which is sometimes maddening because it is indefinable. It is, perhaps, Poe's versatile use of the grotesques that introduces the atmosphere of hysteria into his tales. The conflicting emotions they arouse—fear and laughter—are the reactions of hysteria. The demoniac laughter that echoes through *Melmoth* is possibly designed only to induce fear, but even it, since it is the laughter of despair, has a hysterical note. Poe's characters, finding themselves surrounded by grotesques, show distinct signs of hysteria and, if the reader is attuned to them at all, he must be at least discomforted in a new way. Poe also makes use of another aspect of the grotesque. It acquired its name from the grottos with fantastic decorations in which the first examples of it were found. Its identifying feature is not the distorted figures per se, but the combination of them intertwined so that they seem to move and writhe about. Small wonder such an art should have been adopted by literature to convey the shifting surface of reality. As Kayser says: "It is our world which has to be transformed. . . . We are so strongly affected and terrified because it is our world which ceases to be reliable."[13] In Poe's tales, the world of his characters ceases to be reliable for them and the decorative grotesque appears in his stories. The frame of the portrait in "The Oval Portrait" (1842) is wrought in "arabesques" (another term for the figures of the decorative grotesque). In "Ligeia" (1838) the curtains that shut out the day from Lady Rowena's tomb-like room are covered with arabesque designs that appear life-like under the continuous rippling movement of the hangings. Poe also peoples his stories with figures from the decorative grotesque. The death skeleton and the whole setting of "The Masque of the Red Death" (1842) seem drawn from this source. The decorations of the rooms, the masked figures dancing through them have the artificiality, the enigmatic movement-in-stillness of a frieze.

Poe's animal figures are also ambiguously grotesque. In "The Black Cat" (1843) the cat with its one eye and its stare, which the narrator, at least, sees as accusing, might be an animated gargoyle. "Hop-Frog" (1849) is a story centered on this use of the animal grotesque. Its figures gain a special symbolic significance because they are not actually animals. They either look like or are dressed up as animals. Hop-Frog is a dwarf and the implacable vindictiveness of his nature makes his deformity seem an outward manifestation of the meanness of a soul too petty to rise above the cruelties inflicted on it. To prevent such a simplified view, however, Tripetta, Hop-Frog's beloved, is of his race and even tinier, but she is physically perfect, undeformed and graceful. Thus, there seems to be no symbolic equation between size of body and soul. Instead, Hop-Frog is equated with the king and his counsellors. Hop-Frog is noted as having a strange ape-like gait, and he dresses them as orangutangs for the costume ball—that is, he and they are both ape-like. It is, of course, Hog-Frog's own view that they had been senselessly mean. Consequently, while the physical sameness between him with his ape-like walk and them in their ape costumes seems to satirize them as petty, cruel, dwarf-like spirits, this also redounds back on him. So the original equation between small stature and pettiness seems to stand after all. In revenge for their mindless cruelty to him and Tripetta, Hop-Frog immolates them by setting fire to the costumes. And Tripetta, little and sweet-tempered as she seems, vigorously assists him in his grisly execution of his tormentors. So, in the end, all appear to share the same bestial characteristics.

Poe has galvanized the illusion of movement in the decorative grotesque into actually moving figures, then used transformations of shape and size to make and unmake equations in a way that leaves us groping uncertainly for a moral position. Such manipulation becomes a simple literary trick played on the reader of "The Murders in the Rue Morgue" (1841). Here, bestiality is contrasted with the purely cerebral. Heavily curtained windows block out the light of day and nature in the house of Poe's Dupin, an all-seeing deductive genius. This setting represents and makes possible intellect in its purest, most abstract form, and

Dupin emerges from it only at night. He is set against a monster that only at the end of the story turns out to be actually an animal. Once again Poe uses a beast closely identified with man, the orangutang or wild man of the woods, as an embodiment of sheer brutishness, and because neither the reader nor the characters know that the murderer is not a human brute, he and they are "tricked" into accepting the possibility of its ferocity as human. Its brutality is thus equated with human brutishness as it would be without the fine cast of the human intellect to overlay and modify it. By setting the clever Dupin in contrast to the doltish police (a device that became, of course, a convention of detective fiction), Poe emphasizes the superiority of his deductive method over their empirical approach. In this first of the detective stories brain is thus set against brutishness in a manner that, through the "trick," reveals the two as aspects of human nature.[14] The bumbling police and other ordinary people, such as the reader, fall between the two as mixed beings of a more everyday reality than either the beast or the brilliant detective. While reading, however, we have been made to suppose that inhuman brutality was human, and that only superhuman intellect could overcome it. However reassuring it may be to learn that the killer is an unthinking ape, the residue of fear of such a human possibility is left. The beast within is frequently represented as ape-like.

The detective story, however, presents the triumph of reason over brutality and the use of science to a good end. Gothic fiction tips the balance the other way and works to undo any pride we may feel in the powers of the human mind. In this respect, Hawthorne is particularly ruthless. In "Rappaccini's Daughter" (1844) science is used to distort and poison nature itself. The monstrously beautiful flowers in Rappaccini's garden might themselves be part of an arabesque border in which plants and animals are often intertwined. Among them, the beauty of Beatrice only makes her poisonousness more hideous. Hawthorne presents her with the usual Gothic equation of beauty and virtue, and yet she is poisonous. Like the flowers in a grotesque border, which are not themselves distorted or ugly, she is a grotesque by context. By the end of the story we can no longer tell who is the monster, however, Giovanni or Beatrice. The easy contrast between Nature and art or science or civilization dissolves into uncertainty.

"The Birthmark" (1843) sports another ambiguous grotesque. Aylmer's pursuit of perfection reverses the relationships of "Rappaccini's Daughter" only to bring us back to the same lack of surety. As in Poe's stories, we have a brilliant mind—at least it is supposed that it is brilliant—in Aylmer, who, like Poe's Dupin, shuts out the daylight by curtaining his wife's room from floor to ceiling. And we again find physical appearance equated with mental state. Aylmer's lab assistant is an animal-like troglodyte who merely does such necessary dirty work as tending the furnace. He is consistently described as a creature of this earth, black from the furnace, with a sardonic laugh. Hence, he is the grotesque in this story. Yet it is he who knows all along what the effect will be of the attempt to remove the birthmark. Ultimately, he seems just a figure of the earth, of nature, and it is Aylmer's sacrifice of his wife in his pursuit of perfection that seems monstrous. Again, though, because for much of the story we have been constrained to believe in Aylmer's brilliance and to at least share apprehensively in his idealism, we cannot easily reverse our attitudes. We are left knowing there is some truth in both the pursuit of perfection and the earthy realization of its futility.

Aylmer's assistant is a grotesque of gnome-like ambiguity but he has a very minor place in the story. In *Dr. Jekyll and Mr. Hyde* (1886) Stevenson makes a similar figure central. Hyde is a combination of a grotesque and a doubles figure. In him the evil aspect of human nature has again become an inherent part of Man's make-up which must be present in all, for he is instinctively recognized for what he is. Characters from the subtle, observant Enfield to the simple housemaid who witnesses the murder are filled instantly with an inexplicable horror at the mere sight of him. All remark on his stunted stature and are struck by the fact that "he gives a strong feeling of deformity," although they cannot say how he is deformed. This instant recognition of evil suggests that, at the end of the nineteenth century, human beings could still be seen as endowed with that Moral Sense that knows good and evil instantaneously.

Nevertheless, although the Moral Sense was a prime tenet of benevolism, the figure of Hyde seems to deny benevolist ideas. Stevenson uses the convention of the physically stunted figure to show Hyde as the warped animal nature of Jekyll, an actual part of him. Jekyll's clothes are symbolically too large for Hyde, who is a veritable id. We are led to believe he should have been kept under, repressed, and in the control of the rational civilized man. Doubt is thrown on this conclusion too, but only after we have lived through the imaginative experience of the breaking out of a repressed aspect of the personality. Throughout the tales featuring grotesques, artists, scientists, and the intellect itself are brought into some kind of conflict with the demons of the physical, the creatures from underground or from the mental below-ground of characters and readers alike. The figures of the intellect, however, also appear frighteningly ambiguous and shifting.

MAD SCIENTISTS AND FAUSTS

The Faustian "mad scientists" of the nineteenth century are male characters. They have female equivalents in many a witch, but these have a slightly different function. An occasional male witch appears, such as the wizard Old Maule in *The House of the Seven Gables,* but more often the Faustian scientists are too human and fallible to be wizards. From Mary Shelley's Frankenstein on, they pursue a forbidden path that cuts them off from their fellow humans and so from virtue, an indication of the continuing influence of Sentimentalism and its concept of virtue as social. When they have thus cut themselves off, they are lost and damned.[15] Gothic fiction uses these figures in its exploration of madness. We find a relationship made not only between madness and crime, but also, in the ancient Faustian theme, between madness and knowledge and/or art. This results inevitably in a third equation between knowledge or art and crime. Frankenstein, it will be remembered, is doomed by his fascination with the alchemists. It is true that he rejects them, but the two contrasted professors of modern science and his relations with them make it clear, nevertheless, that the earlier inclination has produced an irreparable distortion of his mind. He seems to make the mistake of measuring inner worth by physical appearance, but the situation is more complicated. First he encounters Professor Krempe "a little squat man with a gruff voice and a repulsive countenance; the teacher, therefore did not prepossess me in favour of his pursuits." So he feels little inclination to pursue modern science. The "modern" scientist no longer seeks "immortality and power," and Frankenstein feels he is "required to exchange chimeras of boundless grandeur for realities of little worth." Then he meets Professor Waldman who is "very unlike his colleague." He has "an aspect expressive of the greatest benevolence. . . . His person was short but remarkably erect; and his voice the sweetest I had ever heard." This man is Frankenstein's downfall. In Frankenstein's willingness to follow Waldman but not Krempe, Mary Shelley uses the equation of beauty and virtue ironically. The seductive power of Waldman's voice leads Frankenstein to pursue in modern science goals as false as those alchemy had seemed to promise. Waldman himself is a good man able to show him the value of modern science: "The ancient teachers of this science," said he, "promised impossibilities and performed nothing. The modern masters promise very little; they know that metals cannot be transmuted and that the elixir of life is a chimera. But these philosophers, whose hands seem only made to dabble in dirt, and their eyes to pore over the microscope or crucible, have indeed performed miracles. They penetrate into the recesses of nature and show how she works in her hiding places."[16] It is Frankenstein's own pride that makes him follow the path pointed out by Waldman only to plunge into pursuits his professor would never have licensed. The symbolic physical appearance of the two men is thoroughly ambiguous. The "squat" dwarf-like Krempe, almost a grotesque, offers no grand vision; Waldman with his "sweet voice" is the siren who lures Frankenstein into his dangerous creation. Neither, in fact, is more than an ordinary professor of science, as their small stature indicates. Only Frankenstein himself is the Prometheus/Faust, not merely defying the gods but putting himself in God's place to create his own wretched Adam.

Hawthorne's scientists come to us fully made and already far along the path to destruction. The lack of a Sentimental background like Frankenstein's makes them more alarming than he. They seem also to have high ideals like his, but we are not given any real assurance of their worth. In "The Birthmark" Aylmer is a brilliant scientist, it is said, although his journal reveals that all his greatest achievements are really failures. He is already wedded to his science when he marries a woman as beautiful as she is virtuous. She has a single blemish, a birthmark shaped like a tiny hand on one cheek. This sign of imperfection Aylmer cannot stand. Clearly, the improbable shape of the mark makes it symbolic of the slight imperfection that is a necessary concomitant of life on this earth. When Aylmer tries to remove it, it turns out to have its grip on the heart of his saintly and self-sacrificing wife. She pays for his passionate perfectionism with her life.

To carry out his experiment Aylmer cuts himself, his wife, and his troll-like assistant off from the world and from nature, not only by excluding the daylight from his wife's boudoir, but also by himself working with his assistant in a dark, infernal laboratory from which even she is excluded. In a previous, less drastic experiment Aylmer first poisons the air of the boudoir in an attempt to destroy the birthmark, desisting only when he sees his wife perishing from the imperceptible fumes. He experiments further, however, until his wife is finally cut off from life.

Strangely, the story's symbolic meaning at first seems very clear. To meddle in knowledge beyond man's limits is to poison the natural life of virtue. The mere blemish, which is the sign of humanity, cannot be removed and the attempt to do so poisons existence and finally kills. The grotesque figure of the assistant, however, throws all in doubt again, for it is he who carries this "moral," if it is the moral, of the tale. If the beautiful virtue of the wife is admirable, however, then Aylmer is wrong only in thinking it can be made perfect. His aspiration cannot be condemned in simple terms. His persistence after the first experiment has endangered his wife's life is the same obsessive pursuit seen in Frankenstein. It is not straightforwardly evil. This we see through the assistant. That creature of the earth sees Aylmer's folly but he only laughs. He says and does nothing to prevent the diastrous consequences of the experiment. Indeed, his laughter suggests a certain glee over it. Hence, Hawthorne finally leaves unresolved the question whether the pursuit of perfection is laudable or damnable and we must conclude that it may be both.

In "Rappaccini's Daughter" it is the two scientists exerting opposite pulls on Giovanni who create the doubt. Unlike Frankenstein's professors, these two, Rappaccini and Baglioni, seem to be presented as standing for directly opposed views. The one follows "false," the other "true" science. From the beginning, however, it is apparent that Baglioni is also guilty of a jealous rivalry with Rappaccini. His envy casts doubt on his motives in denigrating Rappaccini in Giovanni's eyes. Beatrice, moreover, is killed by the antidote provided by Baglioni. Even though she, like the flowers she tends in the walled garden, is grotesque in her poisonous beauty, she is consistently shown to be innocent throughout the story. What then of her father's art, which has made her and the flowers poisonous? Is Rappaccini a Faustian figure deforming nature, or is it Baglioni's envy and lack of imagination that see him so? Giovanni has the evidence of the bouquet of flowers and the insect that wither in Beatrice's poisonous breath to show that Rappaccini is all that Baglioni says he is. Rappaccini, nevertheless, has created something beautiful and infinitely alluring to Giovanni. Himself becoming poisonous, he tries to "cure" her. For a number of reasons, however, the reader is left in a state of uncertainty about this cure. What, for instance, does "poisonous" mean? The question is left unanswered. If Giovanni had understood the answer, could he, and should he, have entered Beatrice's realm instead of trying to draw her back into the ordinary world? We cannot avoid the Dantean allusion in her name and the suggestion it leaves that she represents a higher spiritual good. And we should note that when, afraid to enter her poisonous world, Giovanni becomes fearful and angry with her and also hopeful of "curing" her, it is said that he is lacking understanding, crudely of this world, and that she is an angel. This takes us back to that exclamation at the beginning of the story: "Blessed are all simple emotions, be they dark or bright! It is the lurid intermixture of the two that produces the illuminating blaze of the infernal regions."[17]

This enigmatic statement takes the story into a world of shifting values of which the main characteristic is instability. "Rappaccini's Daughter" has been given a strictly Freudian interpretation, which would make Giovanni's and Baglioni's fear of Rappaccini, his garden, and his daughter a fear of the voluptuous, a fear of the sexual woman, who is perceived as poisonous to the higher life of abstraction. Another possibility is left open here too, however. Rappaccini appears very little in the story; usually, like Giovanni, he is in a window watching Beatrice. May we not see in this the jealous father seeking to keep his daughter to himself by keeping her "innocent" and the equally jealous lover afraid of the power of the father to destroy him if he approaches the daughter too closely? Is Rappaccini "guarding" his daughter against her own natural sexual development, as the father in *Carmilla* or Jonathan and his friends in *Dracula* try and fail to do?

Even more than in the vampire tales, the ambiguity is complete. Hawthorne, with his scientists, has added to the sexual question the split between the voluptuous beauty of the garden and the austere life of intellectual discipline. Giovanni is apparently condemned for his unwillingness to enter the poisoned world while, at the same time, it is clearly shown to *be* poisonous and deadly to everyday life. The reader is not left with the idea that what is good under some circumstances may be bad under others. Rather, an idea beyond that is presented. Giovanni has penetrated to a realm that asserts one cannot know at all. Good and evil have one and the same source; the pursuit of intellectual knowledge may destroy the simpler human relationships of love and marriage, or it may not, and, whether it does or not, it may still have value in and of itself. Would Rappaccini have been less a jealous father if he had not been a scientist, Giovanni less a timid lover if he had not been a student, Baglioni less a man of principle if he had been more brilliant? The central point of the story is that these questions cannot be answered.

In addition to the ambiguous moral issues that they raise, these scientists are all mad in that they follow their investigations and experiments obsessively, unable to stop themselves. Their madness is not emphasized, as the derangement of Poe's central characters is. That, however, only makes clearer the concept of it as a distortion of their natural state. In their passionate natures these male figures are closely connected with the female witch figures of Gothic fiction. There is a further connection, in that their knowledge of life's secrets comes, as Frankenstein puts it, from dabbling in dirt—or worse. The false, or ambiguously false, science of Frankenstein, Rappaccini, and Aylmer and the grotesque figures associated with them connects them to the infernal brews of Vathek's mother Carathis or the incantations of Ambrosio's Matilda. These scientists are all intellect, and they are also violators of Mother Earth and her secrets. In a rather different way, the female figures of Gothic fiction are also double-sided. This can already be seen in the female element in the stories of artists who, in their pursuit of an intellectual ideal, seem to deny the life of ordinary man and are thus closely allied to the Faustian scientists. When, in Poe's "The Oval Portrait," the artist is said to have been married to his art before his wife, as Aylmer was to science before his, art and science have figuratively been made female. In Hoffmann's stories when the artist or poet is torn between figures of art and life, the figure of art may be a mere automaton or it may be the enchanting green snake, but it is female, as is the woman who represents life. Repeatedly the male characters are torn between two kinds of female enchantment.

EARTH MOTHERS AND WITCHES

The double aspect of the female side of human nature in the Gothic novels does not split the female figures in half as it does the male characters. Woman as gentle inspiration or as seductress seems to be two forms of a single image. In either case, she is in touch with the earth and, whether she is gentle or fierce, this contact makes her stronger than the male characters because she is not torn. For good or ill, she asserts a unity between things earthly and extraterrestrial aspirations. In its positive form, the female spirit ties the male to the earth, keeping him in touch with it however high his spirit soars. In its malignant aspect, it is anomalous; it tempts, seduces, lures men to inevitable destruction, and draws its power from that same tie with the earth.

This view of woman is also seen in the Sentimental

novel. Paul's Virginia and Werther's Lotte become earth mothers through their identification with Nature. Paul and Virginia are like twin children of nature, yet it is she who sits like a young goddess in their special grove and he who gathers fruit to bring to her there. Paul's love for her takes on a mystic quality. She is the informing spirit of the nature with which the two live in such harmony. The same is true of Lotte. Werther seeks in her the peace he has sought in nature and she truly is what he seeks. She is both the highest inspiration and the tie with this earth and she is denied to him partly by worldly circumstances, partly because his idealism is too extreme, too unworldly. Even figures like Miss Walton and Julia in Mackenzie's novels, who do not have the same tie to the earth, are nevertheless the center of the hero's aspirations. They again are the strong figure, the fixed foot of the compass.

In the Gothic novel such characters begin to merge with the figure of the witch. In *Otranto* the women are still Sentimental heroines and Matilda is an ideal figure of inspiration for both men and women. In *Vathek* things begin to change. Carathis and Nouronihar form a sort of balance to each other; they are not just a contrast. The caliph's mother constantly dabbles in magic and witchcraft. Like the Faustian scientists, she is consumed with a desire for illicit knowledge. But she is an integrated personality, pursuing her aims with gusto; she is not torn. She despises Vathek for his sensuality and his infatuation for Nouronihar, which distracts him from the pursuit of hellish knowledge. Nouronihar, however, is the interesting figure here. The leader of the Sentimental pair she makes with her little cousin Gulchenrouz, she also leads Vathek back to the pursuit of knowledge. Vathek is drawn to hell, albeit quite willingly, by the apparently innocent Nouronihar, as well as being driven there by his fearsome mother. A similar situation occurs again and again in other works.

In *The Monk* Antonia and Matilda represent the extreme opposites in female figures. Yet both contribute to

Ambrosio's downfall. The witch-demon Matilda undoubtedly brings about his destruction. Yet it is also true that Elvira's care for her child's virtue and her courage in defending it and Antonia's complete innocence and natural virtue cause Ambrosio to commit his two most monstrous crimes. The two women are in no way culpable, but the very naturalness of their virtue makes them rock-like in resisting evil, and they are a part of his fall. Ambroiso, villain though he is, is reflected in his sister. Also a trembling, fated victim, he is weaker than she, the victim of his own passions and of the crimes he commits. He is a child in the hands of Matilda. Ambrosio and Antonia are thus potentially a pair like their Sentimental counterparts.

Matilda herself is a clear example of the evil seductress. As sexual temptress, as enchantress with occult powers, as agent of Lucifer, she manipulates Ambrosio with ease. She seduces him by taking the bold and heroic measure of sucking the poison from his wound and appearing to be willing to die for him. Once he is seduced, she quickly abandons all appearance of female softness and exercises control over him with ferocity and scorn. She is strong and decisive; he is weak and easily led. And her powers are drawn directly from the underworld, as her incantations are performed in the underground vaults.

In the Sentimental relationship of Frankenstein and Elizabeth she is both all goodness and the victim of violence, like Antonia, while he is the torn male parallel to the female witch figure. Her goodness is his inspiration in the beginning; her spirit spurs on his pursuit of evil in the end. Yet, here again, the paradoxical duality of the woman appears. Elizabeth, the companion of Frankenstein's idyllic childhood, is quite blameless in his downfall. And yet, his very aspirations that led to that fall were inspired by her goodness. The spirit that spurs him on to hunt down the monster in the end is again the spirit of goodness, he says, encouraging him to pursue evil. But he dies in the pursuit. Frankenstein has drawn inspiration from Elizabeth, but he has distorted it into false aspirations that cut him off from nature and from her. Elizabeth is an innocent "cause" of Frankenstein's transgression and destruction, but she remains the steady force that would have tied him to virtue and to the earth simultaneously. If he had had the wisdom not to desert the life of sensibility for the life of the mind, he would not have fallen into that distortion of the tie to the earth, the unhealthy robbing of the grave's secrets.

Even Immalee in *Melmoth* plays the dual role of the female figures. Pure child of nature, she too is the female force that attaches the male to the earth. Because she is innocence personified in complete harmony with nature, she alone can, for a short while, bring the demon Wanderer back to his humanity. In his relationship to her he is transformed from a figure of death to a demon lover. Here, however, all is inverted. Melmoth being a grotesque figure already in the grip of Hell, Immalee's power draws him back to the earth and nature from a lower, darker power. His original aspiration was Faustian, like Frankenstein's, but he has already destroyed himself. She is an influence to draw him back from the abyss.

These ambiguous heroines, then, are more closely allied to the real witches than at first appears. A witch, having supernatural power, is always close to being a grotesque, like Carathis and such figures of Hoffmann's as the apple-woman-witch-nurse and the green snake in "The Golden Flower Pot," or the Furstin-gypsy-woman with her raven in "The Doubles." They are at one and the same time shifting, changing grotesques and witch figures with magic at their fingertips. They exercise a good-evil power that symbolizes man's need to reconcile his idealism with his attachment to the earth. This same combination in a shape-changing female figure appears in tones more somber than Hoffmann's in Kleist's *Michael Kohlhaas* (1808). There Kohlhaas' martyred, virtuous wife is also a prophesying witch, an instrument in the destiny of the principal characters.

In other stories there is no need for such a figure because the earth itself is a female power. In Hoffmann's "The Mines of Falun" primeval myth is re-enacted as the seafaring man is drawn from the arms of his bride into the jeweled bowels of the earth, where, in the service of the earth Queen, he suffers petrifaction. His return to the service of Mother Earth is a choice that cannot be reconciled with human love. Earth reclaims him and the living body, in becoming a stone image of itself, also becomes a part of the earth. This form of return to the earth also appears in Hawthorne's stories "The Man of Adamant" and "Ethan Brand." In "The Man of Adamant" the character is turned to stone and, in becoming dead to life, yet achieves a sort of immortality by becoming a part of the earth. In "Ethan Brand" it is Brand's heart alone that is converted to glowing stone; in "The Man of Adamant" the whole figure is gradually transformed. In both stories the petrifaction is the symbolic price of sinfulness. Both central figures have "hardened their hearts" and so undergo literally what the reader understands metaphorically, as, in *Vathek,* the hearts of the damned burn in their chests in the underground Halls of Eblis. The power of the female earth to envelope men and make them part of itself corresponds to the strength of the virtuous women and the witches who draw their power from the earth, in contrast to the male scientists who try to wrest her secrets from her.

Nowhere, perhaps, is the tie to the earth in a central female figure used with more subtle effect than in *Wuthering Heights.* Heathcliff is a being from outside made dark and demonic by his uncertain origins and his abrupt entry into the world of the Yorkshire moors. The apparently more ordinary Cathy, however, is truly the *spiritus loci.* Even though Heathcliff is a fierce, enigmatic figure, he, too, is a mere child in the hands of Cathy. When they are actually children she leads their expeditions on the moors; she instigates their little rebellions. Later, however complicated his revenge, it is she who is the still center of his tempestuous world. For her, he leaves to "better himself"; for her, he returns. Once she is dead, his entire life is a search for reunion with her, a tormented wait for her to call him. Only when she does, does he find peace. When they are reunited, she has allowed him to rejoin her as the spirit of the moors. The bond between them is a dark, occult communion between kindred spirits. Nature and the natural have become a paradoxical source of the fiercest, the meanest, but also the most profound emanation of the human spirit. This is why, when Heathcliff longs for death, he does not think of rejoining his beloved in the afterlife, as Werther does, but of reunion with her in the earth, in the grave. Cathy's enigmatic remark, "I am Heathcliff," is not a woman's subordination of her selfhood to the man she loves. Ordinary human love, marriage, motherhood—these belong to Edgar. When Cathy says she is Heathcliff, she states that she is his very soul, the force that orients him. She binds him, a being divorced from his origins, in union to the earth. Cathy is unusual for a female character in that she undergoes the split usually experienced by the male. Even in this, however, she is typical of the feminine spirit in Gothic fiction. The men from Frankenstein to Dr. Jekyll are lured into a pursuit which divides one part of the human personality from the other. Cathy is caught between two worlds, each of which claims her, and her indignation is unbounded at their attempt to split her in two, at the desire of each to deny the other's world. Entering civilization when she marries Edgar, she protests that her feelings for her husband have nothing to do with her natural, permanent, and unbreakable attachment to Heathcliff. She does not make herself sick and die out of perversity, as Nellie thinks. She cannot, and will not, live divided. In her, Emily Brontë has made something new out of the paradoxical involvement of virtue in evil seen in other novels. In Cathy, the indomitability of the light-filled human spirit rests in its tie to the dark demonic forces of the earth. The identity of the two shows this. The spirit world into which Cathy draws Heathcliff must be part of that same universal demon realm from which he came and which surrounds the domains of man, civilized and savage alike. The union of Cathy's spirit and Heathcliff's out on the moor parallels the tie between the younger Cathy and Hareton, destined to live in Thrushcross Grange, the seat of civilization.

James is equally subtle in *The Turn of the Screw.* He divides again the figures of the heroine and the witch, but he does so only to confound them the more. We cannot know ultimately if there is any difference between Miss Jessel and the governess, since the one may inhabit the mind of the other. If we could keep them separate, moreover, we still would not know whether Miss Jessel were evil or only seen as evil. James's presentation of them in two separate figures determines the relationship between him as ultimate narrator and his novel, which differs from Emily Brontë's relationship to hers. Because he does not present the ghost-governess and her living counterpart in one figure, he as "implied author" stands back from the tale and leaves the reader to work out the puzzle. Emily Brontë, on the other hand, may give a dual view of every moral value, but the spirit Cathy represents remains one and there is no ironic distance between herself as author and her work. Thus, the split in Cathy is healed in "higher truth." The governess/Miss Jessel, however, being split symbolically, remains on a more mundane level where the reader must try to puzzle out the problem of moral values, self-delusion, and sexual repression with very little help and with no appeal to an ultimate value.

Witches, earth mothers, Faust figures, grotesques—all these tend to push Gothic fiction toward the enigmatic and the ambiguous. They work to confuse the reader rather than supplying him with answers. The exploration into human evil seems less and less able to draw a line between it and the good. This movement in Gothic tales probably reflects the general tendency for moral absolutes to give way before moral relativity in the modern world. But in literature's inquiry into the mind it led eventually to a more objective view of man's mental make-up. Before that happened, however, the prime features of Gothic fiction—its dream-like ambience, its paired heroes and heroines, its doubles figures, and its houses, portraits, mirrors, statues, and paintings—all also took on increasingly tenuous, slippery meanings.

DREAMS AND NIGHTMARES

All Gothic tales are to some extent dreams. Real dreams being themselves manifestations of mental material, their figures and settings are a natural choice for fictional explorations of the mind. Both *The Castle of Otranto* and *Frankenstein* originated, of course, in actual dreams. For these dreams to have given rise to works of Gothic literature, however, the authors must have been predisposed to see the dream material itself as suited to furnish a fiction and have felt a compulsion to make the dream manifest and so give it a general and less personal application.

Walpole gave expression to imagery from his subconscious mind in a manner that was new to his contemporaries, who greeted it as a welcome innovation. His successors recognized a new literary method and in short order made it a convention. They varied greatly from individual to individual in the extent to which they wrote under direct personal pressure to put their subconscious minds on paper. But whether neurotic or objective, the relation between the interest in the mind and the use of dream imagery is direct.

Walpole tells of writing at white heat under a compelling impulse. He records that he remembered only the mailed hand on the staircase of the actual dream itself and that in the process of writing he unconsciously gave the castle architectural features of his Cambridge college.[18] The symbolic construct which gives the novel its main force as a piece of fiction, its themes of incest, violence, and usurpation, the way these are couched in mythic fairy-tale patterns are sufficient reason to see it as coming in some sense from his subconscious mind. It is not a transcription of the dream itself, however, and too much should not be made of its origins in his subconscious, since the imagination is compelled to draw much of its imagery from the subconscious, on the one hand, and, on the other, no piece of fiction is a simple transcription of unconscious thought processes. The important fact about Gothic fiction is that the division between its imagery and its subject matter is slight.

Like Walpole, Beckford and Matthew Lewis claimed to have written their novels at great speed under an inner compulsion. All three had their heads full of Gothic materials, Walpole living at Strawberry Hill at a point in his life when he was anxious to escape from the great world and banish politics from his mind; Beckford immersed in oriental literature; Lewis agog with the weird tales of the German *Schauerromanen*. None of them seems to have thought of his work as a fictional delineation of his own subconscious mind, yet the compulsion to write suggests a need for self-expression. This was, of course, a fashionable attitude among the Romantics and Lewis had some financial compulsions as urgent as his psychological ones, but these are not reasons to doubt they wrote fast and fervently.

The pattern of nightmare in *The Castle of Otranto* and *The Monk*, which compels a sense that they are drawn from the depths of the authors' own minds, and the similar impression left by Beckford's *Vathek*, makes these works seem unlike the novels of Clara Reeve and Ann Radcliffe. In *Frankenstein* this impulse to make manifest in fiction the emotional life of the author is strangely melded with a more intellectual embodiment of the ideas of the age. The pattern of nightmare is fitted into an exceptionally complex, self-conscious structure. In this, the novel may perhaps reflect the role of the intellectual ideas in the emotional life of a young woman whose parents and husband in their very persons and in their actions stood for the ideas they lived for.[19] It is ideas that Mary Shelley embodies in her fiction, though in all likelihood they are colored and shaped by the configuration of her subconscious mind.

Both Poe and Hawthorne are known to have drawn deliberately upon the material of their dreams, shaping it into fictions, but leaving the ambiguous, symbolic dream atmosphere intact in a manner that resists interpretation. The most striking difference, perhaps, between their tales and those of their predecessors lies here. They are conscious of the importance of dream material and deliberately delineate the mind through its own raw materials. Their stories are not dreamlike; they are dreams—and nightmares at that. Both authors induced in themselves a "hypnagogic state" which, as Richard Wilbur describes it, is one between waking and sleeping "in which the conscious mind is conscious of the subconscious, and can, as it were, look down into the dream which is shortly to engulf it."[20] Hawthorne's tales are set out with a surface calm and detachment. One's sense of the "implied author" is of an observer setting down his observations in a fiction. With Poe, on the other hand, the frantic and exclamatory voice suggests complete involvement. The reader is tempted to equate the narrators with the author, despite the fact that they are often self-avowed madmen and either criminals or great sinners and that their hysteria is seen in the laughter forced from horror that is evoked by the grotesque within the tale. Poe's stories, beyond all others, stand out as the direct evocation of the atmosphere of a dream while the dreamer is experiencing it, rather than a dream remembered in a waking state.

Directly or indirectly expressive of dreams, the closed worlds of the Gothic novels are themselves symbolic and dream-like. They also frequently contain accounts of the dreams of their characters. Often these are no more than convenient foreshadowing devices, entirely improbable as dreams. Edmund's dream in *The Old English Baron,* for instance, slightly diminishes the need for the supernatural effects Clara Reeve so wished to minimize. We may believe the dream was inspired by the haunted room, but we are not told so. Similarly, Lorenzo's dream at the beginning of *The Monk* gives us a lurid foretaste of the whole Ambrosio/Antonia plot, doing little more than set the atmosphere of the novel.

Even such foreshadowing dreams, however, sometimes have the haunting quality of real nightmare. Frankenstein's dream after he has created the monster presages the final destruction of all he loves and throws a lurid light on any interpretation of the novel, but it is enough like a real nightmare to make the correspondences subtle. He dreams that, as he clasps Elizabeth, she becomes a corpse in his arms, which he then finds is the already rotting body of his dead mother. The dream thus foretells the dire consequences of the "foul creation," since the monster will destroy in the end all Frankenstein's family. By embodying all that Frankenstein loves in Elizabeth and then identifying her with his mother, however, the dream looks backward as well as forward to the paradoxical causes as well as the consequences of Frankenstein's making the monster. On her deathbed the mother joins Elizabeth's and Frankenstein's hands, bequeathing her to him as his bride. She dies, moreover, of the fever she caught while nursing Elizabeth back to health from the same illness. Thus, the mother and Elizabeth—the source of Frankenstein's Sentimental upbringing and the Sentimental heroine of the novel—have already been closely identified with each other. This identification is confirmed by the horrible nightmare in which Elizabeth *is* the rotting body of the mother. Thus the paradoxical part played by the Sentimental upbringing in Frankenstein's corruption is symbolized in the dream. Frankenstein's nightmare is induced by his completion of his creation. His sleeping self knows that the idealism inspired in him by his mother and Elizabeth, which aroused the desire to greatly benefit mankind, has in turn become pride and overweening ambition to transgress human limits and thus led to the creation of the monster.

The mother's death, taking place just before Frankenstein leaves for the university and, in fact, delaying his departure is, through the equation of the mother and Elizabeth, a presage of what is to come. The macabre dream does more than foreshadow the events of the novel; by its parallels, it indicates the significance of the symbolism. It shows at an early point that, in breaking the bounds of knowledge, Frankenstein has destroyed the goodness and virtue of his nature. As soon as the monster is created the reader is thus told through the dream that it is a projection of Frankenstein's personality and that that personality is "fated," as he puts it, to destroy all that he values. At the same time the identification of Elizabeth with the mother tells us, again symbolically, that she reflects the nature with which Frankenstein was born and that, as a character, she is an embodiment of the Sentimentalist view of human nature. The dream also intensifies suspense in the novel because the reader, consciously or not, waits for the terrible nightmare to be realized.

Melmoth is dotted with dreams along with every other Gothic device but, except for the Wanderer's final dream, which is a summons from the devil, they are simple foreshadowing devices. In Hoffmann, on the other hand, each tale itself is turned into a dream. His stories are filled with constantly shifting changing figures that appear and disappear without notice. His central characters appear in one setting, then another, without traveling between the two, and they are themselves bemused, dreamy types, more acted upon than acting. The stories are peopled with tall thin figures like Dr. Dappertuto, Peter Schlemihl, and Herr Dapsul von Zabelthau, and their short fat counterparts. The tall figures, at least in one shape, are often magicians, to accompany the shape-changing witchwomen. Snakes are also beautiful girls, and beautiful girls, mechanical dolls. Trees tinkle with music and sparkle with jewels, and doorknobs become faces. Such a variegated cast is not necessarily dream content, but the constant shifting and changing, the way the central character suddenly finds himself in new surroundings without knowing how he got there, reproduces the feeling of a dream.

Poe's stories, too, are themselves dreams. They are not, like Hoffmann's, cheerful and sparkling reveries, but full-blown nightmares. Their dream atmosphere is so compelling that it has caused a good deal of critical controversy. The dream is frequently said to be the narrator's, perhaps because, if it is not, it is hard to say whose it is—unless it is the reader's.

One way in which Poe keeps the identity of the dreaming mind obscure is through his means of creating the closed world, and this adds a great deal of uncertainty to his tales. The closed world becomes a tomb, and the tomb is the self. In "Ligeia" and in "The Masque of the Red Death" a world is closed off within the story by the central character himself. Prince Prospero deliberately cuts off the palace from the outside world and himself decorates his self-contained seven rooms. The narrator/central character of "Ligeia" also decorates the bridal chamber with phantasmagoric arabesques, marble sarcophagi, and a black coffin-like bed. He creates within the abbey, which itself has a remote and unspecified location in the English countryside, an even more remote and confined world, a world which, in fact, is a tomb. Roderick Usher, of course, also entombs his sister, as Prince Prospero does his courtiers, albeit with different intents. When to this is added all the murder victims who, in Poe's stories are bricked up in walls, stuffed into chimneys, and buried under floors, it can be seen that these effects all manifest a major theme. The closed world of the self has become a symbol of death. But the character himself is also in a closed world, so ultimately he is part of the dream and, consequently, it is always problematical whether he can also be the dreamer. By keeping the center of consciousness uncertain in this way, Poe effectively makes everything else unsure—what, if anything, happens? Are the events mental only? Whose is the guilt and for what?

Poe repeatedly uses these techniques, along with first-person narration, to prevent the reader from exculpating himself by extricating himself from the story. None of Poe's tales is less amenable to exact interpretation than "Ligeia," but this fact only increases the reader's sense of involvement. The narrator's having himself created a closed world affects the reader's view of it and of the part of the narrative that precedes it. The reader's sense that he is experiencing or sharing a dream is determined from the opening by the vagueness of the introduction the narrator provides. He cannot remember where Ligeia comes from, he says, or where and when he first knew her, and he is almost sure he never knew her family name. He does know that she comes of an ancient house and has a mind imbued with the wisdom of centuries. This may be an indication of his madness, as has often been suggested, but his confused, amnesiac opening also serves to alert the reader at once to the kind of reading expected. He has to keep his mind in suspense, waiting for a clarification that, in fact, never comes. Whether the narrator is mad or recording a dream state or both, his vagueness here and in other tales contributes more than anything else to the sense of their ambiguity. The dream-like uncertainty may be an uncertainty of perception in the character but, if it is, the reader is forced to share it.

Since the feverish, hallucinatory mental state of Poe's protagonists frequently leads to criminality, there is a decided feeling of a continuance of the Sentimentalist/Gothic view of evil as a distortion of human nature. When, however, the story is told in direct, first-person narration without a frame, the narrator's confused state leaves this very premise open to question. Is man naturally good or is he perverse by nature? The narrator of "The Imp of the Perverse" avers that man is perverse by a deep principle in his nature, just as Dostoyevsky's Underground Man does. As in Dostoyevsky's work, the narrator first sets forth his ideas and then, in the sharply disconnected second half, provides a narrative account. Dostoyevsky's narrative illustrates the perversity expounded in the first half. Poe, however, creates a different, surprise effect. Unlike Dostoyevsky, he has not included in his opening sections clues to the peculiarities of his narrator's personality. The first part reads like an essay and the narrator is invisible. In the second part, when he bursts upon us, he turns out to be criminally insane. The reader is thus forced to go back and re-assess the first part, now that he knows the mind that has produced it. But he is still given no clue as to how he is to take it.

The narrator of "The Black Cat," equally confusingly, describes himself as having started out life as particularly good, gentle, kind, and sensitive—a typical Sentimental hero, in fact. For unspecified reasons he has taken to drink and become the epitome of criminal perversity. Is he, then, a naturally good man gone bad for reasons that are unspecified but could be defined? Or, unhinged as he is, is his characterization of himself as a virtuous and sensitive man false? Because of Poe's narrative technique, it is impossible to answer these questions and so a major part of Poe's meaning must be that they are unanswerable.

Poe may, indeed, have had personal grounds for pondering this problem. The connection between his own experiences and the exacerbated sensibilities of his characters under the effects of drugs and alcohol is, however, largely irrelevant to a discussion of the Gothic tradition. The ambiguity of his tales and the sense they give of a dream relayed directly are literary illusions and the doubts about human nature the ambiguity suggests, however personal their origins, continue the exploration of the psychology of evil in general.[21] For this very reason they are written according to Gothic conventions. Poe's characters, with their extreme sensibility, their special lineage from an ancient family degenerate through its very inbred refinement, their addiction to opium or alcohol, are typically Gothic. These character traits maintain the fuzziness of their outlines. They are trapped in their own nightmares and the reader with them.

"Ligeia" strikingly has the atmosphere of a dream. It is conceivable that, in a dream, the dreamer might suppose himself married to a woman whose appearance is vivid and precise and yet know only that he does not know her origins. This aspect of the vagueness seems more important than the question of whether he is mad or not. For if Ligeia is a dream figure in the narrator's mind, then the story can be interpreted to the extent that a dream can be interpreted. Liegeia may, in part, "stand for" the intellectual pursuits to which he is wedded before he marries the real-life Rowena, who herself may be a real-life figure within the narrator's dream, rather than a "person." The violent substitution of Ligeia's spirit for Rowena's life would then be the destruction of the communion between human beings by the restless, probing life of the mind, a theme that reappears in "The Oval Portrait."

It would be wrong, however, to take such a simple, allegorical interpretation as complete. Poe is suggestive rather than precise. The tormented, opium-eating narrator tries to fulfill his duty to Rowena, sitting by her bedside, ministering the drink into which the drops of poison fall, keeping a death watch. Yet he has built that tomb-like room in so remote a turret that help cannot be summoned and he hands her the poison. The story must remain vague as an expression both of the tormented conflict in the narrator's mind between the life of the intellect and Life, and of his own inability to understand the nature of the conflict. To this must be added Poe's intuitive understanding that such a conflict, when not admitted to consciousness, will force itself into symbolic expression in the subconscious mind.

The narrator equates his beloved with "Nature," a word which he uses in the sense most common in the eighteenth century, to mean the universe, its spirit and its order. He explains this in that famous passage in which he describes himself as looking into Ligeia's eyes and feeling on the verge of comprehension of some great truth that refuses to yield itself to him—another equation between his state and the reader's. The passage ends with the quotation from Glanville that seems to make Ligeia the force of the will itself, that force by which man opposes God and Nature and himself wrests food for his spirit from the universe. The Faustian conflict has become in Poe a deadly psychological struggle in which the life of the mind must destroy or be destroyed by the life of the body. Poe seems to equate this with the will to live, to oppose death, making this impulse a part of man's spirit. By a peculiar twist, the spirit that will not let the narrator live an ordinary life in this world stretches back through the centuries, very much a part of this earth. It is not surprising then to find that Ligeia is a witch-like, earth-mother figure equated with Nature.

The conflict seen in "Ligeia" finds different and quite extraordinary expression in "The Fall of the House of Usher."[22] The narrator rides into the closed world of the House of Usher, making this a first-person mediated narration like *Paul and Virginia* and *Frankenstein*. The narrator does not understand the world of the Ushers and once again we must assess just how reliable his story is. The story proper has many qualities of a dream. The extreme and unexplained illogicalities of Roderick's actions, and the very fact that the narrator does not comment on them, create the same dream-like ambiguity seen in "Ligeia." Against this, however, stands the fact that we are told the story as fact, as an experience, by the narrator and, unlike the narrator of "Ligeia," this one is not the central character but, rather, a figure like Lockwood in *Wuthering Heights,* who has been into the closed world and then left it again and so is the only witness to what happened there. Poe, then, must have wanted the dream atmosphere but not wanted the reader to take the story as the record of a dream as such. The structure thus seems to make us accept dream material as an important aspect of reality, the images of the subconscious as providing vital information about life.

The dream world the narrator enters is a gradually intensifying nightmare. For him, it is a nightmare situation; for Roderick, the nightmare of his own mind; for the reader, plain nightmare. From the start, the narrator rides to the house through gloomy weather; the house itself has an air of dejection; and when he looks in the tarn, hoping its reflection will be more cheerful, he finds it even worse. Poe thus uses the technique of the frame to assert that the world of the House of Usher is "real," creating the same effect of strangeness that has appeared in other Gothic novels. Because it is a dream and yet no dream, the story becomes an exploration of the human mind in general. Attention is focused, not on the narrator, but on Roderick, and, even though he is the last of a delicate and inbred line, the ambiguity between the dream state and the waking world makes the story applicable to all men and, therefore, frightening.

The rather wooden unimaginativeness of the narrator is important to the story. In not understanding what is happening, he is, like Lockwood, an inhabitant of the same world in which the reader lives. His involvement in Roderick's terror, which is shared by the reader, culminates in a feeling that the unknown, incomprehensible, and frightening is, once again, within all men, not external to them. Clearly, the supernatural happenings in this story are unreal and so must be seen as symbolic—houses, the reader knows, do not crack open and fall apart. There are inconsistencies, however, which are not supernatural. They lie in Roderick's illogical, irrational behavior. The most glaring of these is the burial of his sister in the vault. She has been liable to cataleptic fits and he does not trust her doctors. So he lays her body in the vault, planning to move it to the family graveyard only when he is sure she is dead. The vault in which he puts her, however, is deep underground, at the end of a copper-sheathed tunnel. It has a particularly heavy door that is difficult to open. In addition, after the narrator and Roderick have taken a last look at Madeline's face and noticed the slight flush of the cheeks that makes her look alive, they carefully screw down the lid of the coffin and return to the main part of the house.

Thus, Madeline Usher is most effectively buried and neither Roderick nor his friend remarks on the strangeness of this method of ensuring that she should *not* be buried alive. To this bizarre situation, so typical of the illogic of a dream, a number of points from the story can be juxtaposed to arrive at an interpretation. Roderick has summoned his common-sensical, relatively impassive friend from the everyday world into the world of the House of Usher, which, it is explicitly stated, is the little world of Roderick himself. On the day of his arrival, Madeline Usher appears once, dressed in white, and passes wraith-like and wordless across the end of the room. From that moment she takes to her bed and appears no more. Roderick paints abstract designs. The narrator can make nothing of any of them, with one exception. He describes it—a passage, a vault, a strange light. The description corresponds very closely to his later description of the vault where they bury Madeline, although he does not make the connection. The two of them bury Madeline together, and it is at this point that we learn that she and Roderick are identical in appearance and have that special form of wordless communication so often attributed to twins. On the night of the terrible storm, Roderick at last shrieks out his terrible confession. He has been hearing his sister's struggles to free herself for days and he has not dared to go to her aid. At this point no mention is made of his original reason for laying her in the vault. Finally, when the doors fly open Madeline, dressed in a blood-stained white robe, falls on top of Roderick in an embrace of death that nevertheless has the form of a sexual embrace, just as the stained robe suggests the deflowering of a virgin. It should also be noted that these two are the last of a family said to be severely inbred because it has descended in a straight line and has no collateral branches. This again seems illogical or at least open to only one interpretation. Inbreeding usually occurs through the persistent intermarriage of cousins. The continuance of a direct line would depend on a constant renewal from outside, which would lessen the inbreeding, except in one case—incest.

If these points are taken together, a nightmare indeed appears. If this story is a dream, it is a dream within a dream, Roderick's nightmare within the nightmare of the whole. Given the quasi-sexual embrace that concludes this story of the last representatives of a possibly incestuous family, we may see Roderick's summons to his friend as an effort to muster the forces of normality and rationality, to bring to bear the values of the outside world in a final attempt to repress the incestuous impulse. The fact that those forces fail only makes the supposition stronger. The story is so ambiguous that it is not possible to decide whether Roderick is resisting his sister's incestuous desires or his own. The fact that she refuses to be buried and falls on him suggests, at least, that the woman here is again stronger than the man, that she is drawing him toward incest, rather than that he is trying to seduce her to it, even while the bloodstained dress suggests a violated maiden. The impulse probably lies in both of them, since he has to struggle so to resist. Art in its three principal forms, painting, music, and literature, is Roderick's last defense. Wild and formless, his art gives expression to formless inner urgings and, when it takes on form, in the painting of the vault, it tells him and the narrator that temptation must be totally repressed, buried. Hence the narrator's understanding of this painting only. They put Madeline's body in the very depths of the house that, it should be remembered, *is* Roderick. The copper lining of the vault, moreover, has been especially designed to protect the house from an accidental explosion among the explosives stored there. Thus, Roderick has buried his incestuous impulses deep within himself, thinking he will be safe from any attempt by the wickedness in him to break out, to explode. Repression does not work, however. In terror and agony, Roderick waits for the reappearance of that which he has buried, knowing that it will indeed come to the surface again. And at least symbolically the incest does occur in the final fall of brother and sister. The House of Usher splits in half with the joining of its two last representatives. It falls into its own reflection in the mirror-like tarn in a final symbolization of the theme of incest. Roderick and his own reflection, Madeline, have also fallen into each other and into destruction. The narrator rides away by the light of the bloodstained moon.

By this interpretation, when Roderick fails at self-understanding and resorts, horrified, to total repression, the result is disaster. Two things need to be kept in mind, however, to avoid making such an interpretation into a too bald, oversimplifying statement. First, these aspects of the story are only suggested through apparent inconsistencies and ambiguities. They are not *the* real meaning but a suggested, underlying meaning. Second, the vagueness, together with the devices used, make the mental state that is hinted at general and not particular either to Roderick or to the narrator. Poe has invoked the brother and sister relationship of Sentimental fiction and the too great sensibility of its heroes and heroines; the Gothic building that crumbles for psychic reasons, a building that *is* its owner in the first place, flawed like him by the ominous crack; a mirror device in the tarn; paintings; a subterranean vault; and weather that corresponds to mental states.

It matters little whether, in thus conjuring up the full splendor of the Gothic literature, Poe was consciously aware of the psychological possibilities of his story. By pushing to its limits the dream symbolism dredged up from his own subconscious (and this would not in itself mean that he was or was not more incestuous than the rest of mankind), he has created a story that, suspended in the most delicate web of ambiguities, entraps all readers. It is not surprising that he should have been an inspiration to the symbolists who, as Gordon Bigelow says, "arouse in the reader a haunting sense that he is in the presence of deep meaning which he *feels* but cannot quite articulate."[23] This state he likens to that of the narrator when he looks into Ligeia's eyes and feels himself on the brink of understanding. Poe's ambiguous, haunting imprecision leaves his readers with a sense of terrible possibilities within themselves. It is not incest as such that matters, but Poe's revelation of the dark recesses of the mind and of the hegemony its demons may hold over it. Whether those demons are themselves evil or are made evil by the fact of represssion does not seem to be a part of the story, as it is in later Gothic tales. The sheer evocation of nightmare itself precludes consideration of moral or abstract questions.

The suggestive complexity of Poe's stories may give them significance beyond the purposes of Gothic fiction. Their importance in the Gothic tradition lies in the dream atmosphere. Poe uses Gothic devices to create it and subordinates all else to it. When we see this, we can also see more clearly that, at least in one of their dimensions, other Gothic tales are also dreams. The fact that other authors do not make theirs only dreams means that their stories have other things to say besides mapping the topography of the dreaming mind. As one moves from Poe to Hawthorne, for instance, one finds stories that also tell of guilt and repression but in relation to life and action. Yet, could not the experiences of Young Goodman Brown or of Reuben in "Roger Malvin's Burial" be their own nightmares and nightmares for the reader as well?

From the beginning the dream-like quality of Gothic tales is evoked through the narrative structure. The fact of a remote world created through the method of narration interposes a mind between the reader and the tale. When the mind belongs to a character within the tale, the effect is intensified. It is the condition of such a story that the reader is told what the narrator thinks or has heard or has seen to be what happened. The concentric narration seen in *Frankenstein* doubles or triples this effect. It was used again by Emily Brontë in *Wuthering Heights* (1847) and by Henry James in *The Turn of the Screw* (1898), each time with a slight difference.

The double narration of *Wuthering Heights* has been pointed out many times. Its use of the two narrators, Lockwood and Nellie Dean, encapsulates the Gothic tale within the ordinary world, as in *Frankenstein*. Lockwood comes from "civilization" in London seeking rest and quiet (which, of course, he does not find). Nellie comes from Gummerton. The world of the moors nonplusses Lockwood entirely and he needs Nellie to explain its strange inhabitants to him. He, in turn, relays what he learns to us. The major difference from *Frankenstein* lies in Nellie's being only a minor character. Frankenstein is the only one who can tell his story, whereas Nellie is an observer who finds the Earnshaws and the Lintons hard to fathom. The fact that the narrators are relaying a story they do not understand gives an abiding sense of the mysteriousness of the impulses that motivate the characters. To the extent that the world is dream-like they also represent the lack of insight (Nellie) and the busyness and preoccupation with social life (Lockwood) that blur man's view of himself even when it is laid out before him in symbols.

Henry James's use of the concentric narrative structure at the end of the century is again slightly different. In *The Turn of the Screw* the outer circles are incomplete. Once Douglas has started to read the manuscript we have only the governess' first-person narration, and Douglas and his listeners never reappear. The governess, like Frankenstein, is both central character and narrator. In this tale we can see most clearly the connection between the mediated narration and the dream and why the dream is so important to Gothic fiction. *The Turn of the Screw* is not presented as a dream, just as even Poe's stories are not explicitly nightmares. The features, however, that make these tales dream-like—the vagueness of the "I" in "Ligeia," the illogicalities the narrator of "The Fall of the House of Usher" fails to notice—set them up as mental worlds. The governess tells us the story of *The Turn of the Screw;* we have only her account and a number of indications that we are reading of her perception of events without experiencing the events themselves. As a result we can hardly avoid seeing everything in the tale as in some sense a product of her mind. At the same time, it is a fiction such as we are accustomed to. It has characters, setting, dialogue, action. It has, in fact, a relationship to the governess' mind analogous to the relationship between a dream and the mental processes of the mind that is doing the dreaming. The concentric narrative structures show clearly how the isolated worlds of Gothic novels are set up analogously to dreams even when they are not, like Poe's, deliberately presented as dreamlike.

This dream quality is most important in setting up the landscape as a mental one. It also works to compel suspension of moral judgment and so gradually increases understanding of the foibles of human nature. This growing objectivity is seen in the intensified ambiguity of the self-reflecting characters as they reappear in Victorian Gothic fiction.

HEROES AND HEROINES

The change from absolute to relative morality was inherent in Gothic fiction from the start. We see its progress not only in the change in the villainous characters but also in the successors to the self-reflecting heroes and heroines. Still sensitive and vulnerable, these characters are now found living in strange worlds of enigmatic and unexplained evil. The sensitive characters who love each other because each is virtue loving virtue in the other become, in Roger and Madeline Usher, a pair whose inbred delicacy and blood relationship is their doom. They are dependent on each other for the very breath of life and, being brother and sister in actual fact, the implication of real incest undercuts the quasi-incestuous Sentimental relationship. In *Wuthering Heights,* on the other hand, hero and heroine are not related by blood, but, as in the Sentimental novels, they have grown up together so that their love as adults has a suggestion of incest about it.[24]

Like Sentimentalism's paragons of virtue, Cathy and Heathcliff are separate individuals who are yet unable to live without each other. No longer, however, are they embodiments of self-reflecting virtue. In Heathcliff and Cathy the lines that separated the Sentimental and Gothic heroes and heroines from the vain, the worldly, and the wicked have become blurred, so that good and evil in human nature are seen as totally intermingled. Heathcliff, like Frankenstein, is human, pathetic, and obsessed into following an evil path. Unlike Frankenstein, however, he is of a dark, mysterious, and unknown origin, more like the demonic companions of the Faustian scientists than like the scientists themselves. He is a mixture of the dynamic, the attractive, and the horrible. And because he remains unexplained and incomprehensible to the other characters there is no indication that his evil is a distortion of his nature.[25] Because he is presented as demonic the cruelties inflicted on him in childhood do not necessarily account for his wickedness. Yet the entire novel is craftily molded to make the reader's sympathies go out to Heathcliff and Cathy, even as he revolts against Heathcliff's cruelty and Cathy's apparent perversity.

Throughout *Wuthering Heights* the traditional symbolism of good and evil, light and dark, is filled with enigmatic, ambiguous meaning. The two children grow up together in the dark and gloomy old house, two wild creatures beleaguered and themselves bedevilling the puritanical Joseph. In contrast, the Linton children grow up in light, airy, sunlit Thrushcross Grange. The contrast between the light and dark houses separated by the wild moor and inhabited respectively by the blond Lintons and the dark Earnshaws is set up, however, only to be broken down again and confused. The characters who seem to represent lightness and dark intermarry with results that at first are disastrous and then later are beneficial. Linton, Heathcliff's son, blond and bearing the name of blondness, is confined to Wuthering Heights. His physical frailty and his inability to withstand his father's sombre violence make him much like Conrad, Manfred's son in *Otranto.* Notably, his mother Isbaella is brought up in the house of light and reduced to a sordid spiritual darkness. She is unable to cope with the dark forces of the other side of the moor. The younger Cathy, on the other hand, child of the Lintons and Thrushcross Grange, but also the daughter of Heathcliff's soul mate, the older Cathy, is able to bring the light of the Grange to dispel the gloom of the Heights. It is she, combining the worlds of light and dark in herself, who relieves the night of ignorance and savagery that Heathcliff has imposed upon Hareton, vengefully making Hareton's childhood worse than a copy of his own. It is she who brings light and cleanliness to the old house, so that at the end of the novel, while it is still imbued with its ancient spirit, it yet admits the sunshine. The Grange by itself is seen to lack the life and spirit of the Heights. The Heights, on the other hand, without light from the Grange, is sunk in nightmarish darkness. Both houses are also actual and seeming prisons. At the end of the novel the people of the Grange no longer inhabit it. It has been taken over at least temporarily by worldly foppishness in the person of Lockwood. But its light has been admitted to the old house, which is inhabited by the younger generation, who have let in the sunlight to bathe its ancient spirit. The younger Cathy and Hareton have, Nelly says, eyes that are "precisely similar, and they are those of Catherine Earnshaw. [Nelly's use of Cathy's maiden name is significant.] The present Catherine has no other likeness to her, except a breadth of forehead, and a certain arch of the nostril. . . . With Hareton . . . it is singular, at all times—

then, it was particularly striking, because his senses were alert."[26]

Cathy and Hareton combine between them the characteristics of all their forebears and of the two houses that symbolically represent what was divided but should be united. At the same time, Hareton, dark and swarthy like Heathcliff and with his "singular" likeness to the older Cathy, seems to incorporate in himself Cathy and Heathcliff, although he is not their child. The combination in him bears out Cathy's assertion of the pair's identity earlier in the novel and is more important ultimately than his marriage to the younger Cathy. Since his name is the same as his ancestor's, which is carved over the door of Wuthering Heights, the title of the novel indicates that the restoration of light to the old house, that is, the light let into Hareton's mind, is the concluding meaning of the novel. He is the reconciliation of the opposed and warring states of mind on either side of the moor. Yet he looks like the pair from the Wuthering Heights side only. Ultimately, then, when light is restored to the old house and to Hareton Earnshaw, the wild spirit of the moors is reestablished in its rightful undegraded state.

This combination of the opposed spirits of dark and light appears to have brought peace. Hareton and the younger Cathy wander fearlessly on the moor at night, causing Lockwood to "grumble" that "together they would brave Satan and all his legions" (p. 266). Yet they, who have brought light to the old house, are planning to move to the Grange, leaving Wuthering Heights to its ghosts. Nelly says at the conclusion of the novel: "I believe the dead are at peace." Lockwood ends his account with his visit to the graves in the yard of the crumbling church on the moor. He says he "wondered how any one could ever imagine unquiet slumbers for the sleepers in that quiet earth" (p. 266).

The reader has learnt, however, to distrust those two

representatives of shortsighted ordinariness. To the extent that Hareton and Cathy carry the spirit of the two restless beings so totally identified with each other, with whom the reader's sympathies and interest remain, the concluding establishment of things-as-they-should-be may be accepted. Yet, with the reconciliation, Hareton and the younger Cathy scarcely hold the reader's interest. A part of him is always willing to pay the price of restlessness for freedom of the spirit, however involved in darkness, even while he hankers for the sunlit kitchen of ordinariness. Consequently, the impression remains that the spirits of Cathy and Heathcliff are still out on the moor, not safely banished underground. "Evil" in *Wuthering Heights* is also the source of deep longings, "good" is also the constraint and limitation against which the spirit chafes. To designate one side of the spirit as good and spurn the other as evil is to destroy a part of the vital self. Little could the eighteenth-century novelists have foreseen that, when the mist lifted over the country they explored, what would be revealed was not the dreadful abyss but the mysterious, wind-swept, open moor on which it is easy to lose one's way.

Even in *Frankenstein,* as has been seen, there is no doubt that the Sentimental love of Frankenstein and Elizabeth represents a positive and realizable good. The inner goodness encrusted with monstrosity, which is Frankenstein's state as manifested in the monster, is to be eschewed as a state of utter misery. The ambiguity in *Frankenstein* lies in the difficulty of making a right choice, the disparity between Frankenstein's motives and the results of his actions, the danger of pride to even the worthily ambitious. The possibilities of happiness and misery, however, are unambiguously contrasted. *Wuthering Heights* shows no such comfortable dichotomy. Its legacy is discomfort, even the possible choice of madness over sanity. What it reveals is not a social picture of nineteenth-century life on the Yorkshire moors, but the restless human spirit that cannot be content with the respectable humdrum of everyday.

Perhaps surprisingly, among the realistic, gently satiric stories of Anton Chekhov, one, "The Black Monk," also explores madness and sanity and the restless human spirit in highly ambiguous terms. Less surprisingly, it uses the techniques of Gothic fiction to do so. The figure of the monk which appears to the hero, Kovrin, is not "real" for Kovrin and symbolic for the reader. Both know it is a hallucination. Chekhov makes Kovrin leave the busy world of the city for the relatively closed world of his foster-father's estate in the countryside. There nature is symbolic: the flowers and fruit trees around the house represent the life of this earth, marriage, love, children, while the river and fields beyond are "gloomy and severe" and "there one always felt one must sit down and write a ballad." Again we find a quais-incestuous love between Tanya and Kovrin, who have grown up together in the house surrounded by its garden, which is Nature ordered and controlled by man. Now that he has returned Kovrin thinks of Tanya that "in the course of the summer he might grow fond of this little, weak, talkative creature, might be carried away and fall in love; in their position it was so possible and so natural!" And Tanya's father, when he broaches the subject of marriage between the two, says: "I will speak plainly: you are the only man to whom I should not be afraid to marry my daughter. [He is afraid any other son-in-law would let the garden "go to the devil," a significant expression when the symbolic value of the garden is considered.] . . . the chief reason is that I love you as a son."[27] Neither Tanya nor her father nor Kovrin himself betrays the smallest sense that Kovrin's brother-son relationship to them could do anything but enhance their happiness or make him anything other than a natural choice as a husband for Tanya. The relationship is exactly the one we find in the Sentimental novels.

Beyond the garden, however, order is threatened. Down by the river Kovrin first sees the monk. He comes in the form of a tornado, a black and whirling cloud. The Gothic elements of correspondent setting and a supernatural figure are used expressly to depict Kovrin's madness, but the story is ambiguous. Kovrin is happy when he is mad, willing to die for learning, for the "Idea," and unhappy when an attempt is made to cure him, for then he feels himself to be a mediocrity. The ambiguity lies in our uncertainty: is he a mediocrity who thinks himself a genius in his fits of madness, or is the price of genius insomnia, unremitting work in the service of the "Idea," and consequent madness? The paradox is deepened by the fact that Kovrin marries Tanya while he is mad and turns against her because she is afraid of his madness and persuades him to undergo a cure. Thus, his exalted state does not cut him off from the world. Rather, her failure to enter that state destroys him. The situation is a little like that of Beatrice and Giovanni in "Rappaccini's Daughter" with the roles of man and woman reversed and, along with them, the place of intellect and sexuality in the dilemma presented. Now it is the woman, the child of orderly nature in the garden, who tries to rescue the man, the intellectual inquirer, from his pursuits, which, because she perceives them as madness, are poisoning her being. All the reader knows, finally, is that in denying the life of earth in the name of the life of the spirit that can save mankind, Kovrin is doomed to die; that, in general, such a state cannot be sustained for long by man. But while he knows this, he still does not know whether it is a true state or a delusion. All the uncomfortable ambiguity of Gothic fiction, now turned to a presentation of the nature of madness and genius presses upon him as before. And, once again, an apparently harmless character, who wishes to save a loved figure from occult forces and the search for forbidden knowledge, is involved in that person's destruction. Here, as in *The Monk* and *Frankenstein,* the gentle and virtuous figure of the heroine is ironically an unwitting cause of the disaster that overwhelms the hero.

Chekhov's story is also similar to Poe's "Ligeia" in its treatment of madness. In "Ligeia," with its possibly mad hero wedded to the spirit of Ligeia, all we are allowed to know is that the dark spirit of Ligeia, whatever it represents, is inimical to life in this world as represented in the blonde Lady Rowena. Thus, in three such different authors as Emily Brontë, Poe, and Chekhov, the paired characters of Sentimentalism are still used to assert a *natural* affinity, but now, through that affinity, moral relativity, physical degeneracy, and madness are portrayed, all of them relating these Sentimental pairs to the Gothic villains and their descendants. Later still, Henry James portrays another such pair, using them as the vehicles of his irony. The two children in *The Turn of the Screw* are an exquisitely beautiful picture of innocence, at least to the governess. Yet they are, also in her view, small imps in league with the Hell-fiends who have returned to haunt Bly. Perhaps they are both. Probably they are neither.

DOUBLES

The melding together of the figures of Sentimental hero and heroine with that of the Gothic villain is a necessary step in the portrayal of the split personality and of madness, through doubles figures. By making Frankenstein both Sentimental hero and Gothic villain Mary Shelley combines the devices of the reflected self and the split personality. Elizabeth, as has been seen, reflects the inner self in Victor that becomes monstrously encrusted by his evil scientific pursuits and is then projected into the figure of his double, the monster. The use of the double here makes the Faustian pursuit of knowledge in itself a sort of madness. Other doubles stories grope after different forms of madness, such as the paranoia in the flight and invidious pursuit in *Caleb Williams.* In that novel, also, though differently, the idea of the double is linked to both Sentimental and Gothic novels. Caleb, in reflecting both the virtuous Falkland in his nobility and sensibility and the fallen Falkland in his growing paranoia, is used to show the split in Falkland's personality. But the division is not a simple one. Falkland and Caleb finally destroy each other so that the split mind may be seen as destroying itself as a result of its conflict.[28]

The double of Hogg's justified Sinner, who is more or less a contemporary of Frankenstein's, splits off the evil side of the Gothic villain. Since the Sinner believes he cannot be damned and so is psychologically incapable of recognizing himself as author of the crimes he commits, the double is a representation both of the split in him, which is the effect of a narrow religious upbringing, and of his own hallucination. This is why the twin narrations contradict each other, informing the reader that the double is and is not a separate person. We are left with two choices—evil as an inner distortion or as caused by an outside, external social situation. In either case, however, there is no doubt about the Sinner's degeneration into madness.

As with other Gothic devices, Hoffmann uses the double with his own special twist in his story "The Doubles," in which the two identical young men are not separated halves of one personality but two quite separate people.[29] Several characters in the story have double identities: Amadeus Schwendy is really Graf von Torny, Graf von Zebes is really Furst Isidore, the old gypsy woman is really the Furstin. The doubles themselves have two names each: Deodatus Schwendy is really the young Furst and George Haberland is really the young Torny—and in addition they are identical to each other. Only the true Furst, Remigius, and Natalie, the beloved of both Deodatus and George, are without an alias. Ultimately, as is so frequently the case in Hoffmann's stories, a choice has to be made between life and art. Deodatus, who is the Furst's heir, gets Natalie and the throne. George, who is the son of Graf Torny, leaves the town, declaring that Natalie, his true love, is the spirit of his art. Thus, Hoffmann uses the device of the double in contrast to the disguises in his story. No one penetrates any of the disguises. Everyone recognizes and is quite sure he knows one or other of the young men, but most of the time a mistake is made. George is recognized as Deodatus and vice versa. Hoffmann uses his doubles and his disguised characters to create a world of shifting mirrors in which, in the end, the painter chooses art over life. Thus, although the doubles are separate characters in the story, in the "reality" the story reflects they represent the conflict in the artistic mind between the service of art and the everyday life of human relations and human love.

Hoffmann's artists are certainly divided, tormented personalities, but the emphasis of his tales is not on madness. Similarly, in stories where a symbolic doubles figure is a good aspect of the character, madness is not portrayed. Poe's William Wilson is a simpler figure than his enigmatic reflecting characters. The part of the self projected into a double is the good half of William Wilson, or his conscience. At first, the familiar ambiguity holds us. We are not allowed to know whether the schoolboy who so troubles Wilson is a separate person or not. As Wilson sinks progressively deeper into wickedness, however, he is periodically haunted by the copy of himself, who appears suddenly and unexpectedly and reproaches him for his evil ways. By this point, then, the double is more clearly a symbolic representation of his conscience. In the culmination of the story, Wilson, no longer able to escape, attacks the double, only to find that the blood-stained figure is his own reflection in a mirror and then that the double's death is his own spiritual death.

In "William Wilson" Poe merely posits the idea that a man, however depraved, cannot obliterate his own conscience without shattering himself. This idea, too, derives from Sentimentalism and the notion of the natural goodness of man. Wilson, however, is depicted as descending to mean baseness, rather than committing violent crime, until he turns on his double at the very end, and only then does he show any sign of madness. James similarly makes the doubles figure the better half in "The Jolly Corner." Here, too, there is no descent into madness. The hero,

Spencer Brydon, pursues a double who turns out to be the man he might have been. The only implication of madness in these stories lies in their presenting as a "real" experience something that cannot be accepted as "real." A man who sees his own conscience walking about or pursues the self he never became must be in a dubious mental state. Even though Brydon and Wilson are portrayed as ordinary sane men, the reader knows that they see as real the doubles that he interprets as symbolic. To this extent they are somewhat mad, after all, or else they are, once again, characters let loose in their own nightmares.

The suggestions of madness associated with the doubles figures in these stories have all involved general concepts of the split personality and so the stories containing them have an overall symbolic ambience. With Dostoyevsky's *The Double* we can see what happens when the split personality is treated as something happening to a specific individual. Fantasy is still used in the figure of the double, but he appears in a story with an otherwise realistic setting. For the reader he is an illusion of the central character and not a figure to be given a symbolic interpretation. The pathetic protagonist, a government clerk named Golyadkin, becomes increasingly irrational as he keeps running into his evil but wish-fulfilling double. Sometimes they encounter each other on the street, two clearly separate men. At others Golyadkin thinks he is looking at the double only to find he is staring at his own reflection in the mirror. At all times, although Golyadkin himself cannot face the fact, the reader is made aware that the double is performing those wicked deeds the timid clerk does not dare to commit.

The clerk is an unassuming, humble man, not consciously in revolt against the society of which he is a lowly member. Consequently, he cannot cope with the resentment and hatred which society's mistreatment creates in him. Constant humiliation has built up in him an unconscious resentment of his superiors and a desire to try to wrest from them the dignity and respect he has been denied. Unable, however, to even imagine one so lowly as himself doing such a thing, he projects the actions he is actually committing onto a separate figure. The moments when he sees the figure as his own reflection are partial glimpses of reality from which he recoils until he is finally carried off to the madhouse, lamenting his cruel fate and society's confusion of himself with his double. Because this story does not have the confusing system of narration of, say, Hogg's *Sinner* the delusion is clearly in Golyadkin's mind and a strong impression is made of his having broken down under outside, social pressures. Here, the general question of the source of madness and evil does not occur. The clerk's anger breaks out in madness and minor violence because he has been oppressed and intimidated. The madness itself becomes the object of objective scrutiny detached from any moral question except the one of society's duty to its citizens. The clerk's name derives from the Russian word for "naked." He has been stripped naked of his defenses by a heartless society and, in his madness, he stands naked before us in his pathos.

With Stevenson's *Dr. Jekyll and Mr. Hyde,* on the other hand, we return to the purely symbolic tale.[30] Dr. Jekyll is horrified at the actions of his evil double and the double is more clearly than ever an objectification of the evil within, since he is not a separate person but a metamorphosis of Dr. Jekyll. He symbolizes Jekyll's own repressed evil, which, once let loose, he cannot control. The doubles figures are a means by which either the character or the reader or both are able to see an aspect of the character's personality. They are reflecting devices, as are the paired figures of the heroes and heroines and as the physical objects of Gothic fiction also are.

HOUSES, PORTRAITS, STATUES, MIRRORS

Just as each Gothic tale is itself a dream and also a mirror showing the reader his mind, everything within these symbolic stories tends to be a reflecting surface. The exterior landscape, the storms and sunshine are reflective of the figures in and beneath them, rounding out the otherwise scanty characterization and keeping personality traits general. The house that is its owner serves the same function. Actual mirrors or works of art that throw back an image of at least the outer person serve a variety of functions as smaller mirrors within the larger mirror of the overall work. To catalogue such reflecting devices would fill a volume, but even a few examples show that they, too, mirror the changes within sameness that mark the entire Gothic tradition. From fairly simple reflectors they become mirrors in which tormented characters catch glimpses of that inner self they struggle with but do not understand.

In *Otranto* the statue of Alfonso, which is an exact resemblance of Theodore his worthy successor, and the portrait of the grandfather of whom Manfred is the degenerate successor are indications to the reader only, of spiritual states. Similarly, in Clara Reeve's *The Old English Baron,* when the portraits of Edward's parents, which have been "turned with their faces to the wall" in the closed and secret rooms, are righted, they reveal that the face of the hero's father, shining out in that of his son, is the face of nobility itself. In *The Monk,* the portrait begins to have a function beyond simple reflection. The likeness of Matilda, which is set up as a blasphemous image of the Madonna, serves to start Ambrosio on his road to Hell. In *Melmoth,* the Wanderer's portrait, with its preternaturally brilliant gaze, bears the same name, John, as his descendant and is a hint to the younger man of the diabolic character to be revealed. Perhaps it also serves to identify the younger man with the Wanderer and so suggest an internalization of the good and evil portrayed. These, however, are still transitory, minor indicators.

Hoffmann uses the mirror, as he does other Gothic devices, with great subtlety. His "A New Year's Eve Adventure" is presented as a "fancy-flight" from the journals of

"The Travelling Enthusiast." In it, the "editor" says, the enthusiast "has apparently not separated the events of his inner life from those of the outside world."[31] The result is a dream sequence of which the section entitled "In the Beer Cellar" uses the mirror device. The little man who "seemed to be driven by springs," is terrified of mirrors, or of any reflecting surface. He also has "two different faces, the pleasant young man's and the unlovely demonic old man's" (p. 111). He has no reflection, just as Peter Schlemihl, who also appears in this story, has no shadow.

The Enthusiast, like the central figures in other Hoffmann stories, tries unsuccessfully to blend art and life through his love for Julia. He tells her: "Your love is the spark that glows in me, kindling a higher life in art and poetry. Without you, without your love, everything is dead and lifeless" (p. 108). This is a vain hope, as usual, and it is when he flees from the party at which he sees Julia that he takes refuge in the beer cellar. There, as in "The Doubles," characters have a shifting identity. "General Suvarov" (the nickname given the little man because he has no reflection) is highly plastic. He first appears as "a short, dried-up-looking fellow . . . engulfed in a cloak . . . which bubbled and flapped around him as he bounced across the room toward us, so that in the dim light it looked as if a series of forms were dissolving and emerging from one another." This little man's constantly interchanging selves become apparent when the Enthusiast offers him a tobacco box with a shiny surface. He notes that "he had become a different person. He had burst into the beer cellar with a pleasant, youthful face, but now a deathly pale, shrivelled, terrified old man's face glared at me with hollow eyes." This double face is partially explained: "In the masquerade of life our true inner essence often shines out beyond our mask when we meet a similar person, and it so happened that we three strange beings . . . looked at one another and knew what we were" (pp. 110–11).

These three—the Enthusiast, "General Suvarov," and

Peter Schlemihl—converse. Schlemihl mentions a portrait painted "with intense love and longing," which is "more than just a likeness, a true image." To this The Enthusiast replies: "So completely true . . . that you could almost say it was stolen from a mirror" (pp. 110–11). In the next section of the story, "Manifestations," The Enthusiast sees "a dark form" floating "from the remote background of the reflection" in a large mirror that he has just uncovered. The form turns out to be the image of Julia, which shortly disappears again. When little "General Suvarov" stands before this mirror, he is not reflected in it. As he explains, he has "given his reflection to Julia." The Enthusiast then tells of a waking dream within the dream sequence of the story. In this, Julia tells him she has "you and your reflection, once and for all." When he awakes, he finds the manuscript that now forms a story within a story and tells of the lost reflection. Forced to part with Julia, the little man, who in this interpolated story is "Erasmus Spikher," acquiesces in her request that he leave her his reflection. Julia "released him and stretched out her arms longingly to the mirror. Erasmus saw his image step forward independent of his movements, glide into Guiletta's [Julia's] arms, and disappear with her in a strange vapor." When Erasmus' wife discovers that he has no reflection, he tries to convince her that mirrors lead only to vanity and "pseudo-philosophical nonsense about the reflection dividing the ego into truth and dream." She, however, rejects him as a demon from Hell and eventually sends him out into the world to try to regain his reflection. The Enthusiast concludes the story with a complaint to Hoffmann that "a strnge dark power manifests itself in my life . . . steals the best dreams away from sleep, pushing strange forms into my life." Thus he "almost half" believes that "the good Julia was a picture of a siren by Rembrandt or Callot—who betrayed the unfortunate Spikher to get his alter ego, his reflection in the mirror" (pp. 122–29).

Hoffmann thus melds together the mirror, the portrait,

and doubles devices to turn life itself into a dream. E. F. Bleiler sums up the psychological significance of his use of them: "It was not simply a mysterious, supernatural double; instead it was associated with the strange phenomena of the mind, with personality fragments, with multiple personalities (a phenomenon which interested early 19th-century psychologists) and with emergence of an unconscious mind. In story technique this meant that a personality complex could assume spontaneous, autonomous life and become a character itself. From a converse point of view, two persons who were physically nearly identical might fuse, to form a single personality, or to create an impermanent, rotating personality which shifts from pole to pole of identity."[32]

In general, the reflections thrown back at the viewer from mirrors and portraits reveal the inner self, as eyes in this literature reveal the soul. The fact that these devices appear in stories dealing with the relation of art to life may be ascribed perhaps to the Romantic view of art. The Romantic writer in pursuit of transcendence becomes a vessel mediating Nature's truth through his own mind; his vision is expressed through the mediating consciousness. What the artist sees, and how, becomes a subject expressed in shifting images of mental instability. When the eyes are turned upon the inner landscape of the mind itself, rather than discerning transcendent truths beyond it, what they see are the fearful outlines of the subconscious—flitting shadows and cornered trolls—which can only be exposed to full daylight at great risk. If art is self-expression, then the self reflected in art becomes a threat to daily existence.

In Poe, as in Hoffmann, art is ambiguously and mysteriously inimical to life. In "The Oval Portrait," the device of the portrait is central. As in so many Gothic tales, the narrator relates the story of the portrait at third hand. He has read it in "a small volume," a sort of catalogue of the pictures, found by chance and written by an unknown hand, but certainly not by either of the two characters in the story proper, the painter and his young wife who sat for the portrait. The room itself is in a remote turret of a deserted chateau, "one of those piles of commingled gloom and grandeur which have so long frowned among the Appennine, not less in fact than in the fancy of Mrs. Radcliffe." The narrator tells us that there is "an absolute *life-likeness* of expression [in the portrait], which at first startling, finally confounded, subdued, and appalled me." He then encloses himself within the black velvet curtains of the bed and reads the legend of the portrait. It is a tiny anecdotal tale of a painter, "having already a bride in his Art," who drains the life from his young wife in creating the perfect likeness on the canvas. As the last touches are put in, the young wife dies. The painting is made in "the dark high turret-chamber where . . . the light which fell so ghastlily . . . withered the health and the spirits of his bride."[33] The portrait device here may be seen as achieving somewhat the same effect as the Black Monk in Chekhov's story and as the doubles, George/Deodatus, in Hoffmann's. In each case a Gothic device brings out the paradoxical conflict between art and life, between man's soaring spirit and his connection with the earth.

Hawthorne's novels may be said to be "less Gothic" than his tales. He makes use of Gothic devices, however, like Dostoyevsky, adapting them to his immediate purposes. Among these are the reflecting works of art. The portrait of old Pyncheon in *The House of the Seven Gables* makes this ancestor a dark spirit weighing on his descendants. Like Dostoyevsky's *The Double,* Hawthorne's novel is in the main a story of individuals, as distinct from a Gothic fantasy. This use of Gothic devices indicates again that the ideas explored in Gothic fiction were accepted as a part of life. That this was a consequence of a greater consciousness of the mental landscape they symbolized seems clear from some of Hawthorne's own discussions of his literary practices. His famous distinction between romance and novel in his preface to *The House of the Seven Gables* throws light on the manner in which these symbolic portraits and mirror images should be interpreted, and it indicates his preoccupation with a subject matter for which the limitations of strict realism are unsuited. He says of the romance that, "while, as a work of art, it must rigidly subject itself to laws, and while it sins unpardonably so far as it may swerve aside from the truth of the human heart—[it] has fairly a right to present that truth under circumstances, to a great extent, of the writer's own choosing or creation. If he think fit, also, he may so manage his atmospherical medium as to bring out or mellow the lights and deepen and enrich the shadows of the picture." This preface, itself using a painting image, introduces the tale in which the portrait is the symbolization of the dominant theme. This, Hawthorne states in the preface, is "the truth, namely, that the wrong-doing of one generation lives into the successive ones, and, divesting itself of every temporary advantage, becomes a pure and uncontrollable mischief."[34]

The description of the portrait corresponds to this statement of the "moral" of the novel, which is so close to Walpole's moral for *Otranto:* "While the physical outline and substance were darkening away from the beholder's eye, the bold, hard, and, at the same time, indirect character of the man seemed to be brought out in a kind of spiritual relief. . . . [Such a painting is] reflecting the unlovely truth of a human soul. In such cases, the painter's deep conception of his subject's inward traits has wrought itself into the essence of the picture, and is seen after the superficial coloring has been rubbed off by time."[35] The portrait haunts the house of the seven gables to suggest the spiritual doom of its pathetic denizens, a family blighted in spirit.

Hawthorne also discusses his use of setting in the Gothic manner. While European Sentimentalists frequently use America as an exotic Romance setting, he uses Europe for the same purpose. In Europe, he writes, the "romancer" is "allowed a license with regard to every-day probability, in view of the improved effects which he is bound to produce thereby. Among ourselves, on the contrary, there is as yet no such Faery Land, so like the real world, that, in a suitable remoteness, one cannot well tell the difference, but with an atmosphere of strange enchantment, beheld through which the inhabitants have a propriety of their own."[36] Hawthorne claims to have chosen Italy as the setting for *The Marble Faun* to avoid the difficulties of the daylight world of America: "Italy, as the site of [the author's] Romance, was chiefly valuable to him as affording a sort of poetic or fairy precinct, where actualities would not be so terribly insisted upon as they are, and must needs be, in America. . . . Romance and poetry, ivy, lichens, and wall-flowers need ruin to make them grow."[37]

His use of paintings as reflections of the soul and of the mysterious likeness of the statue in *The Marble Faun* are further indications of the way Gothic imagery is employed in novels of social life. This is equally true of Wilde's *The Picture of Dorian Gray.* Wilde combines the device of the mirror with that of the portrait. The perfect likeness of youthful purity in the portrait gradually grows hideous as Dorian's spiritual state degenerates. When, himself still beautiful, he finally rends the likeness with a knife, it is he himself, in that deformed likeness, who is found dead with the knife through his heart, while the portrait again shines forth in all its goodness and beauty. Here, as in "William Wilson" and Dostoyevsky's *The Double,* the reader is forced into considerable gymnastics. Appearance and reality do not merely shift to give a sense of uncertainty about perception and the possibility or impossibility of knowing what is objectively external to ourselves. Rather, they are made to change places abruptly and bewilderingly. William Wilson stabs his double, then turns away, only to find himself faced with his own reflection, which, he then realizes, is not his reflection but the double after all, only to learn that the double is himself, or a part of himself that he has killed. Dorian Gray, still beautiful, faces the degenerate portrait and plunges his knife into it. This is the asserted reality. Yet, immediately, just the opposite, the normally possible, turns out to be the real. Dorian has stabbed the degenerate self he has come to loathe and the portrait is as it was in the beginning. With such rapid switching back and forth between contradictory images successively presented as "reality," the reader is enticed into looking behind the canvas on which these stories are painted. As long as William Wilson and his double are separate figures, we go along with the concept that a man and his conscience are separate. When, however, we are tumbled abruptly in and out of this "reality," in the final scene, we see the author's more complex view. Wilson sees his conscience as separate, and it is separate to the extent that he can kill it and still remain standing. It is also not separate, however, but a part of the self that is seen in reflection, in a mirror, and cannot be killed without maiming the self.

The other stories open themselves up to the same manner of interpretation. Wilde uses the convention of the portrait to present the moral problem of corruption in Dorian Gray. Without this device—and the portrait is, after all, the title character—his novel would be a lightly satirical story of the *fin-de-siècle.*[38] With it, it is a symbolic fantasy. On one level, it is once again a tale of human evil, or corruption from within and its effect in driving mad an initially good soul. On another, it may be, as has been suggested, a covertly homosexual love story.[39] As with the social satire, however, this dimension is deepened and complicated by the general moral application, which is not altered by it; the moral question would be the same for heterosexual love.

Wilde plays specifically with the convention that equates physical appearance and spiritual state. Because, in the opening pages, Dorian's beauty and innocence are one and the same, his depravity results in increasing ugliness. Wilde gives the convention an extra twist by combining it with the device of the mirror double, Dorian's portrait. The setting of the tale is the small, exclusive, but real world of upper-class London society. In part, this world simply provides the corrupting Lord Henry to seduce Dorian out of his innocence and the sane, decent man's commentary of the painter Basil as a balance. But Basil has another function. It was he, after all, who inspired by Dorian's unearthly beauty, painted that magic portrait. In a sense, he is like Poe's painter who kills his sitter by draining life from the human subject into the painting itself. We may wonder whether, in painting him so, Basil has not stolen Dorian's soul and thus become the initial cause of his life of vice, as well as the means for its safe continuance. Dorian cannot resist the power that his apparent beauty gives him. The world literally takes him at face value, leaving him "free" to plunge into vice. For the society of "beautiful people," appearances are the criterion of acceptability, not real worth. Dorian has been able to sin with impunity just because the world, seeing the beautiful face, thought him virtuous. The story accuses society of moral blindness, which makes it not only corrupt but corrupting. And the decent, quietly observant Basil is the instrument of that corrupting power. His painting provides Narcissus with his reflection. We are not allowed to set up a simple dichotomy between upper-class degeneracy (Lord Henry) and middle-class decency (Basil). Basil's inadvertent involvement in the ruin of Dorian echoes the "innocent" responsibility of Antonia in Ambrosio's downfall and Elizabeth in Frankenstein's.

In the scene of Dorian's death, Wilde reveals great psychological insight. Dorian's soul is in the portrait and narcissism has caused his downfall. When he tries to rend the portrait he is really stabbing himself, as we see, for the knife ends up, supernaturally, in his own heart. The body disfigured by vice that lies on the floor is Dorian's. Released from it, the portrait, which is his soul, shines forth again in the beauty of its original perfection. In this complicated symbolic maneuver, Wilde has gone beyond depicting merely the self-hatred of the depraved—he has shown how self-loathing projected outward away from the self results in violence, often murder. Dorian, in fact, kills himself. By having him strike out at the portrait, however, Wilde reveals the possible connection between self-hatred, suicide, and murder. The Other here is the portrait, the self, but Dorian is in the psychological state of a man striking out at another who displays the same marks of vice and so makes him visible to himself.

Dorian Gray, published in 1891, shows a heightened degree of analytical consciousness in dealing with psychological phenomena. Other works at the end of the nineteenth century show this new awareness.

THE ARRIVAL AT CONSCIOUSNESS

The integration of Gothic effects into social novels is an indication of the integration of "Gothic ideas" with general ideas about life and society. The increasingly scientific study of psychology and the wide general and particular acceptance of determinism led to characterizations of individuals, as in Dostoyevsky, or families, as in Hawthorne, or society, as in Wilde, which used Gothic devices to show the determining effects of environment, without falling into the over-simplifying trap of making the environment the sole and simple cause of the features presented. By the end of the century Gothic novels show a conscious awareness in their authors of the implications of the tradition. Two novels of that period, in particular—*Dr. Jekyll and Mr. Hyde* and *The Turn of the Screw*—are remarkable in different ways for their display of this awareness.

Stevenson's *Dr. Jekyll and Mr. Hyde* contains an explicit explanation of its own symbolism. It uses such Gothic features as the strange house, multiple narration, and, above all, the doubles figure, one who, like Frankenstein's monster, is the product of the Faustian spirit of the scientist. By 1886, however, the conventions of the detective story had been developed and Stevenson uses some of its techniques. We have seen how Poe in "The Murders in the Rue Morgue" sets pure mind against pure animality, creating suspense by making the reader wonder and wait till Dupin solves the crime for him. An important feature distinguishing his story and its successors from the Gothic tales lies in the nature of the suspense aroused. The Gothic tales, seeking to arouse terror and horror, use various means to shock the reader—ugliness, brutality, the awesomeness of great heights. Suspense lies in the reader's hope that the hero and heroine will escape these horrid threats, or the fear that they will not. The traditional detective story, on the other hand, although it may use these means to chill its readers' blood, must also create the suspense of curiosity through an appeal to the reason. There is a crime to be solved. The central feature of the story is the uncovering of "what really happened." A prime means of creating this kind of suspense is the cumulative technique that we have already seen used by Clara Reeve and Maturin to create a sense of the gradual uncovering of the truth. This technique Wilkie Collins used for the mystery story, rediscovering the method for himself.[40] It appears again in the narrative structure of *Dr. Jekyll and Mr. Hyde.* Stevenson presents his novel as a series of strands of evidence from a succession of witnesses.

Dr. Jekyll and Mr. Hyde contains a crime—a brutal act (Hyde's trampling on the little girl)—and characters—Utterson and Enfield—with a burning curiosity to get to the bottom of it. Thus, the tale is set up as a mystery story. Mr. Hyde is seen; he disappears behind the blank wall of the house. Scraps of information begin to filter through to Utterson and he tries to fit them together into a coherent explanation: Dr. Jekyll's greater or lesser sociability, his strange will, the reappearances of Hyde, the murder. The pieces, however, refuse to fit together. It takes first Dr. Lanyon's account, and then Jekyll's own, before the full story is out. Thus, these written accounts are forms of mediated narration combined with the cumulative technique to make a narrative structure typical of Gothic fiction. The reader is first presented with the action, then with two fuller accounts. At the same time, the strangeness is emphasized by the story's being mediated to him through the minds of the two scientists who, it is supposed, are needed to make it understandable. The very combination of these two techniques shows that the exploration of the psychology of human nature has now become a matter of conscious speculation. With Frankenstein, for instance, the critic must interpret the concentric narrative structure to show that it gives the novel a certain meaning that would be missing without it. In combining this structure with the technique of cumulative evidence, however, Stevenson shows a clear awareness of the nature of his exploration. Indeed, his two doctors make quite explicit, in their accounts, the psychological truths that have been uncovered. At the same time, because it takes two scientists to explain the matter to the reader, Stevenson maintains a nice balance; he is portraying psychological reality, but that reality is so strange that Lanyon dies of the intolerable shock of its unveiling.

It is no longer necessary for the reader to interpret the symbolism; Dr. Jekyll, in effect, explains it himself. He says explicitly that man has a dual nature and that part of it (what might now be called the id) must be controlled or the individual will be split and eventually destroyed. If the libidinous, passionate part of man's nature is indulged, it will grow stronger and become increasingly difficult to hold down. At the same time, however, the attempt to suppress totally this libidinous nature leads it to break out into monstrous crimes and eventually to overwhelm the good and civilized side.

Stevenson uses explicit statement of this sort to back up and clarify the symbolization of his ideas. While speaking of man's dual nature, Dr. Jekyll explains how he discovered the potion by which he could transform himself into Mr. Hyde and Hyde back into himself again. The potion itself, it should be noted, is neutral. Had he taken it when his good nature was uppermost he would have been an angel, for it would have freed the good part of him from the animal part. Jekyll's version seems to throw a retrospective light all the way back to *The Monk* and *Frankenstein.* Again, we have high aspirations, great sensitivity, intellectual brilliance, and the imaginative daring that leads to pride, transgression, and disaster. Once more, the very efforts to repress evil exacerbate its effects and we are left to consider whether the evil is absolute or whether the trouble is caused by the perception of certain impulses as evil. All these themes, which had been appearing in Gothic fiction for a hundred years, recur in *Jekyll and Hyde* and are made manifest through Gothic devices. Now, however, they are also explained within the work.

Stevenson, like Hawthorne and Mary Shelley before him, sets up two scientists in his story. One, Lanyon, eschews the mystical and keeps within the limits of the strictly materialist, as Jekyll calls it, scientific approach. The other, Jekyll, is willing to dare, to explore beyond human limits, destroying himself, but despising the caution of Lanyon. Here again, we have the ambiguity of the Faust figure and, here again, there are interesting differences within the sameness. Hyde's deeds are horrifying. The story states specifically that Jekyll is led into his daring researches by his desire to live a double life, the indulgence of the senses being inconsonant with the dignity of a respectable doctor in the eyes of Victorian society. The result of these researches is the total destruction of the self. But the pathos of Jekyll's sufferings as he is overwhelmed by Hyde is also shown, as is the frightening attraction of his scientific daring. Utterson and Lanyon are good men, properly balanced and controlled, but can the reader, closing the book, feel a yearning for their lives rather than Jekyll's? If he cannot, it is again because the tale will not let him. The double narrative, first Lanyon's, then Jekyll's, has a purpose beyond that of providing a sense of increasing revelation. Utterson reads Dr. Lanyon's account after Lanyon has died of sheer horror and despair over what has been revealed to him. Lanyon does not wish to live in a world in which men's natures are revealed as containing, each and every one of them, a Hyde. Consequently, while the reader's sense of the horrible is intensified, his view of Lanyon and Utterson as cautious types less admirable than the romantic Jekyll is also increased.

Jekyll lays great stress on the fact that he remains throughout a double personality. He is always the man people know, the bundle of good qualities others may or may not recognize, plus Hyde. Hyde, on the other hand, is just Hyde, without the rest of Jekyll. When he is on the loose, the rest of Jekyll does not exist and Hyde revels in his passions without scruple or remorse. Jekyll not only suffers from the pangs of conscience and the admonitions of principle, he also has Hyde and all that Hyde stands for within him at all times, though in varying degrees of quiescence. This is what Lanyon cannot face. That is, a respected and successful doctor, pursuing a useful and constructive life, when faced with the "reality" of human nature, breaks down and dies. The fact that the reader learns all this at third hand and twice over creates a sense of strangeness through the same techniques that are used in *Frankenstein* and in Hogg's *Sinner.* Again, the scientist has to tell his story to a fellow scientist who must relay it further, because the knowledge is beyond the ordinary mind to grasp. Again the story is told and then told again by a second narrator.

Stevenson could hardly have stated more compellingly the need to face "the facts" nor, incidentally, have shown more clearly why literature was still needed to reveal them. To this may be attributed his setting. No longer remote in time or place, his story occurs in the heart of contemporary London. He uses the London fog to good effect, as Dickens had used it and as Iris Murdoch still uses it today. The streets have the values we have come to expect, the quiet prosperous setting for the blank-walled house, the dingy misery of Soho. Stevenson adapts the convention of houses, too, to convey his ideas of psychological evil. The mysterious blank into which Hyde disappears houses Jekyll's laboratory and is in fact the back part of his house, separated from it by a court. Thus, the house on the square that people know is the public Jekyll, the laboratory is the concealed aspect of his personality. The building now delineates the split man. The street in Soho also has all the slovenly sordidness of Hyde. It is brutal, dirty, insensitive, Hyde's rooms, however, rented and furnished by Jekyll, are, ironically, a little oasis of civilization.

The identity of Jekyll's house with the state of Jekyll/Hyde's soul is emphasized the first time Jekyll wakes up to find Hyde's hairy hand on the sheet. When he realizes that he has involuntarily changed into his evil alter ego during his sleep, he rushes to conceal himself in the laboratory, that is, the part of the house that represents his hidden mental life. It is interesting to see how specifically Stevenson notes that the repressed personality comes increasingly to the surface during moments of relaxation and especially during sleep. Yet this view of the operation of the subconscious mind is combined with ideas that still hark back to Sentimentalism. In making Hyde a Gothic monster of pure evil who fills all who come in contact with him with instinctive revulsion, Stevenson seems to reassert the concept of the Moral Sense through which men instantaneously recognize evil. In making them perceive Hyde as deformed in some unspecified way, he seems to present the idea of evil as a distortion while slyly denying the usual equation with the physical. Hyde *seems* deformed but no one can say how. Stevenson continues, too, the idea that the soul is reflected in the eyes so that, for instance, during the two months after the murder, during which Jekyll is able to repress Hyde completely, "his face seemed to open and brighten."[41] Virtue is still happiness; while evil is misery. This concept, however, is considerably weakened by the complete amalgamation of the central character and his evil double. Because Jekyll is not separate from Hyde, when virtue shines out on his face, it is the virtue of an ordinary man. He is not a personification of virtue itself. In fact, with Hyde within him, he is like Frankenstein's Monster inside out. And once he has become aware of Hyde, he is never entirely happy again.

Stevenson certainly presents Hyde as horrifying evil itself and his novel seems to suggest that men should suppress their libidinous nature. But perhaps, after all, he is more subtle than this. It is respectable society, represented in dull figures like Lanyon and Enfield, which has made the imaginative, daring Jekyll believe that his desire for pleasure is reprehensible and must be indulged only in secret. Society makes unreasonable demands that result in his presenting it with a stuffy and respectable front. As a consequence, when he does let loose, he goes on a rampage. Or so we may suppose. We cannot be sure, since we have Enfield's, Lanyon's, and Jekyll's views, but not Hyde's nor any ironic indication from the author as to how to balance them. The novel reads, however, like a battle between the superego and the id in which the ego is destroyed. The double was from the beginning an ambiguous device, but Stevenson's use of it shows a new light has been thrown on the mind. It is a far cry from Ambrosio to Jekyll/Hyde.

Other works at the end of the century also recast some of the principal themes of Gothic fiction through their use of its devices. Bram Stoker's *Dracula,* which appeared eleven years after *Jekyll and Hyde,* is also set in England. But, once again symbolizing an unspecifiable evil, Stoker goes back to the old Gothic use of the exotic setting in the opening section. His hero journeys into remote Transylvania and to the castle isolated within it, where he meets Dracula. Only when he has established the existence of his vampire in this strange setting can Stoker bring the evil home to England. However, once there, Stoker uses modern disbelief in the supernatural to enable the vampire to move around in the ordinary world. The scientist's efforts to defeat this monster are greatly hampered because he cannot make the struggle public for fear that it will meet with disbelief. Thus the reality of the vampire is presented as almost beyond belief. This does more than increase the suspense. The suggestion that this creature of ancient superstition is not credible to modern minds implies that what it symbolizes may also correspond to a somewhat outdated belief. The vampires, we have seen, suggest not marauding sexual assault so much as awakening sexuality. They may be seen as evil if the dormant sexuality of the young virgin is seen as an inviolable purity and the forces that resist the inevitable change are accepted as virtue and respectability. But this "if" questions the absoluteness of the evil. In making science bring the force of religion, specifically Catholicism, to its aid to defeat the occult power of evil, one might suppose that Stoker wished to right the balance after Gothic fiction had presented such a succession of evil monks, ghostly nuns, and mad scientists, but at the same time, the use of religion also suggests that the church, like the old-fashioned sentimental scientist, is one of those forces of society that sees a young woman's awakening sexuality as evil.

In *The Turn of the Screw,* which appeared in 1898, one hundred and one years after *The Monk,* these ironic questionings all seem to come together. The subtlety of James's novel lies in its much discussed ambiguity. That ambiguity, however, no longer carries the feeling of psychological phenomena intuitively grasped but beyond comprehension. James's nightmare presents a gigantic paradox as a psychological reality. After a hundred years of literary exploration, the dilemma of those who would protect innocence by keeping the innocent in ignorance and who thereby expose them to evil is finally resolved in James's short novel. The very idea of childhood innocence is rejected, but not by a return to the concept of Fallen Man and inevitable human depravity. Instead, the concept of human nature is divorced from moral value judgments. James's novel looks at the question objectively. He combines ambiguous irony with the use of convention to question each value assumed in that convention. And because he leaves his paradoxes unresolved, the questions he raises remain without answers, forcing an objective view.[42] In his use of the devices that had occurred again and again in earlier Gothic works, James brings the knowledge for which his predecessors had groped into consciousness. Where earlier works left ambiguous that which was felt more than understood, the ambiguity for which *The Turn of the Screw* is famous is the instrument for restating the innocence/ignorance paradox.

In his narrative structure James extends to the full the means of creating a closed world. He has a triple mediation—through the governess, to Douglas, to his companions around the fireplace, and hence to the reader (the listeners' eager curiosity equals the reader's own)—of the strange events of a world completely closed off from the everyday. This triples the reader's sense that he depends entirely on the reliability of the governess' account, since only her words tell anything at all about Bly and what happened there. She turns out to be highly unreliable, leaving a sense that nothing can be certainly known.

The world of Bly is not only made into a closed one through the literary device of narration. It is deliberately cut off from the outside by the uncle, who stipulates that he wishes to hear nothing about it. Hence, into this world, there intrude from outside only the forces of the supernatural—the ghosts—and, of course, the governess herself. The uncertainty about the reality of the apparitions serves to lay bare the different degrees of ignorance and innocence in the inhabitants of this world. Those inhabitants have many ancestors in earlier works. The two children, as they are first seen, are blond, blue-eyed, innocent and angelic. They are brother and sister, orphans, with a close secret understanding and communication, a heightened sensitivity, and a solidarity against the rest. In them, James presents the equation of beauty and goodness as one of the clues to the governess' unreliability. It is she who insists that the children must *be* innocent because they *look* like angels. James relies on the reader to look on the conclusion with suspicion. Then there are the ghosts who, at first, seem to represent a malignant evil intruding into the children's world. Their existence and their wickedness are real for the governess, but problematical for the others, suggesting symbolically to the reader that the question of evil may be one of perception.

The children have been looked after by the housekeeper of symbolic name, Mrs. Grose, who, having no children of her own, loves them as her own. She thus stands in the same relation to them as the nurse in *Julia de Rubigné* who is "mother" to the hero and heroine. Like Nelly Dean in *Wuthering Heights,* she is both nurse and housekeeper and interpreter of the situation to the narrator who comes in from outside. There are significant differences, however. Mrs. Grose is unlettered, a state representing an inability to understand the beings she cares for, and the further inability to explain to the governess, even factually, the events that have taken place before the young woman arrives to take charge. Mrs. Grose is able to tell the governess about Quint and Miss Jessel in life. She is ignorant of the cause of their deaths and, as an informant, she is more unreliable than Nelly. She is, first of all, reluctant to tell even what she does know, and she has no coherent story to offer, only scraps of information elicited under the pains of fear and compassion. She also cannot see the ghosts. It is significant that her assurance to the governess that she "believes" comes only after Flora, in talking of the governess, not of Miss Jessel, says things that shock her into giving credence to the governess' ghosts.

She is horrified by Quint and Miss Jessel on a very mundane level. Their behavior was shocking. They carried on an affair while in charge of innocent children, endangering the morals of the young. They violated, furthermore, the proprieties of the class structure. Miss Jessel, a lady, lowered herself in carrying on with a gentlemen's "man." The reader knows simultaneously that it is not of such problems that James wishes him to take cognizance and that they are, nevertheless, the key to the question the novel does discuss. The governess' reaction to Mrs. Grose's revelations is also unreliable, as Mrs. Grose's account is, in the sense that both reveal character for us, but do not inform us what the real situation is. Our uncertainty about "reality" within the story is, nevertheless, a key to understanding the novel. The fact that both women are so intent on the shockingness of Quint's and Miss Jessel's behavior serves to show that the children, whether or not they are innocent by the standards of the two women in charge of them, are innocent in a sense that is broader than the meaning the women attach to that word.

The narrative structure, too, although designed to give the same sense of a strange closed world, shows some difference from that of *Wuthering Heights.* Here, the governess, the central character, is the narrator. She is not an observer, like Lockwood, but is involved in the action; her account is no more likely to be accurate than, say, Cathy's would be, if she were the narrator of *Wuthering Heights.* Like Lockwood, the governess goes into and then comes out of the strange world. Lacking a coherent account from Mrs. Grose, however, the governess has herself no adequate mediating narration to explain the world she has entered. This is an important difference, since in this story, the narrator on whom the reader must depend is herself bewildered and leaves the closed world, to judge by her account, without having understood it at all, not even to the extent that Lockwood has fathomed the mysteries of Wuthering Heights. Throughout the story, the reader's main task is to assess for himself the nature of reality. This he knows through the very ambiguity with which the ghosts are presented. Are they there or are they figments of the governess' imagination? Mrs. Grose is not skeptical about their existence but reluctant to believe in it, so that even in the scene by the lake, when the governess sees Miss Jessel and she does not, the reader still cannot be sure.

Now, the governess is herself an outside force that has

intruded into the closed world. The reader, when he begins to question her exclamatory horror at the supernatural intruders, begins to suspect her of imagining them. If this is the case then, in a sense, it is she who has brought the ghosts with her into the peaceful world of Bly. Thus, in questioning their reality, the reader begins to question the reality of the evil from which the governess wishes to protect the children. The problem is not whether the children have been in some way influenced by Miss Jessel and Quint, but whether the influence is evil, what "evil influence" means, and whether the governess, like Mrs. Grose, is the product of a society that sees as evil something it cannot accept. The governess is given the necessary background to make the reader suspect that what she calls evil may not be so. She is young and ignorant, the daughter of a country parson, with ideas that cause her to construct a romantic fantasy about her employer. It is entirely possible that she has grown up to believe that, beneath the surface of human beings, a beast that must be kept caged is trapped, as Mr. Hyde is trapped inside Dr. Jekyll. This is certainly not an unusual theme in James's writings. Here, it can be seen reflected in the way in which the house is shown to be a prison, a cage, for Miles.

Much of what the governess relates, if taken together with the way James uses the Sentimentalist convention in Miles and Flora, forces an answer to this question. Like Mrs. Grose, she is shocked over the affair between Quint and Miss Jessel. She shares the housekeeper's view of the social impropriety of their breach of class barriers, and condemns the relationship in itself as shocking, using the bad influence on the children as justification of her condemnation. The young should be shielded, she believes, from all knowledge of such goings on. She sees herself as a screen between the children and the world. She cannot imagine them growing up and going out into life, but envisions a fairy-tale future in which they live at Bly forever, like a prince and princess, fenced in from the society outside. The reader's speculations are centered on the governess' attitude toward the children by the very vagueness of her statements. What do Quint and Miss Jessel tell the children? "Horrors!" What does she mean when she says they have come to get their former charges? They want them to share the miseries of Hell! Never does the governess talk in simple terms about social improprieties or the education of children. All is diabolical evil and unnameable horrors.

The language in which she recounts her relationship with the children, particularly with Miles, is unconsciously libidinous. Although at first she speaks of them as little angels, she constantly talks of their exerting their charms on her and of herself as overcome by those charms. Increasingly, she sees their charming ways as diabolical, their beautiful eyes as false, "their more than earthly beauty, the absolutely unnatural goodness" as "a policy and a fraud." The tenderness and affection that she expresses for and to them from the first seems extravagant for a newly arrived governess. The language in which she describes her encounters with Miles, moreover, is markedly sexual. Dressed up in his Sunday suit, he is, in her eyes, a little man. She hestitates to enter his bedroom, describing the "risk" of shocking him, if he is "innocent," as "hideous." Yet, on the two occasions when she does do so, she sits on his bed, and, on the second, throws herself upon him to kiss him. She sees herself as a "gaoler," keeping him always under surveillance, and it is "freedom" that he demands when he does, as she puts its, "rebel."

The subject that she dare not broach to the children, she thinks, is the possible existence of ghosts. It is, she believes, against her pedagogical principles to introduce superstition into small minds. Yet her fears go much deeper than this. She insists the ghosts "can destroy" the children and describes their sudden appearances in what are now commonly accepted sexual images: "they're seen . . . in strange places and on high places, the top of towers, the roof of houses, the outside of windows, the further edge of pools." These images become a part of the reality of the final scene with Miles. The child keeps peering out of the window through which, on two separate occasions, the reader has previously seen Quint and the governess peer in, alarming the person within who sees them. When Miles peers out, the frames surrounding the glass panes like prison bars are emphasized, rather than the window itself, and his desire to "see" is associated with his caged restlessness and his desire for "freedom." The governess' most surprising depiction of the relationship between herself and Miles introduces this scene: "We continued silent while the maid was with us—as silent, it whimsically occurred to me, as some young couple who, on their wedding-journey, at the inn, feel shy in the presence of the waiter."[43]

Such an incongruous simile perhaps suggests the real state of the governess' mind. Although she does not know it, the view of Bly as the inn on a wedding journey fits into her fantasy about the children's uncle. From the beginning, her heroic view of herself as earning her employer's gratitude by "managing" without disturbing him is tied to her sexual fantasy about him. It is a fantasy, of course, safely wrapped up in romantic terms. When she first sees Quint staring malignantly at her from the tower (then and at the window, she points out, he is visible only from the waist up), she has been wandering in the garden at twilight imagining to herself, as she turns a corner, "some one" who "would appear . . . and smile and approve. I didn't ask more than that." When, instead, Quint appears, a man above and a tower below the waist, she feels "the scene had been stricken with death" (pp. 15–16).

It seems no oversimplification of James's subtlety to see the governess projecting her sexual desires on to a safely remote and romantic object, the children's uncle. Nothing else, at least, can account for her strange reaction when Mrs. Grose implores her to send for the "master." If she writes, she thinks, he will see her letter, with scorn, as "the fine machinery I had set in motion to attract his attention to my slighted charms." This comes from a young woman borne down by the responsibility of protecting two innocent children from evil, who has, in fact, seen her employer only once.

Throughout the story, the governess has repeatedly measured people by the ability to see. She herself can *see;* Mrs. Grose cannot. The children *see,* to her horror. They *know.* In the final scene her triumph lies in her realization that Miles cannot see. The child's feverish suffering does not deter her determination to have "all my proof" as she persists in questioning him: "Whom do you mean by 'he'?" She sees his answer as "his supreme surrender" and "his tribute to my devotion," but that answer has been: "Peter Quint—you devil!" The sequence of the dialogue and the syntax both insist that the "you devil!" is addressed, not to Quint, but to the governess, and at this point, as in all Gothic tales, the abyss appears: "He uttered the cry of a creature hurled over an abyss, and the grasp with which I recovered him might have been that of catching him in his fall. I caught him, yes, I held him—it may be imagined with what a passion" (p. 88). But Miles is dead in her arms. Like Giovanni giving the antidote to Beatrice in "Rappaccini's Daughter," like Victor's wife saving him from madness in Chekhov's "The Black Monk," the governess as savior has turned out to be destroyer.

The elaborate narrative frame with which *The Turn of the Screw* begins is not taken up again at the end. We are left with the stark puzzle of the child's death. James's deliberate ambiguity should not be denied, but the hints given throughout by the imagery also cannot be ignored. It is the governess who, all unaware of the sexual force of her romantic desires, is full of unconscious fears of contaminating the children, who, by her ideas, are innocent and, therefore, sexless beings. Hence, in describing her contacts with them, she uses sexual imagery, whereas, when she is aware of sexuality—in Quint and Miss Jessel—she is all vaguely expressed condemnation and shock. In part, it is she who is the intruder into the children's world, and the supernatural beings who enter it with her are projections of her guilty feelings. From this point of view, Miss Jessel and Quint are libidinous doubles of the governess and her "master," with their respective class ranking ironically reversed, so that the governess, like Quint, is the sexual predator.

This interpretation, however, does not account for the children's behavior. The reader need not doubt the governess' word that Miles really was on the lawn at night or that Flora did venture across the pond. Here again, James uses his ambiguities to good purpose. Flora's violent turning away from the governess in the second scene by the pond and Miles's feverish anguish just before his death, even his use of the names of Quint and Miss Jessel, indicate James's view of the innocence/ignorance dilemma. As long as the governess' own inhibitions prevent her from forcing her fears into the open, the reader is left unsure of what the children do or do not know. When the governess most suspects them of being in contact with the ghosts, they are serene, charming, and cheerful. When she brutally brings things into the open they are full of fear and anguish. Surely, in this, James is using the governess' own projections symbolically, to suggest that small children are indeed sexual beings, but that adult sex, especially accompanied by the gamut of adult suggestions of wickedness and forbidden knowledge, is frightening to them. The death of Miles at the end may suggest possible symbolic deaths—his death as a normal sexual being in his capitulation to the governess' twisted views; the death of his innocence in the real sense, not the governess' sense, as a child; even that ancient "death" which is literature's term for the sexual climax.[44]

It seems quite reasonable to say that in *The Turn of the Screw* James has brought to fictional resolution the dilemma Lewis had posed so long before. How, Lewis asks, is innocence to be safeguarded if ignorance is both necessary to it and its greatest danger? James seems to answer that the real danger may lie in twisting human nature into the weird shapes of monsters that feed on superstition. It had taken many a work between the two to bring this knowledge to the surface.

EPILOGUE

THE TWENTIETH CENTURY

"You are, so to speak, the brute existent by which they define
themselves. The exile, captivity, death they shrink from—
the blunt facts of their mortality,
their abandonment—that's what you make them recognize,
embrace! You are *mankind, or man's condition:*
inseparable as the mountain-climber and the mountain."
The dragon to Grendel, *Grendel* by John Gardner

IN THE Gothic fiction of writers like James and Stevenson and Wilde, we can see a high degree of awareness of psychological phenomena and a deliberate use of Gothic imagery to embody them in literature. This awareness was, of course, the consequence of advances in psychology itself, which, with the writings of Freud, was shortly to become a subject of general knowledge. Born in 1856, Freud belonged to the same generation as James (b. 1843), Stoker (b. 1847), Stevenson (b. 1850), and Wilde (also born in 1856), and his researches and their literary works belong to the same cultural era.

The development of the study of the mind into the science of psychology has continued to affect concepts of human nature and their reflection in Gothic literature. The course of the Gothic tradition in the twentieth century merits a study of its own for this reason alone. In addition, there has been a great proliferation of forms as a result of the upsurge in popular literature, the introduction into our culture of films, television, and comic books, and the appearance of a "youth culture." These together change the nature of the study needed. A glance at the kind of Gothic tales that have appeared in our century reveals, nonetheless, something of the direction the tradition has taken in its expression of man's fears and fancies.

The widespread general knowledge of psychology is reflected in the melding of Gothic fantasy and realistic fiction that can already be seen in the late nineteenth century. The tales and novels of Joseph Conrad, a contemporary of James, Stevenson, Stoker, and Wilde, are an example of the amalgam. Conrad regularly sets up a closed world, for instance, by isolating his characters on board ship, but, because, in real life, a ship forms a small world of its own, he presents it as a miniature of the larger society on land, using realistic techniques. In this way, in *The Nigger of the Narcissus,* for example, Conrad deals with the relations of man-to-man and man-to-society, encompassing both external social and internal psychological reality. Even his most famous doubles story, *The Secret Sharer,* portrays both the captain's mind and the social problems of responsibility and leadership by making the two figures embody the conflict in the captain over his dual role—as captain and as man.

When, on the other hand, Conrad turns to a direct symbolization of the mind in *Heart of Darkness,* he chooses to build his story with the narrative structure that we have found in *Frankenstein, Wuthering Heights,* and *The Turn of the Screw.* It is a frame story, one of those told by Marlow, who recounts it to a group of hearers among whom the reader finds himself. Conrad also uses other Gothic devices. His heroine is a typically pale and simplified Sentimental figure, kept out of the action so that she can be an embodiment of ignorance identified as innocence. The tale, like so many of its Gothic predecessors, is one of vague horrors taking place in a closed and impenetrable world—darkest Africa. All is unspecified evil and dread, which becomes an inner dread for the reader as well as the characters.

The twentieth century's smiths of the well-wrought tale

frequently present blood-curdling supernatural events in a realistic social setting. The tales of Saki (H. H. Munro), Graham Greene, and W. Somerset Maugham introduce the terrifying into social scenes in a way that asserts that the fears to which they correspond are indeed a part of everyday life. Franz Kafka goes one step further, turning the technique topsy-turvy and using the most meticulous realism, not to convey an illusion of "real life," but to evoke the atmosphere of a nightmare. With great precision the execution machine in "In the Penal Colony" is made as solid and tangible as any real gallows, yet the penal colony and the people in it are all imbued with the quality of a dream, just as the settings through which K. and Joseph K. wander in the novels are dream landscapes.

In *The Metamorphosis,* a Gothic device is used to make psychological truth a part of reality. Characters, setting, tone, plot—all are treated realistically. Everything about the Samsa family and their lives is as ordinary as can be—except for the one startling fact that Gregor is a beetle.[1] And in this tale we can see a twentieth-century view of human nature. Through his use of a grotesque (Gregor as beetle) in an otherwise exact rendering of everyday life, Kafka presents a horrid possibility that would not have appeared before our era—the belief that, psychologically, a man may really be a beetle. No longer are we shown a central, indestructible core of the self, however encrusted over with ugliness, like Frankenstein's monster, or an outer body of civilized decency, like Jekyll, controlling and diminishing the uncivilized id projected into Hyde. Gregor just *is* a beetle, and nothing else, actually, potentially, or in any other way. He may have been reduced to that state—we cannot tell—but, if so, the reduction is complete and permanent. Gregor is a monster of despicableness, rejected even by those who loved him—and he is nothing more than that.

Kafka's vision, of course, leans toward the abiding nightmare of the period immediately before and after the second World War—the chilling apprehension of the meaningless, Absurd universe. The staring figures of the grotesque, contorted into frozen movement, which only reluctantly yield up meaning, are particularly suited to the embodiment of meaninglessness. They can consequently be used in the literature of the Absurd itself. They have also been used in the twentieth century, however, as they were in the middle ages and the renaissance, to oppose the emptiness of malignancy and evil to the truth of a higher, transcendent Good. In Par Lägerkvist's allegorical fantasy *The Dwarf,* the dwarf symbolizes the evil in man in a "historical" setting. The Prince's dwarf, a grotesque, is the central character and also the narrator, like Frankenstein's monster when it tells its story. The dwarf, who is like Stevenson's Hyde, except that the prince is aware of him only as separate from himself, tells us that all men have dwarfs, but they do not know it, because these stunted beings are concealed within them. When the dwarf is in high favor, the Prince leads his nation to war and disaster threatens to overwhelm the state. When the dwarf is chained up in a deep, dark dungeon, the Prince shows the better side of his nature and rules well and beneficently.

Flannery O'Connor, too, uses the grotesque to present a society that lacks the transcendent values in which she believes, as she explains in her discussion of her methods.[2] She portrays very ordinary human beings as fantastically idiosyncratic, rendering them as grotesques. She does not suggest that beneath their weird and loony exteriors her characters have, after all, a sterling spirit or a good heart, nor does she demand sympathy for them because they might have been different. Rather, her vision demands acceptance and compassion for her people as they are, not despite what they are. This is the traditional use of the grotesque—to confront the demonic and fix its nightmares in art so that we ultimately accept our own nature as Fallen. In among O'Connor's grotesques, however, an occasional Gothic device probes beneath the surface to add a psychological explanation of a character's condition. In

"You Can't Be Any Poorer Than Dead," the dead man's eyes hound the boy Tarwater in a rare glimpse of the supernatural used, in the Gothic manner, to symbolize guilt. And the artificial leg of Hulga/Joy in "Good Country People" reminds us of Hoffman's automata and is used for a similar purpose—to convey the conflict between intellectuality and the ordinary concerns of life. This is a common theme in O'Connor's stories, but, in this one, the leg, which threatens to dehumanize its wearer, paradoxically deepens her human pathos for us. Here, as we will see happening in other twentieth-century Gothic works, the grotesque and the normal figures have been joined into one. In Hoffmann, the artist and the automaton were separate; in O'Connor, the intellectual is the automaton, suggesting, as Kafka's Gregor Samsa does, that the diminution of a human being may be absolute.

Gothic techniques also appear in works depicting the psychological aspects of alienation, the most prevalent of human conditions in an Absurd universe. Carson McCullers, for instance, uses them in "The Ballad of the Sad Café," a tale of the nature of human love and the destructiveness of self-isolation. The closed world of a small town into which we are led by the narrator; the cross-eyed, mannish female giant, Miss Amelia, and the small and womanish crook-backed dwarf, Cousin Lymon—these are Gothic devices; and the café itself, for all its fragile and delapidated state, is a recognizable Gothic "castle" that becomes the center of warmth and caring when Miss Amelia opens herself out to others, and gray and shuttered when she closes herself off from the world.

McCullers' discussion of her writing could well describe the techniques of Gothic writers ever since Walpole. "Writing," she says, "is a wandering, dreaming occupation. The intellect is submerged beneath the unconscious—the thinking mind is best controlled by the imagination." And speaking of one of her major themes, she explains that "love, and especially love of a person who is incapable of returning or receiving it, is at the heart of my selection of grotesque figures to write about—people whose physical incapacity is a symbol of their spiritual incapacity to love or receive love—their spiritual isolation." This kind of symbolism is the same as that used by earlier authors in portraying Gothic villains as stormy giants or embodying a sense of guilt in the deformed figure of a double, as is clear from McCullers' elaboration of her point: "The fact that John Singer . . . is a deaf-and-dumb man is a symbol, and the fact that Captain Penderton . . . is homosexual, is also a symbol of handicap and impotence. . . . Symbols suggest the story and theme and incident, and they are so interwoven that one cannot understand consciously where the suggestion begins."[3] McCullers' "Ballad" uses its Gothic devices to explore the nature of human love—not only sexual, but love as the only true relationship—and the self-isolation which is its opposite. In Truman Capote's *Other Voices, Other Rooms,* we again find Gothic characters used to present once more the problem of ignorance and innocence in a boy seeking his sexual identity. And in Eudora Welty's *The Robber Bridegroom,* a girl's coming to maturity is presented in a combination of American tall-tale and the fairy-tale form, which Bruno Bettelheim has identified as a traditional vehicle for such subject matter.[4]

Other twentieth-century works have used the convention to present sexual orientation—the attraction of men and women to each other, of men to men, and of women to women—and also to present the sexual aspect of human nature itself—the concept of androgyny.[5] We find the first in Isak Dinesen's *Seven Gothic Tales* and her other collections of stories, and the second in Hermann Hesse's *Demian,* in which the androgynous figure of Demian's mother is represented as a giantess. The successive novels of Iris Murdoch play continually on themes of sexual orientation and sexuality in human nature, as well as androgyny, and she, too, employs Gothic techniques. In *A Severed Head,* which weaves an extraordinary tangle of relationships, she uses the London fog as Stevenson uses it in *Jekyll and Hyde*, and portrays the character who represents the "horrifying truth"—the revelation of the central character's subconscious fears—as a grotesque, a pagan idol, threatening castration as a punishment for incest. *The Unicorn* opens with the heroine's difficulties in entering a closed world. Like the central character of *The Turn of the Screw*, she comes as a governess and enters the world with romanticized expectations. Once there, she finds two contrasted houses, one of them the closed, secretive expression of long-standing guilt, and a symbolic bog that draws men beneath its surface. These Gothic devices are used to explore twists of human nature, as Marian learns, much like Emily in *The Mysteries of Udolpho*, the difference between her perceptions colored by her imagination and the "reality" of the situation.

Both these novels deal with sexual relationships. *The Bell* is concerned with androgyny, and it displays the full panoply of Gothic devices. The house in the closed world, Imber Court, is its owner, Michael. A walled convent represents forbidden Woman. There is an earthy figure, Dora, contrasted with Michael's spirituality. There is an ignorant/innocent, Toby, who must find himself as a sexual adult, who wonders whether he is a "natural homosexual" and tries to assert his heterosexuality with the earth-mother Dora. Then there are fraternal twins, each denying the sexual self, who represent the male and female aspects of human nature, the two split halves of a potential, androgynous whole. The house and characters, especially Toby, who is trying to see himself, are all reflected in the great central mirror of the lake, and, throughout, all are haunted in different ways by the twin bells, perfect symbols of androgyny with their phallic clappers inside their great, round, cavernous bellies. The characters are unable to deal with their problems or with the difficulties that arise over the bells, just as they are unable to cope with their monosexual lives, whether hetero- or homo-, or recognize the possible dualities in themselves. They immure the bells safely out of sight, one in the convent, one in a museum. We, as readers, however, can note the narrator's remark that "we all participate in both sexes" and see that, although, in life, most people choose, on balance, one sex or the other, the drag of the other, if it is immured within and unrecognized, will set up strains and conflicts, rending our inmost natures apart.

Such explorations of human nature and the nature of human sexuality form a natural extension of the themes of the earlier Gothic tradition. They use Gothic devices to turn our eyes inward in the continued exploration of the self. But the view of the universe as absurd threatens such explorations with meaninglessness. Science fiction, horror stories, films, television shows, and the comics have filled the modern consciousness with monsters, mutants, and creatures from outer space, all designed to represent, not the self, but the alien Other, the altogether different, alien presence.[6] Such figures are in themselves difficult for the human imagination to devise and their creators draw on the long tradition of the grotesque to delineate them. Writers like Tolkien, on the other hand, use traditional figures from fairy tales and medieval romance and epic to depict Otherness in fantasies related to the Gothic tradition that invent a world—geography, inhabitants, and all—or, like Richard Adams, portray "animal" societies. Perhaps this plethora of grotesques, some of them presented as attractive, indicates a new familiarity with the demonic in our age, which has also given rise to tales that naturalize it. Rochester's mad wife in *Jane Eyre* has reappeared, changed from a vague, sinister presence to a suffering woman, the central character of *The Wide Sargasso Sea* by Jean Rhys. Heathcliff is now the center of his own novel, an epistolary historical novel presented through a mediating frame narration by Lockwood, via Nelly. Even more interestingly, John Gardner has drawn Grendel out of the middle ages and made him the narrator of his own tale, like the monster when he narrates his own section of *Frankenstein*. There is, however, no central core of good human nature to Grendel, such as Frankenstein's monster has. On the contrary, the ferocious, ravening savage is the basic being of the "brood of Cain." Yet, Gardner's vision of Grendel is as different from, say, Stevenson's view of Hyde as it is from Mary Shelley's concept of her monster. Grendel weaves a web of language—very poetic language—which he throws out between the harsh world and himself, and he cannot prevent himself from adopting the "lying" perceptions of the bard, who turns the bloodthirsty irrationality of the thanes into the beautiful heroism of epic poetry. Grendel turns to really savage violence only when his encounter with the dragon (a comic, Lewis-Carroll figure in the midst of all the gloom) leaves him bereft of hope. To that extent he resembles Mary Shelley's monster, but Gardner's fantasy, with its Gothic monster and medieval setting, presents a twentieth-century view of perception as an imaginative structure projected onto chaos to give it meaning.

Leslie Fiedler has attempted to show that the Otherness of "freaks" has come to be perceived as the reflection of the secret self. Radu Florescu has explored the legends and brought forth the "real Dracula," still dripping blood but now analyzed for his place in the popular imagination as a symbol of subconscious impulses, and Leonard Wolf, who has also edited *The Annotated Frankenstein,* has traveled from research into the real Dracula of medieval Hungary to a search for living vampires in contemporary San Francisco, which brought a case that might be described as "psychological vampirism" to his living room.[7]

The vampire presented realistically, as one of us, also appears in Anne Rice's novel *Interview with the Vampire,* a work that again explores the forms of human love and the nature of its relationships, in a first-person, mediated account from the mouth of the vampire himself. The Otherness of this figure, which is beyond human nature in that it does not die and feeds and finds its satisfactions in non-human ways, is dissolved in the "reality" of the living, breathing creature sitting quietly and talking into the tape recorder, recounting a tale of passions that we recognize. But this novel leaves us, as so many earlier Gothic tales do, on the edge of a quicksand of uncertainty. What kind of credence is demanded of a realistic account transmitted by one whom we know to be a creature of the fancy only? Is this vampire, like James's governess, seeing evil where there is only the natural? Having experienced his story and learned what it is to be a vampire, we cannot dismiss him, any more than we could dismiss Frankenstein's monster, as a narrator. Throughout the novel we have given imaginative assent to the vampire's account. We have been in the position of the boy who has taken his tape recorder and interviewed the very figure of the threatening evil within, but now that boy has himself taken on the nature of a vampire and gone to seek further. Do we wish to follow him? Perhaps he is another Frankenstein, pursuing forbidden knowledge to the destruction of himself and others? Or is no knowledge forbidden? The novel uses the supernatural, as the Gothic tradition has always done, to present new views of human nature ambiguously, so that we are forced to ask questions about it. Because the twentieth century is not yet in a position to answer those questions and others concerning the inner self, Gothic literature will continue to appear.

Within the universality of the human condition there is always a particularity, the aspect of the dilemma, the paradox of that condition, that presents itself to any given age. Anne Rice's novel, like its predecessors in the Gothic tradition, is a fulfillment of literature's inexorable function to show life's complexities. Gothic fiction symbolizes the unresolvable, shifting, but perpetual paradox of human nature. Until the human condition changes, we will need such fantasies to embody the dilemma of our existence, to face us with it, so that we, too, may face the dark.

NOTES

1. Introductory: Gothic Literature—What It Is and Why

1. For a discussion of the expression of psychological concerns in Western fairy tales see Bruno Bettelheim, *The Uses of Enchantment.* Gothic literature is part of the larger field of Romance. For a delineation of Romance itself, see Northrop Frye, *The Secular Scripture.*

2. Even major studies have hampered themselves by this characterization. J. M. S. Tompkins, in *The Popular Novel in England,* seems to equate popular and bad; Devendra Varma and Montague Summers in their studies of Gothic literature, and James Foster in *The Pre-Romantic Novel* put themselves through a Purgatorial circle littered with third-, fourth-, and fifth-rate examples in order to supply plot summaries of novels which their readers would not themselves read. It is small wonder that these chroniclers of the genre should as a result indulge in a good deal of pained sarcasm at the expense of their own subject. Problems also arise in deciding what literature is "popular." Q. D. Leavis, for instance, in *Fiction and the Reading Public,* makes numbers her criterion. As a result, Scott, Dickens, and Charlotte Brontë are popular, Emily Brontë is not. See the appendix to her study. Lionel Gossman, on the other hand, in discussing the place in folk literature of Robert Burns's poetry concludes that the same poetry in the "literate" and "folk" traditions constitutes "two different bodies of work." See "Literary Scholarship and Popular History," p. 138. The net result is to make these works studies of the history of the genre while neglecting its significance as a genre.

On popular literature see Russel Nye, *The Unembarrassed Muse.* Also David Madden, "The Necessity for an Aesthetics of Popular Culture." Both Madden and Frank Kermode in *The Sense of an Ending,* discuss the static, "formulaic" works of popular literature, which are simply imitative, and those works that carry forward the "myths" of their age by modifying and changing them. The works discussed in this study fall into the latter category.

In dividing popular literature in this way, it is important to avoid a condescending view of the formulaic. Leslie Fiedler, for instance, defines Gothic literature as "avant-garde" and "anti-bourgeois" and complains that the "popular success of Frankenstein . . . has obscured the fact that . . . one of [its] functions was to shock the bourgeoisie into an awareness of what a chamber of horrors its own smugly regarded world really was." See *Love and Death in the American Novel,* p. 135. Fiedler, however, calls the "popular" form of Gothic fiction an appeal to the prurient subconscious of the same bourgeoisie. He is led to this confusing position by his rejection of the Sentimental novel as the product of "female scribblers," with the result that he obscures the very link he is looking for. There is no need to rescue Frankenstein from the populace in order to take it seriously. The "chamber of horrors" is everyone's. See, on this point, Frye's remarks on popular literature, including Gothic, in *The Secular Scripture,* pp. 28–29. See also Richard Poirier, "A Literature of Law and Order," pp. 12–13, where he notes the bearing of popular culture on "even those experiences we think the most private and original," and discusses the efforts of writers from Melville to Mailer to struggle against "contexts that impose a self and a destiny."

3. A collection of essays specifically discussing Gothic literature as Romantic art is G. R. Thompson, ed., *The Gothic Imagination.* Northrop Frye also treats Gothic literature as part of Romanticism in *A Study of English Romanticism,* as well as alluding to it in *The Secular Scripture.* That it has important links with Romanticism is undeniable and the above works are useful explorations of them. Although related to Romanticism, Gothic works differ from those of the Romantic mainstream in their concern with human psychology in this world, as opposed to Romanticism's primary interest in a transcendental, mystic view of Nature and mankind's yearning for things not of this world. A recent study that recognizes the difference is John V. Murphy's *The Dark Angel.* Murphy shows that Shelley uses the Gothic conventions only when he is plumbing the psychological depths to reveal human feelings, and not when he is dealing with transcendent subject matter. See, especially, pp. 184–85. A recent work that discusses the transcendent interests of Romanticism is Thomas Weiskel's *The Romantic Sublime.* Mainly, though, Gothic fiction cannot be defined as Romantic because, although some Romantics wrote Gothic work, most Gothic authors are not Romantics. A different source of obscurity lies in the inclination to group a number of works together under one rubric without defining their common ground. For instance, so recent a study as Robert Kiely's *The Romantic Novel in England* discusses *Otranto* and *Melmoth* along with *Waverley* and *Nightmare Abbey* without explanation of the overriding principle by which they are united.

4. Lowry Nelson, "Night Thoughts on the Gothic Novel," and Robert Hume "Gothic versus Romantic," discuss the need to see Gothic literature as a "kind" of its own. Hume's statement that, unlike Romanticism, Gothicism is not transcendent is, despite Robert Platzner's denial of it, an important one (see note 7).

5. See Erich Kahler, *The Inward Turn of Narrative,* pp. 65–66, where he notes that the symbolic quality of narratives "inheres in their capacity to extend the range and horizon of human reality because . . . they change that reality. They create a new form of reality with which consciousness thereafter has to deal." This concept is related to Mark Schorer's idea of "technique as discovery," see "Technique as Discovery."

6. See Dan J. McNutt, *The Eighteenth-Century Gothic Novel.* The major early studies combine a history of the Gothic novels and a tracing of their literary origins. These are: Edith Birkhead, *The Tale of Terror;* Eino Railo, *The Haunted Castle;* Montague Summers, *The Gothic Quest;* Devendra P. Varma, *The Gothic Flame.* Two histories of wider fields that provide extensive information on Gothic and Sentimental novels are: J. M. S. Tompkins, *The Popular Novel in England, 1770–1800;* and James R. Foster, *History of the Pre-Romantic Novel in England.*

7. Some important more recent treatments of Gothic literature are: Lowry Nelson, Jr., "Night Thoughts on the Gothic Novel"; Robert D. Hume "Gothic Versus Romantic"; which was followed by a critical controversy between Hume and Robert Platzner in *PMLA* (March 1971), 86:266–74; and James M. Keech, "The Survival of the Gothic Response." These studies show the need for an expanded study of Gothic literature, but do not supply it. Mario Praz, in his "Introductory Essay" to Peter Fairclough, ed., *Three Gothic Novels,* touches upon the psychological implications of the genre. His more important work, *The Romantic Agony,* deals with it indirectly. Julia Briggs', *Night Visitors,* discusses the nineteenth-century ghost story, but she notes that the category more properly includes other stories of the supernatural, which she finds, are concerned with the nature of man's evil.

Francis Hart in "Limits of the Gothic," and Frederick Garber in "Meaning and Mode in Gothic Fiction," attempt to place Gothic literature more accurately in its historical setting.

Such works as *The Werewolf* by Montague Summers, who has also made studies of vampires and witches, are of related interest but are not directly on the subject of this literary study. Radu Florescu's *In Search of Dracula,* and *In Search of Frankenstein* are also of related interest.

Some less extensive or peripheral discussions are: E. F. Bleiler in his "Introduction" to *The Castle of Otranto* by Horace Walpole, *Vathek* by William Beckford, and *The Vampyre* by John Polidori; Leslie A. Fiedler, in *Love and Death in the American Novel* and *Freaks;* Paul Zweig, *The Adventurer;* Leonard Wolf, *A Dream of Dracula;* and Ellen Moers, *Literary Women.*

8. W. S. Lewis, *Horace Walpole,* p. 118.

9. This preface is included in W. S. Lewis' edition of Walpole, *The Castle of Otranto.*

10. W. S. Lewis draws conclusions that favor such a view and he quotes Dr. Mannheim the psychiatrist in support (*Horace Walpole,* pp. 190–91); R. W. Ketton-Cremer in his *Horace Walpole* opposes it.

11. In a letter to Mme. du Deffand, Walpole writes: "I have given reins to my imagination till I became on fire with the visions and feelings which it excited. I have composed it in defiance of rules, of critics, and of philosophers; and it seems to me just so much the better for that very reason." Quoted in Walter Scott, "Walpole," *Lives of the Novelists.*

12. Walpole described Strawberry Hill as a house "built to please my own taste, and in some degree realize my own visions." Quoted in R. W. Ketton-Cremer, p. 121, and W. S. Lewis, p. 101, from Walpole's Preface to *A Description of Strawberry Hill.* See also W. S. Lewis, Introduction to Walpole, *The Castle of Otranto* for Walpole's statement about the influence of the medieval atmosphere of his house and for his description of the night when he wrote till his fingers were numb, indicating the intensity and absorption with which he wrote *Otranto.*

13. See John O. Lyons, *The Invention of the Self,* on this subject.

14. See "Preface to the Second Edition," Walpole, *The Castle of Otranto,* p. 7.

15. Richard Hurd, Letter x, *Letters on Chivalry and Romance* (vol. 4 of *Works*), pp. 321–22.

16. Scott, "Walpole," p. 191.

17. Hurd, Letter iv, pp. 348, 350.

18. Edgar Allan Poe, *The Fall of the House of Usher and Other Tales,* p. 115.

19. For extended discussion of "Sentimental" and related terms see, in particular, Edith Birkhead, "Sentiment and Sensibility in the Eighteenth-Century Novel," and R. F. Brissenden, *Virtue in Distress.*

20. Works recording and explaining the religious and philosophical ideas behind Sentimentalist literature which have been drawn upon here are: R. S. Crane, "Suggestions Toward a Genealogy of the 'Man of Feeling' "; and Donald Greene's recent "reconsideration" of Crane's article: "Latitudinarianism and Sensibility"; Walter Francis Wright, *Sensibility in English Prose Fiction, 1760–1814;* Basil Willey, *The Eighteenth-Century Background;* Northrop Frye, "Towards Defining an Age of Sensibility"; Ernest Lee Tuveson, *The Imagination as a Means of Grace;* Louis I. Bredvold, *The Natural History of Sensibility.* The latest and most complete discussion of "The Novel of Sentiment" is R. F. Brissenden's *Virtue in Distress.* Kiely does not agree with this traditional view of Gothic fiction as deriving from Sentimentalism. Necessarily, the contributors to *The Gothic Imagination,* because they do not differentiate between the Gothic and the main

trends of Romanticism, as this study does, also tend to take a different view. (See note 3 above.)

21. Bredvold, *The Natural History of Sensibility.* Quotations are on pp. 9–10. See also Crane, "Genealogy of the 'Man of Feeling,' " pp. 223–26, concerning the unnaturalness of evil.

22. See Willey, Wright, and Crane. "Human nature" is referred to constantly in eighteenth-century works. *OED* definition I. 2.b: "The general inherent character or disposition of mankind" is the appropriate one in these contexts. (There are citations from 1526 to 1872.)

23. See Willey, and also Wright, who explains Shaftesbury's belief that the Moral Sense in combination with the judgment will produce a man "virtuous in impulse and act" since the Moral Sense leads to love of one's fellows, courage, gratitude, pity. This group of related ideas was very widespread and many examples could be cited. All show the influence of the central Benevolist idea: that a benevolent Creator did not mean life to be always a vale of tears, that life on this earth could be good.

24. See Ernest Tuveson, "The Origins of the Moral Sense," and Crane, pp. 214–20.

25. See Willey, pp. 108–9, 121.

26. Adam Smith, "The Theory of Moral Sentiments," in Trawick, ed., *Backgrounds of Romanticism,* p. 116. "It is he ["the man within"] who shows us . . . the deformity of doing the smallest injury to another, in order to obtain the greatest benefit to ourselves." (The date of this work is 1759.)

27. See Edmund Burke, *A Philosophical Enquiry into the Origin of our Ideas of the Sublime and Beautiful.* Ideas of obscurity and lack of clarity appear throughout Burke's *Enquiry.* See particularly part 2, section 4, pp. 60–64. The importance of the sublime to Gothic literature lies in its ability to arouse the reader's "passions," that is, to appeal to him through his feelings.

28. R. D. Hume, for instance, who regards Gothic literature as "one kind of treatment of the psychology of evil," nevertheless sees the Sentimental novel as exhibiting "feeling for its own sake." See "Gothic vs. Romantic," p. 283. Tompkins, Foster, Birkhead, Fiedler, and Brissenden are all less than flattering in their remarks on the Sentimental novel.

29. Smith, "The Theory of Moral Sentiments," p. 111.

30. See, for instance, Fiedler, *Love and Death in the American Novel,* p. 84: "Neither inwardness nor character . . . interested the scribbling ladies at all"; p. 93: "The genteel, sentimental, quasi-literate female audience . . . and a product which satisfied it"; p. 95: "A tale in which female suffering is portrayed from a female point of view in order to stir female sympathy." Fiedler, naturally, finds it "baffling" that men repeated "in their own books the formulas of feminist sentimentality" (p. 90). He

regrets the use of "the cheapjack machinery of the Gothic novel" in what he considers the masculine novel, but he regards the Gothic novel, nevertheless, as "revolutionary" and as "itself a Faustian commitment" (p. 134). Of course, much has been done since Fiedler wrote to seriously delineate the cultural and psychological factors that really differentiate women authors from men. See, for instance, Patricia Meyer Spacks, *The Female Imagination.*

31. See "Mackenzie," in Scott's *Lives of the Novelists,* p. 171. Scott says that Mackenzie's principal object "has been to reach and sustain a tone of moral pathos, by representing the effect of incidents, whether important or trifling upon the human mind." Brian Vickers also quotes this passage from Scott in his Introduction to *The Man of Feeling* by Henry Mackenzie.

32. See Vickers, "Introduction," *The Man of Feeling,* pp. vii–viii. Vickers notes that "Mackenzie was in tune with the taste of the age rather than expressing a purely personal reaction." He quotes, in support, Scott's *Journal* where Scott notes that Mackenzie was nothing like his heroes (p. viii, n. 2). Jean Hagstrum refers to Mackenzie's novel as "Robert Burns' bosom favorite," in " 'Such, Such Were the Joys': The Boyhood of the Man of Feeling," p. 49.

33. As Northrop Frye notes, "The romancer does not attempt to create 'real people' so much as stylized figures which expand into psychological archetypes." This is true of Sentimental and even more so of Gothic fiction. See *The Anatomy of Criticism,* p. 304.

34. See in particular Brissenden, *Virtue in Distress,* Foster, *Pre-Romantic Novel,* and Tompkins, *Popular Novel.*

35. Preface, *David Simple* by Sarah Fielding. The novel has by now been well established as Sarah Fielding's own work in form and content. Henry Fielding's revisions were not so sweeping as to make it less than her own. Quotations are from pp. 6, 5, 8.

36. Preface, p. 7.

37. Two recent discussions of treatment of contemporary themes in *Evelina* are Waldo S. Glock, "Appearance and Reality," and James B. Vopat, "*Evelina:* Life as Art."

38. T. C. Duncan Eaves and Ben D. Kimpel have done much to counteract the common and rather condescending view of Richardson as an author of "female sensibility" too nervous and inhibited to have been conscious of the import of his own work. See their *Samuel Richardson.* See also Elizabeth Bergen Brophy, *Samuel Richardson: The Triumph of Craft.*

39. Concerning Gray, see W. S. Lewis, "Introduction," *The Castle of Otranto* by Horace Walpole, p. vii. Warburton is quoted by Varma in *The Gothic Flame,* p. 64, as saying in his notes to his edition of Pope's *Imitations of Horace* that in *The Castle of Otranto* "a beautiful imagination supported by strength of judgment, has enabled the author to go beyond his subject,

and effect the full purpose of the Ancient Tragedy." Varma also notes Warton's admiration for *The Mysteries of Udolpho* (p. 96).

40. Scott's *Lives of the Novelists* is proof of this.

41. Clara Reeve, *The Progress of Romance through Times, Countries, and Manners,* pp. 6–7; 108–12, especially p. 111.

42. From Congreve in 1692 to Clara Reeve in 1785 and beyond the romance is defined as "fabulous" and then differentiated from the novel, which is a "picture of real life." See Ioan Williams, "Introduction," *Novel and Romance.* She notes that Congreve is writing of the "nouvelle," or novella, while Clara Reeve means the social novel proper. In general, by "romance" is meant any work that departs from the depiction of the real world in the direction of fantasy, allegory, or the fictional embodiment of ideas. Boswell, for instance, refers to Johnson's *Rasselas* as a "philosophical romance." See *The Life of Samuel Johnson, LL.D.*, George Birkbeck Hill, ed., L. F. Powell rev. (Oxford: Clarendon, 1934), 3:356.

43. See Crane, "Suggestions Toward A Genealogy of the 'Man of Feeling,' " pp. 220–21.

44. John Milton, *Paradise Lost* IV.75 and XII.537, respectively, in *Complete Poems and Major Prose,* Merritt Hughes, ed. (New York: Odyssey Press, 1957).

45. *Miscellaneous Pieces in Prose,* by John Aikin, M.D., and Anna Laetitia Barbauld, originally published as by John and Anna Aikin, Barbauld being Anna Aikin's married name. In "On Romances," they insist on the value of these works on the grounds that "they please the imagination and interest the heart"; that we enjoy their scenes of woe because "so far from being indifferent to the miseries of others, we are, at the time, totally regardless of our own"; and that "they teach us to think by inuring us to feel: They ventilate the mind by sudden gusts of passion" (pp. 45–46). Arthur L. Cooke, in "Some Side Lights on the Theory of Gothic Romance," p. 432, attributes this essay to Anna Aikin. "Inuring" may be defined according to Sense 1 in the *OED:* "To bring (a person, etc.) by use, habit, or continual exercise to a certain condition or state of mind, to the endurance of a certain condition, to the following of a certain kind of life, etc."

46. Aikin, "Pleasure derived from Objects of Terror," *Miscellaneous Pieces,* pp. 119–20. Cooke, in "Some Side Lights," p. 431, attributes this essay to John Aikin on the grounds that it is not included in the edition of his sister Anna's *Works,* published under her married name of Barbauld. As Cooke notes, Summers and Edith Birkhead attribute it to Anna Aikin.

47. Aikin, "An Enquiry into Those Kinds of Distress which excite agreeable Sensations," *Miscellaneous Pieces,* p. 193. In the eighteenth century, "mere" was in the process of changing to its current signification

from the meaning "complete," "entire." Here, a modern author would probably have written "utter" or "complete." The eighteenth-century meaning of "pity" is approximately that of the modern "compassion."

48. "An Enquiry into Those Kinds of Distress," 194–95. In eighteenth-century texts "complacency" is frequently found with the signification of meaning 1 in the *OED:* "The fact or state of being pleased with a thing or person; tranquil pleasure or satisfaction in something or someone."

49. In the eighteenth century "disgusting" is often used to convey a less forceful meaning than the word has today. It frequently appears as a modification of something for which one lacks a taste rather than something for which one feels a strong aversion.

50. Samuel Monk, *The Sublime.* The most famous eighteenth-century source is, of course, Edmund Burke's *A Philosophical Enquiry into the Origin of Our Ideas of the Sublime and Beautiful.* The contribution of the poet James Beattie to this subject is discussed in this chapter. The concept of the sublime is, of course, extremely complex and is only touched upon here in its direct relationship to Gothic literature.

51. See *The Sublime,* p. 54, for a list quoted from Dennis which ranges from gods and demons, through torrents and earthquakes, to lions and tigers, and ends in pestilence and famine, as objects evoking the sublime. Hartley is still expressing similar ideas later in the century. (See "Observations on Man," Trawick, ed. *Backgrounds,* p. 73.) Even Dennis' view is not as simplistic as it seems, for he emphasizes the psychological effect that "ravishes and transports us" (*The Sublime,* p. 53), and Hartley's formulation also indicates why the Sentimental and Gothic authors put such emphasis on the picturesque, for he compares the more immediate effect of a painting with the wider compass of written description in creating sublime effects ("Observations on Man," p. 78).

52. *The Sublime,* p. 74.

53. Nathan Drake, *Literary Hours* vol. 2, Essay XXIV, "On the Evening and Night Scenery of the Poets as Mingled or Contrasted with Pathetic Emotion."

54. Drake, Essay XXXII, "Agnes Felton, a Tale," pp. 263–64.

55. Drake, Essay XL, "On The Farmer's Boy of Bloomfield," p. 464.

56. Aikin, "Pleasure derived from Objects of Terror," p. 120. They first suggest that sheer curiosity keeps us reading despite the pain caused by the story (pp. 123–24), but then go on to note that scenes of terror are read eagerly even when there is no suspense (p. 125).

57. "Pleasure derived . . . ," pp. 122, 125.

58. "Enquiry into . . . Distress," p. 193.

59. Reeve, *The Progress of Romance,* 2:23.

60. *Ibid.*

61. *Ibid.,* pp. 24, 25.

62. Beattie, "Illustrations on Sublimity," *Dissertations Moral and Critical,* p. 655. This improvement is in particular effected through the delineation of virtuous characters, which will "animate us with the love of virtue and honour" (p. 620).

63. "Illustrations on Sublimity," p. 620.

64. Johnson had, of course, warned against mixed characters in novels in general as dangerous, especially to the youthful reader, and Beattie repeated the protest that had so distressed Richardson against the seductive charms that made Lovelace a villain of questionable didactic value.

65. Hume discusses the moral relativity of the Gothic in "Gothic vs. Romantic."

66. Summers quotes Warburton, for instance, as praising *Otranto* (in his edition of Pope), because it can *"purge the passions by pity and terror"* (W.'s italics). See *The Gothic Quest,* pp. 184–85. See note 39 for a similar citation by Varma. Scott also says that Walpole has the ability "to excite the passions of fear and pity," in "Walpole," *Lives of the Novelists,* p. 196.

67. Frye, "Towards Defining an Age of Sensibility," p. 316.

68. "Preface to the Second Edition," Walpole, *The Castle of Otranto,* p. 7.

69. Drake, *Literary Hours,* Essay VIII, "On Gothic Superstition," 1:140–41, 142–45.

70. Drake, *Literary Hours,* Essay XXX, "On the Superstitions of the Highlands of Scotland," 2:208, and Essay XXXI, "The Same Concluded," 2:256–57.

71. See John L. Greenway, "The Gateway to Innocence." Greenway says the Ossianic poems legitimized "the values of sentimental primitivism through a mythic narrative . . . which showed that sentimental views of human nature, virtue, and vice were really present at the dawn of Northern *non*-classical civilization" (p. 162). "Sympathetic imagery (where nature is an extension of character or mood) to integrate landscape into the action" is also "legitimized" by Ossian (p. 165).

72. Drake, *Literary Hours,* Essay XVII, "On Objects of Terror," 1:354.

73. Varma has suggested that the placing of these contemporary eighteenth-century characters in medieval settings makes the Gothic surrealistic. See *The Gothic Flame,* p. 70.

74. It should be noted here that, although the Gothic villain is at war with himself and is maddened by his sense of his own evil, it is theories of human nature and the unnaturalness of evil to it that these works reflect, not eighteenth-century views of insanity, such as are discussed in Michael V. DePorte's *Nightmares and Hobbyhorses,* and Max Byrd's *Visits to Bedlam.* It is, however, also true that nineteenth-century works, because they derive from early Gothic fiction and its ideas of the unnaturalness of evil tend to abound with mad criminals, and it seems regrettably possible that

these tales are at least partly responsible for the tendency in real life to associate insanity with criminality.

2. Characters—The Reflected Self

1. Mackenzie, *The Man of Feeling,* p. 9. "Consciousness" is frequently found in such contexts where in a modern work the redundant "self-consciousness" has become necessary to distinguish this meaning from others. In this context the word means "Internal knowledge or conviction; knowledge as to which one has the testimony within oneself; especially of one's own innocence, guilt, deficiencies, etc." (*OED,* Sense 2).

2. Albert J. Kuhn, ed., "Introduction," *Three Sentimental Novels* (New York: Holt, Rinehart, and Winston, 1970), p. xii.

3. *The Man of Feeling,* pp. 17–18. Page references are hereafter given in the text.

4. For examples of eighteenth-century views opposed to Harley's, see A. O. Aldridge, "The Pleasures of Pity," *ELH* (1949), 16:76–87.

5. *The Lounger,* No. 20, 1785, in Ioan Williams, ed., *Novel and Romance, 1700–1800.*

6. What Walter Wright says of Henley and Anna in Thomas Holcroft's *Anna St. Ives* is true of many others: "[They] really succeed in perfecting only their own souls. They cannot reform mankind; yet by their own lives they reveal that man is perfectible to the extent that he is able to let his instinctive goodness express itself." Wright, *Sensibility in English Prose Fiction 1760–1814,* p. 444.

7. *Atala* and its companion piece *René* both appeared in 1801 and as part of *The Genius of Christianity* (1802), which was not translated into English until 1856. The two tales did not appear separately in English translation until 1952.

8. François-René de Chateaubriand, *Atala & René,* p. 84.

9. *Ibid.,* p. 48.

10. Goethe, *The Sorrows of Young Werther,* pp. 50, 64.

11. *Ibid.,* p. 27.

12. Jean Hagstrum sees in these childlike Sentimental characters evidence of regression. He suggests that Mackenzie's Harley is consumed by a death wish and is a case of arrested development: "The melting feelings that drench the handkerchief of Harley remind one of what Freud called love with an inhibited aim—that is, normal, adult, physical love diverted to sentiment by an inability to cross what persisting childhood continues to regard as forbidden frontiers." In *Vathek* he sees Beckford as presenting only two alternatives: childhood innocence and "the horrible experience of passionate love." This view, however, seems to treat the characters as actual persons. Indeed, Hagstrum cites Rousseau's *Confessions* as

if the subject of the autobiography could be treated on the same level as the character Werther. In such a discussion, the views of the author seem to get entirely lost. See "Such, Such Were the Joys," especially pp. 49 and 50–51. Similarly, Dickens' characterization would perhaps have been less severely criticized if the Sentimental tradition had been more clearly discerned in his novels. See, for instance, Aldous Huxley, "Vulgarity in Literature": "There was something rather wrong with a man who could take this lachrymose and tremulous pleasure in adult infantility"; George Orwell, "Charles Dickens": "Even sexual love is almost outside his scope. Actually his books are not so sexless as they are sometimes declared to be, and considering the time in which he was writing, he is reasonably frank"; or Angus Wilson, "The Heroes and Heroines of Dickens," in which he asserts that "The contemporary absolute demand for sexual purity . . . did, in fact, reduce the great Victorian novelists in the sexual sphere to a childish status beside their continental contemporaries." All appear in Stephen Wall, ed., *Charles Dickens, A Critical Anthology,* pp. 281, 312, and 435, respectively.

13. Frye, *English Romanticism,* p. 18: The myth "becomes a recovery of the original identity. For the sense of an original unity with nature, which being born as a subjective consciousness has broken, the obvious symbol is the mother. The lost paradise becomes really an unborn world, a pre-existent ideal. As a result something of the ancient, mother-centered symbolism comes back into poetry. . . . In the myth of recovery we often have a bride whose descent from a mother-figure is indicated by the fact that . . . she is frequently a sister as well." Mario Praz on the other hand treats the two kinds of incest as one. Tracing the course of Romanticism toward Decadence, he is surprised to find this Decadent feature in the Catholic Chateaubriand. See *The Romantic Agony,* p. 109.

14. Brissenden, *Virtue in Distress,* p. 270.

15. See Elizabeth MacAndrew and Susan Gorsky, "Why Do They Faint and Die?" pp. 735–45. And also W. J. Harvey, *Character and the Novel,* particularly his discussion of Dicken's Esther Summerson, pp. 93–97. The young heroines embroiled with an older man in the Victorian novel may also grow out of the depiction of Sentimental characters as childlike.

16. See Frye's *The Secular Scripture.* In this work Frye relates the death of Walpole's Matilda to the Romance tradition of the sacrificed virgin. See p. 143.

17. Beckford, *Vathek,* in Fairclough, ed., *Three Gothic Novels,* p. 207. An edition appeared in 1972, edited by Robert J. Gemmett, which contains the standard English text of *Vathek* in Henley's translation and the two French editions of 1787 put out by Beckford. The *Episodes of Vathek* in Sir Frank T. Marzial's 1912 translation, also edited by Gemmett, appeared in 1975. See also Kenneth W. Graham, "*Vathek* in English and

French," for a discussion of the differences between the French and English versions. The specific description of Gulchenrouz as girlish ("his arms, which twined so gracefully with those of the young girls in the dance, could neither dart the lance in the chace, nor curb the steeds . . . ," p. 207) may be surreptitiously homosexual. The affair between Alasi and Firouz in the "Episodes" is explicitly so. In *The Monk,* too, there may be some covert allusion to homosexuality. Ambrosio becomes attached to Matilda disguised as Rosario and later the figure of Lucifer raised by Matilda's incantation is that of a naked young man of surpassing beauty. If so, the presentation of disguised homosexual love, which Richard Ellmann sees in *Dorian Gray, The Turn of the Screw,* and some other works of the 1890s, was no new theme. See "A Late Victorian Love Affair," particularly pp. 6–7. The question is irrelevant here. It should be noted, however, that Maturin also insists on Everhard's having "too much beauty for his sex," and on "his delicate and brilliant complexion, his slender and exquisitely moulded form, and the modulation of his tender and tremulous voice" in "The Tale of Guzman's Family," in *Melmoth the Wanderer,* p. 309. This is an interpolated Sentimental story. Cultural clichés about "feminine" and "masculine" characteristics are interesting. The greatest compliment Fanny Burney's Evelina can think to pay her beloved Orville, for instance, is to say that he has a "feminine sensibility." The context shows that this is what makes him a superior being. It would be difficult to separate the symbolic delineation of moral delicacy in the physical features of male Sentimental characters from delicate male beauty described as a covert expression of homosexuality and little other than possible biographical information would be gained by doing so, especially when an author could have had both reasons for his description.

18. *Vathek,* in Fairclough, ed., *Three Gothic Novels,* pp. 235 and 254.

19. As Leonard Wolf notes in *The Annotated Frankenstein,* p. vi in the original edition of 1818, Elizabeth was Victor's cousin. This was changed in the 1831 edition, according to Wolf, "to avoid the slightest suggestion of incest."

20. *Frankenstein, Three Gothic Novels,* p. 290.

21. *Ibid.,* pp. 293 and 297.

3. Characters—The Split Personality

1. This is a very general view in the eighteenth century. It is stated explicitly, for instance, in Johnson's *Rasselas:* "When we consult our own policy, and attempt to find a nearer way to good, by overleaping the settled boundaries of right and wrong, we cannot escape the consciousness of our fault; but, if we miscarry, the disappointment is irremediably

embittered. How comfortless is the sorrow of him who feels at once the pangs of guilt, and the vexation of calamity which guilt has brought upon him!" Imlac says this and goes on to say: "This at least . . . is the present reward [i.e., in this world] of virtuous conduct, that no unlucky consequence can oblige us to repent it." In the next chapter we are told: "Nekayah being thus reconciled to herself, found that no evil is insupportable but that which is accompanied with consciousness of wrong." *Rasselas,* pp. 72–73.

2. This is why they are so often taken as clumsily mimetic. As Frye notes in *The Anatomy of Criticism,* p. 305: "There is hardly any modern romance that could not be made out to be a novel, and vice versa." Only if the distinction is made, however, as Frye himself makes it, can techniques such as the methods of characterization be understood. Much of the criticism of *Wuthering Heights* as a novel with weak characterization resulting from Emily Brontë's inability to portray "real" people would be obviated if, in Frye's terms, the work were treated as a "romance" rather than a "novel" (*Anatomy,* pp. 304–5). Instead of seeing the characters as limited by Brontë's personal idiosyncracies and her isolated life on the Yorkshire moors, readers should see that they are the special kind of characters needed in fantasy. George Eliot's characters are without doubt more realistically portrayed than Emily Brontë's, but Maggie Tulliver would be as much of an anomaly in a Gothic tale as an ape-like double would be in *The Mill on the Floss.*

3. "Preface to the Second Edition," Walpole, *The Castle of Otranto,* p. 8. "Mere" is used here in the second of the adjectival senses given by the *OED,* meaning: "That is what it is in the full sense of the term . . . absolute, entire, sheer, perfect, downright."

4. Francis Russell Hart in "The Experience of Character in the English Gothic Novel," disputes the view of Frye and others that Gothic characters have a symbolic, allegorical quality. He insists that they are "novelistic" because "the question of the demonic in nature is referred to *social* relationship" (p. 105). "It is not . . . 'natural' for characters in Gothic novels to find themselves thrust into a world of 'romance.' The shock is theirs," Hart writes (p. 91). He even refers to "the final authenticity" of Frankenstein's monster residing in "his human pathos" (p. 97). These observations are accurate in themselves but they do not make Gothic characters "novelistic." The monster, for instance, is only an approximation of the human. His pathos is human because that is the only kind a human can depict or understand. It does not make him a human character. Similarly, the shock of entry into the Gothic world is a feature of narrative structure not directly of characterization (see chapter 4). And the social relationships are an indication of the benevolist view of all virtue as social virtue. Most of the ordinary transactions of social life do not take place in these novels, whereas they are the very stuff of social novels.

5. Bram Stoker, for instance, risks ruining the effect of his monster Dracula. He carefully sets the scene in the inaccessible castle in Transylvania and introduces Dracula surrounded by the necessary mystery and bad weather. Then, however, his concern with probability leads him to worry about a castle lacking domestics. So he has Dracula making Jonathan's bed and cooking his meals. The whole tone of the novel and the elaborate structure that has helped create it is seriously threatened. Fortunately, the tale quickly moves on to dark corridors, rapacious female vampires, Dracula's superhuman means of leaving the castle, and the like. After this one slip, domesticity is confined to ordinary characters and Dracula lives the life of a proper villain.

6. *Otranto,* p. 35.

7. Eino Railo sees incest as a device for inspiring terror. It "is the kind of motive that an author with a cool and passionless conception of beauty [one wonders who these authors might be] would avoid as violent and unnatural, whereas a mind fired by romantic defiance of the limits of art and bent upon evoking horror would be secretly drawn to it. When Walpole began to create a 'Gothic' literature, it was only natural that . . . he should chance upon the idea of incestuous relations" (*The Haunted Castle,* p. 271). The view of Walpole as a Romantic secretly drawn to the idea by defiance of the limits of art hardly needs refuting. What does need to be seen is that both Walpole and Lewis use this "violent and unnatural" motive because they wish to demonstrate the unnaturalness of violence. Incest, incidentally, is a theme in novels of all kinds, e.g. Fielding's *Joseph Andrews* and *Tom Jones.*

8. After the second, only expurgated editions appeared until this century. A major and quite different reason for society's outrage was Lewis' treatment of the Bible. See John Berryman's Introduction to the Grove Press edition.

9. Matthew G. Lewis, *The Monk,* p. 39.

10. Peter Grudin in "*The Monk:* Matilda and the Rhetoric of Deceit," demonstrates that Matilda is a demon and notes many hints in the earlier sections of the novel of her malevolent and supernatural knowledge.

11. Mario Praz has pointed out that "with Milton, the Evil One definitely assumes an aspect of fallen beauty, of splendour shadowed by sadness and death" (*The Romantic Agony,* p. 56). He then goes on to cite Ann Radcliffe's Montoni and Schedoni as examples of "grandsons of Milton's Satan." He even quotes the description of Schedoni. It is evident from it, however, that there is nothing of the beauty of the fallen angel about him. Even more strangely, Praz includes Ambrosio among these "metamorphoses of Satan" (see p. 60). It is Lucifer, however, who first appears with the satanic features Praz describes, and not Ambrosio. Similarly, in *Vathek,* Eblis has them, not Beckford's caliph. Thus Lewis and

Beckford make a clear distinction between demonic figures and guilt-haunted men. As for Ann Radcliffe—what has she to do with devils?

12. Railo sees Ambrosio as evil by nature but notes the division in him that presages later use of the doubles figure: "The evil that has hitherto slept in the depths of the monk's soul [expands] at the first opportunity into a second personality, thereby cleaving his spiritual being in two. This feature of a double inward and outward existence was to prove fruitful for the romanticism of terror . . . leading at length to that strangest invention, the conception of a division of the ego into a good and an evil being." *The Haunted Castle,* p. 183.

13. Francis Hart in "The Experience of Character," p. 84, and A. Walton Litz, whom Hart cites, in *Jane Austen,* suggest in passing that Jane Austen may not have entirely rejected Ann Radcliffe and romance after all. Actually, there is a definite affinity between *The Mysteries of Udolpho* and *Northanger Abbey.* Whatever Jane Austen thought, Ann Radcliffe's central theme is, like the central theme of *Northanger Abbey,* the heroine's need to balance sensibility with common sense. There is a real contrast as well. Catherine Moreland lives in the real world and tries to act in a Gothic one. Emily St. Aubert lives and acts first in the world of Sentimental fiction and then in the world of a Gothic tale. Jane Austen deals with life, Ann Radcliffe with attitudes of mind. *The Mysteries of Udolpho* is nevertheless to some extent a novel of development and it is when Emily moves from the Sentimental to the Gothic world that she suffers that "shock" of entering a strange world that Hart claims is an indication that Gothic characters are "novelistic." Possibly with Jane Austen in mind, he calls Emily "an enlightened heroine, a paragon of sense and sensibility." For a study of Ann Radcliffe's works that purports to show that all her novels work out her personal oedipal complex and her repressed feelings about her relationship with her uncle, see Pierre Arnaud, *Ann Radcliffe et le fantastique.*

14. Gerard A. Barker in "Justice to Caleb Williams," points out Caleb's growth in moral stature in the course of the novel. He shows that Godwin changed the ending to make it more consonant with this theme. He sees Caleb when he is confronted with the wreck of Falkland, however, as "overcome by gratuitous remorse." This may be so on the social level, although Godwin's tone does not suggest it. If the two are seen as doubles, then Caleb's regret is a recognition that the punishments of conscience are greater than anything the law can do and so it is not gratuitous. At this point, the whole question of the reputation is ironically turned around. As C. R. Kropf puts it, "It is no longer clear who has been persecuting whom." See his "*Caleb Williams* and the Attack on Romance." Kropf sees the subtitle (originally the main title) "Things as They Are" as an allusion to the controversy over novel and romance as effec-

tive didactic vehicles. He sees both Falkland and Caleb as "the victims of their reading in romance." If they are, they must be added to Emily St. Aubert and Catherine Moreland as bearers of this theme. This conclusion would also increase the sense of them as doubles figures.

15. James M. Keech in "The Survival of the Gothic Response," sees Gothic literature as "attempting to evoke a particularized response"—fear. This response "carries the reader to the realm of nightmare" (p. 131). Keech calls this fear response the defining characteristic of Gothic literature whether of the eighteenth, nineteenth, or twentieth century. He notes the "moral ambiguity" introduced by the mixed character of the hero-villain (p. 134) as a major factor in inducing this fear.

16. *Frankenstein,* pp. 297–98.

17. In "Night Thoughts on the Gothic Novel," Lowry Nelson notes that "Frankenstein and his monster have much in common . . . they are objectified parts of a single sensibility, and . . . represent the intimate good and bad struggle in the human personality" (p. 247).

18. Nelson is apologetic about his own demonstrations of the psychological significance of Mary Shelley's work: "To say flatly that the monster is Frankenstein's id on the rampage and that he subconsciously desires his family's extermination would be pretentious and anachronistic" (*ibid.*). It is certainly desirable to use caution in "psychologizing" about Gothic literature. John A. Duninger, for instance, seems to indulge in anchorless speculation in his psychoanalytic interpretation of Frankenstein in "Kinship and Guilt in Mary Shelley's *Frankenstein,*" and Arnaud's study of Ann Radcliffe is based on simplistic assumptions. Norman N. Holland and Leona F. Sherman in "Gothic Possibilities," combine the drawbacks of "psychologizing" with those caused by disdain for popular literature (see chapter 1, note 2). They define all Gothic literature from *Otranto* on by the characteristics of the pulp Gothic romances of the 1970s, then claim that Gothic fiction opens up certain possibilities for response by readers, each reader projecting his own response onto an otherwise apparently meaningless work.

4. Setting and Narrative Structure— "Far Other Worlds and Other Seas"

1. Mackenzie, *Julia de Rubigné,* p. 124.

2. *Ibid.,* p. 218.

3. *Ibid.,* p. 195. In eighteenth-century texts, "devoted" is frequently found in the *OED* Sense 3: "Formally or surely consigned to evil or destruction; doomed."

4. An interesting contrast is the first reaction to Bly of the governess in *The Turn of the Screw.* She has been expecting a gloomy structure and

finds a cheerful one. James has reversed the convention, because he wishes to emphasize the governess' lack of awareness. The eighteenth-century idea that evil is immediately sensed is countered in his novel. The idea had survived for a long time, however, as can be seen in the more than ordinary fear evoked by the portrait in *The House of the Seven Gables,* by the malignant gazes of Le Fanu's ghost demons, by the universal repulsion felt by everyone who comes in contact with Stevenson's Mr. Hyde. See chapter 5.

5. Jacques Henri Bernardin de Saint Pierre, *Paul and Virginia, Great European Short Novels,* 1:165.

6. *Otranto,* pp. 7–8.

7. Quoted by Walter Scott in "Walpole," *Lives of the Novelists,* p. 184. The quotation has been translated from Walpole's French.

8. Scott's "Introduction," included in Horace Walpole, *The Castle of Otranto,* Marvin Mudrick, ed. (Longon: Collier-Macmillan, 1963), pp. 120–21.

9. *Otranto,* pp. 7–8.

10. *Ibid.,* p. 121.

11. "Walpole," p. 191.

12. Reeve, *The Old English Baron,* pp. 3–5.

13. Quoted by James Trainer, "Introduction," *The Old English Baron,* p. viii, n. 3.

14. Published posthumously in *The New Monthly Magazine* (1826), n.s. 16:145–50 and 532–36.

15. *Ibid.,* p. 145. Here, as in many eighteenth-century texts, "terrific" appears in its primary sense of "causing terror." See *OED,* sense 1.

16. *Ibid.,* pp. 147–48. See also Frye, *The Secular Scripture,* pp. 40–41, for a discussion of the plausible explanation for events presented as supernatural in Ann Radcliffe and other authors.

17. *Ibid.,* p. 149.

18. *Ibid.,* pp. 149–50.

19. Robert Hume suggests that Ann Radcliffe's distinction between the evocations of horror and of terror distinguishes those novels that explore the mind and are morally ambiguous from those that retain a sense of moral absolutes. ("Gothic vs. Romantic," p. 288. See also Varma on the horror/terror distinction.)

20. The edition used here is that of Bonamy Dobrée, ed.

21. *The New Monthly Magazine,* pp. 532–33.

22. See Trainer's "Note on the Text," *The Old English Baron,* p. xvii.

23. *The Old English Baron,* pp. 18–19.

24. *Ibid.,* p. 153.

25. Robert Kiely sees Beckford as "the first of the romantic novelists whose subject is always and irrevocably himself. The Orient is . . . an imaginary region, authentic in some details, but constructed to his own

specifications for his own occupancy." *The Romantic Novel,* p. 44. Because they draw on the imagery of their subconscious minds, all Gothic novelists probably use themselves as subjects as least to some extent. The psychological analysis of their works, however, is the realm of the biographer and is largely irrelevant to literary analysis.

26. Brissenden, *Virtue in Distress.*

27. Robert Kiely finds that the "rational and benevolent view of life represented by Emily St. Aubert's father . . . [is] unconsciously challenged but still respected by Mrs. Radcliffe." *The Romantic Novel,* p. 51. The conclusion, however, belies this view.

28. As Kiely puts it: "Emily half-creates her own Udolpho" (p. 74).

29. See Ann Radcliffe, *The Italian,* Garber, ed., notes to p. 1, p. 148, where Garber, noting that the Inquisition is anachronistic, says it "had to be there. . . . Her business was to shape a world."

30. See Garber's Introduction, pp. xiii-xiv for a discussion of this character. He writes of Schedoni: "With this character [Ann Radcliffe's] blacks and whites become complicated and grey."

31. See George Woodcock, "Things as They Might Be: Things as They Are," for a discussion of Godwin's novels and of *Caleb* in particular. Woodcock sees Falkland as "a forerunner of Dr. Jekyll-and-Mr. Hyde."

32. For a different view on this subject, see Francis Hart's "Limits of the Gothic: The Scottish Example."

33. See Lowry Nelson, "Night Thoughts," for the importance of Walton as a scientist to the system of narration. He writes of him that he tells the story "with all the defensive incredulity of an eyewitness" (p. 243). This method of maintaining credibility is used, as will be seen, in *Dracula,* where the hunt is hampered by the fear of provoking disbelief and derision.

34. See Nelson, p. 243.

35. The *OED* Sense 2 of "enthusiasm" specifies, as an eighteenth-century usage, "ill-regulated or misdirected religious emotion, extravagance of religious speculation."

36. Railo notes that "the loneliness of the Byronic hero approaches that state of mind so tempting to the terror-romanticist with all its potential horrors—insanity" (*The Haunted Castle,* p. 308). For a discussion of cultural attitudes toward madness see Michel Foucault, *Madness and Civilization.*

37. Maturin, *Melmoth,* pp. 43 and 42.

5. The Victorian Hall of Mirrors

1. Dmitri Chizhevsky has made a full study of Dostoyevsky's use of doubles figures in "The Theme of the Double in Dostoevsky."

2. See Toby A. Olshin, "'The Yellow Dwarf' and *The Old Curiosity Shop*," *Nineteenth Century Fiction*, and Wolfgang Kayser, *The Grotesque in Art and Literature*, p. 184, where Kayser distinguishes between the fairy tale and the grotesque. The fairy tale is also closely related to Gothic fiction. Like the grotesque, its themes and motifs are used by the Gothic authors for their own purposes. (See chapter 1, note 1, for a reference to Bruno Bettelheim's study of fairy tales.)

3. His title in Russian is *The Demons*, and he makes symbolic allusion to the biblical tale of the Gardarene swine.

4. *The Grotesque in Art and Literature*, p. 181. Page references are hereafter given in text.

5. In his preface to *Cromwell* (1827), quoted in *The Grotesque*, p. 57.

6. Quoted in *The Grotesque*, p. 53.

7. Nicholas K. Kiessling, "Demonic Dread," pp. 37 and 41.

8. See Christopher Small, *Mary Shelley's Frankenstein*, p. 132. Jack Sullivan notes, however, that in the Edwardian age, T. S. Eliot and others claimed that belief in the supernatural was necessary to the writing of good stories of the supernatural. Otherwise, such literature becomes degenerate and inferior (see *Elegant Nightmares*, p. 4). Sullivan's study is of ghost stories, in which, it is true, a ghost will often appear as a malignant Other. The ghosts of Le Fanu, for instance, are like this. See p. 166.

9. Kayser, *The Grotesque*, pp. 57–58. Kayser makes this point in relation to Hugo's discussion.

10. See Guy Chapman, *Beckford*.

11. Maturin, *Melmoth the Wanderer*, p. 410.

12. See E. F. Bleiler's Introduction to *Three Gothic Novels*, pp. xxxi–xl, for an account of Polidori's authorship and the relationship of his novel to Byron's *Fragment* published with *Mazeppa* and included in this collection of Bleiler's.

13. Kayser, *The Grotesque*, pp. 184–85.

14. It is not surprising that Poe, an author of Gothic tales, should also be the father of detective fiction. Detective fiction implies a belief that criminal psychology is caused by circumstances working on man's nature and so can be understood rationally and scientifically. Such a belief comes out of the same trend of thought that produced the psychologizing Gothic tales. Albert D. Hutter asserts that critics who find a "purely literary genealogy" for detective fiction in "the gothic or some combination of gothic romance and detailed realism" fail to see that this type of literature is related to "the historical rise of the detective police" in Victorian society. It seems to me essential, however, to allow for both constituents. That is, both Gothic and detective fiction arose as a result of a change in generally current ideas, and so did society's formation of "detective police." To ignore the common link between changes in literature and society is to increase the already regrettable gap in our perceptions of litera-

ture and life. It is also, after all, somewhat of a truism to note that if there are no police detectives in life they will not appear as characters in fiction. See Albert D. Hutter, "Dreams, Transformations, and Literature," p. 194.

15. Peter Hays, in *The Limping Hero,* associates these figures with a new Prometheus/Faust archetype. He equates the lame figure in literature with impotence and castration and then, taking the archetype back to the earliest myths of fertility gods who are seasonally dismembered and resurrected or re-embodied, associates them with those figures who, throughout time, have defied the gods in the name of knowledge. Hays quotes Nietzsche on this subject in a statement that uses the imagery of the Gothic: "It is as though the myth [of Oedipus] whispered to us that wisdom . . . is an unnatural crime and that whoever, in pride of knowledge, hurls nature into the abyss of destruction, must himself experience nature's disintegration" (p. 127).

16. *Frankenstein,* p. 307.

17. "Rappaccini's Daughter," *The Complete Novels and Selected Tales of Nathaniel Hawthorne,* p. 1051.

18. Walpole consciously gave Otranto features of Strawberry Hill and based the portrait that steps out of its frame on "the portrait of Lord Falkland all in white in my gallery." He was surprised to find, however, that he had delineated "the towers, gates, chapel, and great hall . . . of a [Cambridge] college." (See W. S. Lewis, Introduction, Walpole, *The Castle of Otranto,* pp. ix, xi.) It has also been suggested that he unconsciously based the description of the giant helmet and parts of the setting on Piranesi's drawings (by Jorgen Anderson, cited by Mario Praz, Introduction, Fairclough, ed., *Three Gothic Novels,* pp. 16f.), Praz's "factual" information should be treated with caution. See, for example, the inaccuracy of his statements about Beckford, Louisa, and William Courtenay, who emerges from Praz's discussion of the relationship as Louisa's five-year-old son, although he was not her son and was considerably older than five even when Beckford first met him. See also chapter 1, notes 11 and 12, concerning Walpole's intensity in writing.

19. Christopher Small has made a convincing case for Frankenstein as an expression of Mary Shelley's complex feelings for her parents and for Shelley and of her fears of inadequacy in the face of the creative effort. See *Mary Shelley's Frankenstein.* See also Florescu's *In Search of Frankenstein.*

20. Quoted in Barton Levi St. Armand, "Hawthorne's 'Haunted Mind,' " p. 4. St. Armand, drawing from Wilbur's studies of Poe, sees Poe as driving his discoveries as far as he could and Hawthorne as drawing back from them, afraid. If this is so, it may go a long way to account for the difference in tone between the two authors.

21. The most striking example is, perhaps, "Ligeia." Roy P. Basler

has interpreted this story in the light of "irrational psychology" and so says it is, therefore, not "a story of the supernatural." Gothic fiction, however, uses the supernatural precisely to symbolize and explore irrational psychology. Poe's particular use of Gothic devices shows an unusual conscious awareness, perhaps, of the workings of the subconscious mind, but he belongs squarely in the tradition. See Basler, "The Interpretation of 'Ligeia.' "

22. Richard Wilbur contends that this story may be seen as a dream of the narrator's. He considers that Poe's writing has an "accessible allegorical meaning" and speaks of the spirals and vortices which appear throughout his work. "The spiral," he says, "invariably represents . . . loss of consciousness, and the descent of the mind into sleep." Noting that Poe's heroes are "always either enclosed or on [their] way to enclosure," Wilbur interprets this recurring feature as "the isolation of the poetic soul in visionary reveries or trance." Thus, the narrator's lack of understanding in "The Fall of the House of Usher" reflects the hypnagogic state whose visions "lie 'beyond the compass of words.' " By the same token the collapse of the house is a symbol of the narrator's having "dreamt himself free of his physical body, and of the material world." This interpretation makes the story a triumphant one, but puts such emphasis on the frame that it neglects the story itself. In addition, it ignores the affinity of Poe's narrator to mediating consciousnesses in the Gothic tradition like Emily Brontë's Lockwood. Above all, if the dissolution of the house is a triumph, the narrator has a strange way of expressing that emotion. If the dream state is "an ideal state, a blessed state," the experience in the House of Usher is a questionable blessing. See "The House of Poe," *Poe,* pp. 99–117. Barton Levi St. Armand sees the collapse of the house as "a catastrophe like the archetypal Gothic climax of . . . *The Castle of Otranto.*" It is not, however, "a description of an apocalypse . . . but of a new genesis." It is hard to see, however, a new genesis in the tone and atmosphere of Poe's tale. From the crumbling of the house, even with a blood-red moon shining through it, no phoenix could arise, no sense of hope is offered. If this is an optimistic story, Poe must have been possessed by his own imp of the perverse while writing it. See Barton Levi St. Armand, "The 'Mysteries' of Edgar Poe."

23. Bigelow, "The Problem of Symbolist Form in Melville's 'Bartleby the Scrivener,' " p. 347.

24. J. Hillis Miller in *The Disappearance of God,* shows that the complete identity of Cathy and Heathcliff gives expression to Emily Brontë's religious beliefs. This is one more example of the way in which a work is simultaneously a manifestation of its author's individuality and a part of a literary convention.

25. Northrop Frye sees him as a version of the Byronic hero: "The so-called Byronic hero is often a Romantic version of the natural man,

who, like Esau or Ishmael, is an outcast, a solitary much given to communing with untamed nature, and who thus represents the potentially expanding and liberating elements in that nature. . . . When he is evil, there is often the feeling that, as with Byron's Cain, his evil is comprehensible, that he is not wholly evil any more than society is wholly good, and that even his evil is a force that society has to reckon with. The greatest of all his incarnations in English literature, Emily Brontë's Heathcliff, has in full the sense of a natural man who eludes all moral categories just as nature itself does, and who cannot be simply condemned or accepted." *English Romanticism,* pp. 30–31.

26. Emily Brontë, *Wuthering Heights,* p. 254. Page references in text are to this edition.

27. "The Black Monk," *Selected Tales of Tchekov,* pp. 316 and 323.

28. Christopher Small suggests the two characters are aspects of one personality. Caleb, in Small's interpretation, is the rational mind, which recognizes and inquires into the deed that the emotional being, Falkland, cannot face. Thus, the pursuit is the attempt to chase away consciousness of evil. If this is so, the doubles figure represents a split between mind and emotion. *Mary Shelley's Frankenstein.*

29. E. T. A. Hoffmann, "The Doubles," *Tales of E. T. A. Hoffmann.*

30. It is important to distinguish such symbolic characters from mimetic ones by seeing that they do not embody strictly individual evil, madness, and mental conflict but, rather, the nature of these afflictions as they occur in the human mind in general. If the distinction is not made, the symbolic figure is assessed by a wrong measure. W. J. Harvey, for instance, writing of *Moby Dick* says: "Melville avoids the great danger inherent in most literary doubles or doppelgangers. In such instances the novelist generally splits a personality in order to objectify some internal moral struggle; the danger is that a crude and simple allegory may result in which the characters are little more than personifications of spiritual or psychological forces. Dr. Jekyll and Mr. Hyde come closer to this." To see this kind of characterization as somehow deficient amounts to regarding the mimetic as a sort of ideal, instead of seeing it as one among several methods. See *Character and the Novel.* This work is generally an excellent study of characterization.

31. E. T. A. Hoffmann, "A New Year's Eve Adventure," *The Best Tales of Hoffmann,* p. 104. Page references given parenthetically are to this edition.

32. E. F. Bleiler, "Introduction," *The Best Tales of Hoffmann,* pp. xxx–xxxi.

33. Edgar Allan Poe, "The Oval Portrait," *Selected Writings of Edgar Allen Poe,* pp. 171 and 173–74.

34. "Preface," *The House of the Seven Gables,* in *The Complete Novels and Selected Tales of Nathaniel Hawthorne,* p. 243.

35. *The House of the Seven Gables,* p. 278.

36. "Preface," *The Blithedale Romance,* in *Complete Novels and Selected Tales,* p. 439.

37. "Preface," *The Marble Faun,* in *Complete Novels and Selected Tales,* p. 590.

38. Mario Praz sees Wilde as a sort of lightweight Decadent. Discussing *Dorian Gray,* he writes: "Wilde's point of view, in fact, is always scenic; he sees things as in stage-perspective; he is all the time arranging his characters, his landscape, his events, and making them pose" (*The Romantic Agony,* p. 345). Seen within the Gothic tradition, however, the conventional devices become more solid, and whether Wilde was a Decadent or not takes second place to his portrayal of exquisite Decadence in Dorian.

39. See Richard Ellmann, "A Late Victorian Love Affair."

40. As J. I. M. Stewart notes in his introduction to the novel: "Round about 1856 Collins attended a criminal trial, and was impressed both by the manner in which a chain of evidence could be forged from the testimonies of successive witnesses, and by the mounting effect of this upon the spectators as the case proceeded; '. . . a series of events in a novel would lend themselves well to an exposition like this. . . . The same means employed here . . . could impart to the reader that acceptance, that sense of belief, which I saw produced here by the succession of testimonies so varied in form and nevertheless so strictly unified by their march toward the same goal.' " Introduction, Collins, *The Moonstone,* p. 12.

41. Robert Louis Stevenson, *Dr. Jekyll and Mr. Hyde.*

42. It is, of course, no coincidence that the age that produced these writings also saw the beginning of Freud's work. See Pamela Kaufman, "Burke, Freud, and the Gothic."

43. Henry James, *The Turn of the Screw,* p. 81. Page references given parenthetically in text are to this edition.

44. It is Miles's complaint that he wants to be with his own "kind" and the behavior that has caused him to be sent home from school that causes Richard Ellmann to see this, like *Dorian Gray,* as a covertly homosexual story. (See "A Late Victorian Love Affair.") Such a view in a way strengthens the interpretation offered here. At the same time, it seems a distracting issue for James to have introduced. Miles may mean he wants to be with other boys and not be seduced from boyhood to manhood by the governess. He may vaguely feel the unhealthiness of the governess' attitude makes her, and the other females he is cooped up with, not his "kind." Certainly, it seems likely that the governess' eager relaying of his words and her "understanding" attitude conveys more about her than about the child. Even more certainly, James means to be vague about the matter.

Epilogue: The Twentieth Century

1. For a discussion of Kafka's use of realism in his fantasy, see M. Elizabeth MacAndrew, "A Splacknuck and a Dung-Beetle."

2. Flannery O'Connor, "Some Aspects of the Grotesque in Southern Fiction," *Mystery and Manners,* pp. 36–50.

3. Carson McCullers, "The Flowering Dream: Notes on Writing," *The Mortgaged Heart,* pp. 315, 311, and 314.

4. Bettelheim, *The Uses of Enchantment.*

5. See Carolyn Heilbrun, *Toward a Recognition of Androgyny,* for a discussion of this subject.

6. Much of the literature concerning this aspect of our culture is itself strange. The attempt to depict Otherness appears in many forms, including elaborate editions, which are part of the "cults" that have grown up around the literature of the strange, whether it be Tolkien or Marvel Comics. Cult literature seems to hover in a realm that is at once intense and non-serious, satirizing and accepting. This strange coexistence of attitudes that have usually tended to squeeze each other out is probably a key to understanding the culture of the 1970s. It may be that, under the threat of meaninglessness, the borderlines between reality and fantasy lose significance, giving fantasy a new dimension. Any bookstore in 1978 will yield examples, some rather expensive editions, of a wide variety of literature of the weird, suggesting a wide and varied audience.

7. See for the works of Fiedler, Florescu, and Wolf: Fiedler, *Freaks;* Florescu, *In Search of Dracula;* Wolf, *A Dream of Dracula.*

BIBLIOGRAPHY

Aikin, John, M.D., and Anna Laetitia Barbauld. *Miscellaneous Pieces in Prose.* London, 1792.

Aldridge, A. O. "The Pleasures of Pity." *ELH* (1949), 16:76–87.

Arnaud, Pierre. *Ann Radcliffe et le fantastique.* Publications de l'Université de Paris-X Nanterre; Paris: Aubier Montaigne, 1976.

Barker, Gerard A. "Justice to Caleb Williams." *Studies in the Novel* (1974), 6:377–88.

Basler, Roy P. "The Interpretation of 'Ligeia.' " In Robert Regan, ed., *Poe.* Englewood Cliffs, N.J.: Prentice-Hall, 1967.

Beattie, James. *Dissertations Moral and Critical.* New York: Garland Press, 1971.

Beckford, William. *Episodes of Vathek.* Sir Frank R. Marzial, tr. Robert J. Gemmett, ed. London: Associated University Presses, 1975.

——*Vathek.* Robert J. Gemmett, ed. Delmar, N.Y.: Scholars' Facsimiles and Reprints, 1972.

Bernardin de Saint Pierre, Jacques Henri. *Paul and Virginia.* In Anthony Winner, ed., *Great European Short Novels.* New York: Harper and Row, 1968.

Bettelheim, Bruno. *The Uses of Enchantment.* New York: Knopf, 1976.

Bigelow, Gordon E. "The Problem of Symbolist Form in Melville's 'Bartleby the Scrivener.' " *MLQ* (1970), 31:345–58.

Birkhead, Edith. "Sentiment and Sensibility in the Eighteenth-Century Novel." *Essays and Studies* (1925), 11:22–116.

——*The Tale of Terror.* London: Constable, 1921.

Bleiler, E. F. "Introduction." *The Castle of Otranto* by Horace Walpole, *Vathek* by William Beckford, *The Vampyre* by John Polidori. New York: Dover, 1966.

Bredvold, Louis I. *The Natural History of Sensibility.* Detroit: Wayne State University Press, 1962.

Briggs, Julia. *Night Visitors. The Rise and Fall of the English Ghost Story.* London: Faber, 1977.

Brissenden, R. F. *Virtue in Distress.* [New York]: Barnes and Noble, 1974.

Brontë, Emily. *Wuthering Heights.* William M. Sale, Jr., ed. New York: Norton, 1972.

Brophy, Elizabeth Bergen. *Samuel Richardson: The Triumph of Craft.* Knoxville: University of Tennessee Press, 1974.

Burke, Edmund. *A Philosophical Enquiry into the Origin of our Ideas of the Sublime and Beautiful.* J. T. Boulton, ed. New York: Columbia University Press, 1958.

Byrd, Max. *Visits to Bedlam.* Columbia: University of South Carolina Press, 1974.

Chapman, Guy. *Beckford.* London: Rupert Hart-Davis, 1952.

Chateaubriand, François-René, de. *Atala* and *René.* Walter J. Cobb, tr. New York: New American Library, 1961.

Chekhov, Anton. "The Black Monk." In *Selected Tales of Tchekov.* Constance Garnett, tr. London: Chatto and Windus, 1958.

Chizhevsky, Dmitri. "The Theme of the Double in Dosteovsky." In René Wellek, ed., *Dostoevsky,* pp. 112–29. Englewood Cliffs, N.J.: Prentice-Hall, 1962.

Collins, William. *The Moonstone.* J. I. M. Stewart, ed. Harmondsworth: Penguin Books, 1966.

Cooke, Arthur L. "Some Side Lights on the Theory of Gothic Romance." *MLQ* (December 1951), 12:429–36.

Crane, R. S. "Suggestions Toward a Genealogy of the 'Man of Feeling.' " *ELH* (December 1934), 1:205–30.

DePorte, Michael V. *Nightmares and Hobbyhorses.* San Marino: Huntington Library, 1974.

Drake, Nathan. *Literary Hours.* New York: Garland Press, 1970.

Duninger, John A. "Kinship and Guilt in Mary Shelley's *Frankenstein.*" *Studies in the Novel* (1976), 8:38–55.

Eaves, T. C. Duncan and Ben D. Kimpel. *Samuel Richardson.* Oxford: Clarendon, 1971.

Ellmann, Richard. "A Late Victorian Love Affair." *The New York Review of Books* (August 4, 1977), 24:6–10.

Fairclough, Peter, ed. *Three Gothic Novels.* Harmondsworth: Penguin Books, 1968.

Fiedler, Leslie, A. *Freaks: Myths and Images of the Secret Self*. New York: Simon and Schuster, 1978.
——*Love and Death in the American Novel*. New York: Dell, 1966.
Fielding, Sarah. *David Simple*. London: Oxford University Press, 1969.
Florescu, Radu. *In Search of Dracula*. New York: Warner Books, 1973.
——*In Search of Frankenstein*. New York: Warner Books, 1976.
Foster, James R. *History of the Pre-Romantic Novel in England*. New York: MLA, 1949.
Foucault, Michel. *Madness and Civilization*. New York: Random House, 1973.
Frye, Northrop. *The Anatomy of Criticism*. New York: Atheneum, 1966.
——*The Secular Scripture*. Cambridge: Harvard University Press, 1976.
——*A Study of English Romanticism*. New York: Random House, 1968.
——"Towards Defining an Age of Sensibility." *ELH* (June 1956), 23:144–52. Reprinted in James L. Clifford, ed., *Eighteenth-Century Literature*. New York: Oxford University Press, 1959.
Garber, Frederick. "Meaning and Mode in Gothic Fiction." In Harold E. Pagliaro, ed., *Studies in Eighteenth-Century Culture*, 3:155–69. Cleveland: The Press of Case Western Reserve University, 1973.
Glock, Waldo S. "Appearance and Reality: The Education of Evelina." *Essays in Literature* (Spring 1975), 2:32–41.
Godwin, William. *Caleb Williams*. New York: Holt, Rinehart and Winston, 1960.
Goethe, Wolfgang Johann, von. *The Sorrows of Young Werther*. New York: New American Library, 1962.
Gossman, Lionel. "Literary Scholarship and Popular History." *ECS* (Winter 1973/74), 7:133–42.
Graham, Kenneth W. "*Vathek* in English and French." *Studies in Bibliography*. Papers of the Bibliographical Society of the University of Virginia, 28:153–66.
Greene, Donald. "Latitudinarianism and Sensibility: The Genealogy of the 'Man of Feeling' Reconsidered." *MP* (1977), 75:159–83.
Greenway, John L. "The Gateway to Innocence: Ossian and the

Nordic Bard as Myth." In Harold E. Pagliero, ed., *Studies in Eighteenth-Century Culture,* 4:160–70. Madison: University of Wisconsin Press, 1975.

Grudin, Peter. "*The Monk:* Matilda and the Rhetoric of Deceit." *Journal of Narrative Technique* (1975), 5:136–46.

Hagstrum, Jean. " 'Such, Such Were the Joys': The Boyhood of the Man of Feeling." In *Changing Taste in Eighteenth-Century Art and Literature.* Clark Library Seminar. Los Angeles: University of California Press, 1972.

Hart, Francis Russell. "The Experience of Character in the English Gothic Novel." In Roy Harvey Pearce, ed., *Experience in the Novel,* pp. 83–105. New York: Columbia University Press, 1968.

——"Limits of the Gothic: The Scottish Example." In Harold E. Pagliaro, ed., *Studies in Eighteenth-Century Culture,* 3:137–53. Cleveland: The Press of Case Western Reserve University, 1973.

Harvey, W. J. *Character and the Novel.* Ithaca, N.Y.: Cornell University Press, 1968.

Hawthorne, Nathaniel. *The Complete Novels and Selected Tales of Nathaniel Hawthorne.* Norman Holmes Pearson, ed. New York: Random House, 1937.

Hays, Peter. *The Limping Hero: Grotesques in Literature.* New York: New York University Press, 1971.

Heilbrun, Carolyn. *Toward a Recognition of Androgyny.* New York: Knopf, 1973.

Hoffmann, E. T. A. *The Best Tales of Hoffmann.* E. F. Bleiler, ed. New York: Dover, 1967.

——*Tales of E. T. A. Hoffmann.* Leonard J. Kent and Elizabeth C. Knight, trs. and eds. Chicago: University of Chicago Press, 1959.

Hogg, James. *The Private Memoirs and Confessions of a Justified Sinner.* John Carey, ed. London: Oxford University Press, 1969.

Holland, Norman N. and Leona F. Sherman. "Gothic Possibilities." *NLH* (1976–77), 8:279–94.

Hume, Robert D. "Gothic versus Romantic: A Revaluation of the Gothic Novel." *PMLA* (March 1969), 84:282–90.

Hume, Robert D. and Robert Platzner. " 'Gothic versus Romantic': A Rejoinder." *PMLA* (March 1971), 86:266–74.

Hurd, Richard. *Letters on Chivalry and Romance.* Vol. 4 of *Works,* 1811; reprinted New York: AMS Press, 1967.

Hutter, Albert D. "Dreams, Transformations, and Literature: The Implications of Detective Fiction." *Victorian Studies* (December 1975), 19:194.
James, Henry. *The Turn of the Screw.* New York: Norton, 1966.
Johnson, Samuel. *Rasselas.* Gwin J. Kolb, ed. Northbrook, Ill.: AHM, 1962.
Kahler, Erich. *The Inward Turn of Narrative.* Richard and Clara Winston, trs. Princeton, N.J.: Princeton University Press, 1973.
Kaufman, Pamela. "Burke, Freud, and the Gothic." *Studies in Burke and His Time* (Spring 1972), 13:2179–92.
Kayser, Wolfgang. *The Grotesque in Art and Literature.* Ulrich Weisstein, tr. Bloomington, Ind.: 1963; reprinted New York: McGraw-Hill, 1966.
Keech, James M. "The Survival of the Gothic Response." *Studies in the Novel* (1974), 6:130–44.
Kermode, Frank. *The Sense of an Ending.* London, 1966; reprinted London: Oxford University Press, 1970.
Ketton-Cremer, R. W. *Horace Walpole.* Ithaca, N.Y.: Cornell University Press, 1964.
Kiely, Robert. *The Romantic Novel in England.* Cambridge: Harvard University Press, 1972.
Kiessling, Nicholas K. "Demonic Dread: The Incubus Figure in British Literature." In G. R. Thompson, ed., *The Gothic Imagination,* pp. 22–41. [Pullman]: Washington State University Press, 1974.
Kropf, C. R. "*Caleb Williams* and the Attack on Romance." *Studies in the Novel* (1976), 8:81–87.
Kuhn, Albert J. "Introduction." *Three Sentimental Novels.* New York: Holt, Rinehart, and Winston, 1970.
Leavis, Q. D. *Fiction and the Reading Public.* London: Chatto and Windus, 1932.
Lewis, Matthew G. *The Monk.* New York: Grove Press, 1959.
Lewis, W. S. *Horace Walpole.* New York: Pantheon Books, 1961.
Litz, A. Walton. *Jane Austen: A Study of Her Artistic Development.* New York: Oxford University Press, 1965.
Lyons, John O. *The Invention of the Self.* Carbondale, Ill.: Southern Illinois University Press, 1978.
MacAndrew, M. Elizabeth. "A Splacknuck and a Dung-Beetle: Realism and Probability in Swift and Kafka." *College English* (1970), 31:376–91.

MacAndrew, Elizabeth and Susan R. Gorsky. "Why Do They Faint and Die?—The Birth of the Delicate Heroine." *Journal of Popular Culture* (Spring 1975), 8:735–45.

McCullers, Carson. *The Mortgaged Heart.* Margarita G. Smith, ed. New York: Bantam Books, 1972.

Mackenzie, Henry. *The Man of Feeling.* London: Oxford University Press, 1970.

McNutt, Dan J. *The Eighteenth-Century Gothic Novel: An Annotated Bibliography of Criticism and Selected Texts.* New York and London: Garland, 1975.

Madden, David. "The Necessity for an Aesthetics of Popular Culture." *JPC* (Summer 1973), 7:1–13.

Maturin, Charles Robert. *Melmoth the Wanderer.* Lincoln: University of Nebraska Press, 1961.

Miller, J. Hillis. *The Disappearance of God.* New York: Schocken Books, 1965.

Moers, Ellen. *Literary Women.* Garden City: Doubleday, 1976.

Monk, Samuel. *The Sublime.* Ann Arbor: University of Michigan Press, 1960.

Murphy, John V. *The Dark Angel: Gothic Elements in Shelley's Works.* Lewisburg, Pa.: Bucknell University Press, 1975.

Nelson, Lowry, Jr. "Night Thoughts on the Gothic Novel." *Yale Review* (1963), 52:236–57.

Nye, Russell. *The Unembarrassed Muse.* New York: Dial, 1970.

O'Connor, Flannery. *Mystery and Manners.* Sally and Robert Fitzgerald, eds. New York: Noonday Press, 1970, pp. 36–50.

Olshin, Toby A. " 'The Yellow Dwarf' and *The Old Curiosity Shop.*" *Nineteenth-Century Fiction* (June 1970), 25:96–99.

Poe, Edgar Allan. *The Fall of the House of Usher and Other Tales.* New York: New American Library, 1960.

——*Selected Writings of Edgar Allan Poe.* Edward H. Davidson, ed. Boston: Houghton Mifflin, 1956.

Poirier, Richard. "A Literature of Law and Order." *The Performing Self,* pp. 3–26. New York: Oxford University Press, 1971.

Praz, Mario. "Introductory Essay." In Peter Fairclough, ed., *Three Gothic Novels,* pp. 7–34. Harmondsworth: Penguin, 1968.

——*The Romantic Agony.* Angus Davidson, tr. London, 1933; reprinted New York: Meridian, 1956.

Radcliffe, Ann. *Gaston de Blondeville.* In *The New Monthly Magazine* (1826), M.S. 16:532–36.

——*The Italian.* Frederick Garber, ed. London: Oxford University Press, 1971.

——*The Mysteries of Udolpho.* Bonamy Dobrée, ed. London: Oxford University Press, 1970.

——"The Supernatural in Poetry." *The New Monthly Magazine* (1826), M.S. 16:145–50.

Railo, Eino. *The Haunted Castle.* New York, 1927; reprinted New York: Gordon Press, 1974.

Reeve, Clara. *The Old English Baron.* New York: Oxford University Press, 1967.

——*The Progress of Romance through Times, Countries, and Manners.* New York: Garland Press, 1970.

St. Armand, Barton Levi. "Hawthorne's 'Haunted Mind': A Subterranean Drama of the Self." *Criticism* (Winter 1971), 13:1–25.

——"The 'Mysteries' of Edgar Poe: The Quest for a Monomyth in Gothic Literature." In G. R. Thompson, ed., *The Gothic Imagination.* [Pullman]: Washington State University Press, 1974.

Schorer, Mark. "Technique as Discovery." *Hudson Review* (1948), 1:68–87.

Scott, Walter. "Introduction." In Horace Walpole, *The Castle of Otranto.* Marvin Mudrick, ed. London: Collier-Macmillan, 1963.

——"Mackenzie" and "Walpole." *Lives of the Novelists.* London: Oxford University Press, 1906.

Small, Christopher. *Mary Shelley's Frankenstein.* [Pittsburgh]: University of Pittsburgh Press, 1973.

Spacks, Patricia Meyer. *The Female Imagination.* New York: Knopf, 1975.

Stevenson, Robert Louis. *Dr. Jekyll and Mr. Hyde.* New York: Bantam Books, 1967.

Sullivan, Jack. *Elegant Nightmares.* Athens: Ohio University Press, 1978.

Summers, Montague. *The Gothic Quest.* New York, 1938; reissued New York: Russell and Russell, 1964.

——*The Werewolf.* New York, 1933; reissued New York: Bell, 1967.

Thompson, G. R., ed. *The Gothic Imagination: Essays in Dark Romanticism.* [Pullman]: Washington State University Press, 1974.

Tompkins, J. M. S. *The Popular Novel in England, 1770–1800.* London, 1932; reprinted Lincoln: University of Nebraska Press, 1961.

Trawick, Leonard M., ed. *Backgrounds of Romanticism*. Bloomington: Indiana University Press, 1967.

Tuveson, Ernest Lee. *The Imagination as a Means of Grace*. Berkeley and Los Angeles: University of California Press, 1960.

——"The Origins of the Moral Sense." *HLQ* (May 1948), 11:241–59.

Varma, Devendra P. *The Gothic Flame*. London, 1957; reissued New York: Russell and Russell, 1966.

Vopat, James B. "*Evelina:* Life as Art—Notes Toward Becoming a Performer on the Stage of Life." *Essays in Literature* (Spring 1975), 2:42–52.

Wall, Stephen, ed. *Charles Dickens, A Critical Anthology*. Harmondsworth: Penguin, 1970.

Walpole, Horace. *The Castle of Otranto*. W. S. Lewis, ed. London: Oxford University Press, 1964.

Weiskel, Thomas. *The Romantic Sublime*. Baltimore: John Hopkins University Press, 1976.

Wilbur, Richard. "The House of Poe." In Robert Regan, ed., *Poe*. Englewood Cliffs, N.J.: Prentice-Hall, 1967.

Willey, Basil. *The Eighteenth-Century Background*. London, 1960; reprinted Boston: Beacon, 1961.

Williams, Ioan, ed. *Novel and Romance, 1700–1800*. New York: Barnes and Noble, 1970.

Wolf, Leonard. *A Dream of Dracula*. New York: Popular Library, 1972.

Wolf, Leonard, ed. *The Annotated Frankenstein*. New York: Clarkson N. Potter, 1977.

Woodcock, George. "Things As They Might Be: Things as They Are: Notes on the Novels of William Godwin." *Dalhousie Review* (1975), 54:685–97.

Wright, Walter Francis. *Sensibility in English Prose Fiction 1760–1814: A Reinterpretation*. Illinois Studies in Language and Literature, vol. 22, nos. 3–4. Urbana: University of Illinois Press, 1937.

Zweig, Paul. *The Adventurer*. New York: Basic Books, 1974

INDEX